PERFORMING AFRICA

AF271253

P A U L L A   A .   E B R O N

Performing Africa

PRINCETON UNIVERSITY PRESS   PRINCETON AND OXFORD

Copyright © 2002 by Princeton University Press

Published by Princeton University Press, 41 WIlliam Street, Princeton, New Jersey 08540

In the United Kingdom: Princeton University Press, 3 Market Place, Woodstock, Oxfordshire OX20 1SY

All Rights Reserved

Library of Congress Cataloging-in-Publication Data

Ebron, Paulla A., 1953–
Performing Africa / Paulla A. Ebron.
p. cm.
Includes bibliographical references and index.
ISBN 0-691-07488-7 (alk. paper)—ISBN 0-691-07489-5 (pbk. : alk. paper)
1. Griots—Gambia—Music—History and criticism. 2. Mandingo (African people)—
Gambia—Music—History and criticism. 3. Music—Gambia—History and criticism.
4. Gambia—Social life and customs. 5. Folklore—Gambia—Performance. I. Title.

ML3760 .E27 2002
781.62'96345—dc21   2001055408

British Library Cataloging-in-Publication Data is available

This book has been composed in Sabon

Printed on acid-free paper ∞

www.pup.princeton.edu

Printed in the United States of America

10 9 8 7 6 5 4 3 2 1

ISBN-13: 978-0-691-07489-4
ISBN-10: 0-691-07489-5

CONTENTS

Where and When I Enter

A convention has marked the opening of ethnographic accounts of the field: the arrival story. More often than not, these stories have posited stable identities for both a Western ethnographer and the "natives" he finds; this difference between the West and its Other provides the window of insight for arrival. Yet my arrival story focuses on a mutual figuring of the field and the identities of those who make the moments of encounter.[1] Here a degree of negotiation over culture and difference takes place. Moreover, this was not my arrival.

In the summer of 1989 I had been in The Gambia for several months, absorbed in the everyday lives of the people in the compound where I lived. I had gone there to learn more about a hereditary group of artisans known in a local language, Mandinka, as *jali*. Jali fill a number of professional roles, including orator, praisesinger, arbiter, political negotiator, matchmaker, genealogist, historian, ceremonial officiator, and entrepreneur. Jali performances of music, however, often assume primacy in current transnational encounters. I had come to The Gambia to study the training jali were expected to undergo to practice their profession, *jaliya*. (*Griot* is a French term for praiseingers, including jali.)

A short visit in 1984 helped me establish the connections that would set the context of the collaborative aspects of my work. Now, five years hence, I had embarked upon a much lengthier stay. Already in the first few months of my research, I had begun to understand social interactions in a society complicated by age, gender, class, ethnicity, and caste differences. These crosscutting, complex social locations were well documented in the literature on the Senegambian region. Yet living there changed my appreciation of the significance of the ways these social categories informed everyday interactions; these categories were no longer mere abstractions that I had encountered in social science accounts, but experiences informing the lives of the people I knew. A few months into my fieldwork I was acutely aware of the difference between the social complexity there and what I was familiar with in the United States.

In the United States, race more often than not takes precedence over other categories in social interactions. Age, gender, class, and national background follow in the wake of the major divide between black and white.[2] This everyday prominence of racial status in the United States contrasted sharply with the multiplicity of social statuses, identities, and languages I found in The Gambia. Furthermore, in the United States I had become used to being perceived as a racial embodiment of subaltern status; strikingly, in Africa, I carried the privilege of status and mobility of my U.S. nationality. To many Gambians, I was an American; to others, my *otherness* appeared as a complicated mystery. Some people assumed I was from southern Africa. This association was commonly made because of the presence of refugees from Namibia, other Others with whom I could easily be categorized. Strikingly, at this time, African Americans were not as familiar to many of the people I met as would later become the case.[3]

Among the many things that fieldwork accomplishes is its providing an occasion to readjust our sense of who we are as we learn to understand different contexts and other ways of constructing personhood. Yet I only appreciated how much my perspective had begun to change when I came face-to-face with African American visitors who reminded me of the ideas and assumptions held by many African Americans about Africa and our relationship to it. Their arrival story provided my moment of insight.

I had gone along with a friend to the airport in Dakar to meet a visitor. The wait took several hours. We sat in the arrival area where, even in the earliest hours of the morning, people milled about. The sun cast rays of dusty light through the windows high above floor level. This gave the waiting area the appearance of an airport hangar: an expansive cave of dim lights and smoky shadows. During this extended period of waiting my mind wandered as I stared out at the passersby; among the things that moved through my consciousness was the question of home and cultural differences.

Sitting down at an airport café, I soon found myself in conversation with three African American men who had come to Senegal as tourists a few weeks earlier, but Africa was not simply a vacation destination for them. The men introduced themselves as "businessmen," not affiliated with a particular company but independent scouts hoping to develop an as-yet-undetermined financial venture with Senegalese entrepreneurs. Initially, I was thrilled to see people from "home." Our conversation was warm and engaging. Slowly, however, I became acutely aware that we were talking past each other, sharing familiar feelings about "home," but not common assumptions about Africa. I realized that my thoughts and their thoughts about Africa differed enormously.

They spoke of Africa and the people they had met with a distant awe, a reverence. Africa was the land of the noblest people. The Senegalese they had only recently met were just amazing, above mortal status. The teachings of U.S. Afrocentric philosophers provided a refrain in my mind that echoed the chorus of praises set off against an Other: "Africans are a spiritual people; Europeans are a materialistic people." Indeed, the travelers expressed their worry that Africa unfortunately lagged behind in material ways. Luckily, they had a solution to the continent's "problems." As businessmen, with a consciousness of course, they would *develop* Africa.

I listened halfheartedly, frankly dubious of their claims. In the previous few months I had somehow muted my awareness of what coming to Africa meant for many African Americans: that juxtaposition between the humble need to learn and connect, a personal quest, and the self-assured desire to be of some assistance, however vague, though seemingly altruistic, that purposefulness might be. On the one hand, African Americans know Africa through the imagery of underdevelopment. Like other Americans, we grew up with various aid campaigns directed toward Africa. The advertisements of international donor agencies such as CARE and Save the Children framed our sense of Africa.

On the other hand, the continent represented more for Africans in diaspora. This "homeland," largely an imagined Africa, created a seemingly timeless sense of connection for many of its long displaced kin. When confronted with contemporary Africa, a compression of time and space occurs where the lives of present-day Africans are blocked out by the overwhelming desire to search for lost kinship ties and belonging. Connection with Africa, it is hoped, will heal the physical and psychological rift created by our departure centuries ago.[4] For many African Americans, Africa was imagined as a potently mythic space of meaning that could embody a fullness absent in the present. But this longing often had little space in which to take in the expanse of present day Africa in all its complexities.

My sense of this "Africa" had been reworked by my interactions with Gambian interlocutors. Some of the Gambians I met were sympathetic to diasporic yearnings, while others, as I suggested earlier, had no notion of the transatlantic slave trade or even of the existence of "African Americans."[5] Still others expressed hostile sentiments: "African Americans were nothing but the slaves of Africans," quipped one Gambian. In this setting, I could not naturalize African American dreams; they suddenly seemed quite exotic.

In our brief conversation, the tourists/entrepreneurs were impressed by my relatively long stay in The Gambia, which seemed to them to indicate deep commitment on my part, particularly when compared to their visit of a few weeks. Yet when they asked me about my work, I sat nervously preparing my defenses. Given my own immersion in the debates about anthropology's history, I thought they would be horrified to hear that I was an anthropologist. From within the discipline, everything about anthropology seemed wrapped up in an intense identity crisis. My training had been absorbed with the dilemmas of reproducing ethnographic stereotypes of non-Western peoples even as one might try to portray people sympathetically. Anthropology, as the recent critiques had urged us to be aware, was intimately tied up with colonial projects.

Yet I should not have worried about these issues in this context. For these African American visitors, my work was immensely important. They believed that as an anthropologist I could offer further accounts of authentic ties of African Americans to the African homeland. After all, wasn't a central part of the anthropologist's task to trace genealogies, to understand a common kinship? To the world at large, this is one of the images of what social anthropologists do. And as I sat bracing for their criticism, I soon learned that they had found Alex Haley's (1976) influential book and television docu-drama, *Roots*, deeply inspiring. They suggested that I, like Haley, could extend a sense of family and kin ties that persisted across the Atlantic against incredible odds.[6]

In part it had been Haley's work that had led me to want to better understand the connections forged between Africans and African Americans. Thus I appreciated the enthusiasm of my compatriots around *Roots*. But I also wanted to know more about the extended contexts in which *Roots* played a part and its significance to a range of audiences. Specifically, I was interested in the transnational context of interaction that enabled both the imagined and material connections between Africa and the diaspora to come to life. I was also interested in the ways that this culture of interconnection was being made into a commodity, and I wondered how the discourse surrounding culture, generated in a peripheral place in Africa, placed The Gambia, one of the smallest countries on the continent, in an international consciousness. What were the implications of this placing for the recasting of ideas about local culture and global processes?

The airport encounter reminded me of deeply held African American commitments to particular visions of "Africa." But it also suggested the need to understand the discursive constructions of Africa within a matrix of visions and encounters in which Gambians could also play a part. In the unfolding of our conversation, the tourists generated powerful images: underdevelopment, home, authentic culture, noble people. Upon reflection, I could not dismiss them easily. These sentiments were not so distant from those of scholars. Scholars and experts of development generate some of the very images of underdevelopment that informed these tourists. Similarly, those interested in cultural production have helped to generate certain images of culture that the tourists found so compelling. In fact, as I noticed later, much of the research on The Gambia falls into these two general classifications: studies either of development or of aesthetic production. The implications of these points of convergence between scholarly and popular interests in aesthetic and economic concerns suggested a productive framing moment for understanding Africa's place within a set of complex projects and debates, not only among African Americans but also within the broader international knowledge industry.

The airport encounter left me with a keen awareness of the role of representation in shaping perceptions of Africa held by those not from the continent. The representations held by African American homeland seekers and by European and Anglo-American lovers of the exotic, brush up against and overlap with those of development experts, journalists, art critics, and, of course, anthropologists. Representations also played an important role in informing the perceptions and receptions of me and others by my Gambian interlocutors. I gained an appreciation of the encounter as offering a series of performative moments in which the ways we had all been "framed" would come into view.

Faced with divergent understandings of Africa and the West, I was pressed to explain my position, to tell it dramatically—indeed, to "perform" it. In turn, my Gambian interlocutors performed their own "African" sensibilities in describing what they saw. Such performances of "Africa" can be appreciated most acutely when pressed up against alternatives and into negotiations. My anthropological work since has tried to address the challenge posed by the place of The Gambia and Africa within multiple imaginative projects. I hope that by opening a dialogue in which we observe the play of multiple agendas at work, we are able to see the way that Africa, and more specifically The Gambia, comes to signify in world politics.

This book is based on a year of field research in The Gambia in 1989 and 1990 and a follow-up visit in 1994. During this period I conducted formal interviews with twenty-nine jali who resided in urban, suburban, and rural areas. I also spoke with other Gambians, formally and informally, devoting my time particularly to patrons, their jali dependents, and the dependents of jali. I also tried to find my way among social groups who had diverse opinions about jali, who, if they were not tied in any capacity to jali or their patrons, were apt to express their ambivalence about jali presence.[7] I attended concerts and learned through careful observation. With the assistance of informed concert goers, I learned something about the aesthetic considerations important to Gambian patrons and performers. Inspired by the attentive enthusiasm and curiosity of my research assistant, Ms. Mariama Jammeh, we learned to accommodate our overlapping and divergent interests in jaliya and still be brave enough to face the next interview (see chapter 5). I used the resources at the Gambian National Archives in Banjul and explored the materials collected in the Oral History and Antiquities Division to become familiar with a range of locally collected materials available on The Gambia.

My research also continued in a number of contexts after my return to the United States. I attended international concerts held in the United States and held informal conversations with people from Africa, both performers and nonperformers, currently living in the United States. Thus I continued to trace the travel of jaliya and its caretakers through promoters and consumers. The central questions explored in this study are: How is Africa produced, circulated, and consumed through performance? How do performance encounters create the place of Africa in the world?

Initially, I imagined my place among jali as a loosely formed apprenticeship. During my earlier visit I had begun to learn to play the *kora*, an instrument sometimes described as a "harp." It is one of the two most important instruments now associated with the Mandinka jali tradition. (The second instrument is the *balaphon*, which resembles the xylophone.) Kora playing is restricted to Mandinka men; women jali sing and play a metal bar called the *neo*, or tap the side of the kora to provide rhythm. During my first visit I studied with a teacher six to eight hours every day, much like a male pupil. My teacher and I sat in the company of his friends and clients, men who during the day-long period of instruction generally went about their business, occasionally interrupting to comment on my practice. At the end of a month, I traveled to my teacher's village and played for the village head and residents. They graciously accepted the foreigner's awkward attempts to play the kora.

Upon my return, I imagined pursuing my project by continuing music lessons. The idea of studying music formally, however, soon dissipated for several reasons that only became clearer in hindsight. I had not fully considered the weight of responsibility one was expected to assume in order to fulfill a notion of apprenticeship during this much longer research period. The relationship between student and teacher in the Gambian context is based upon more than just going for an hour of musical instruction once a week as is the common practice in the United States. Yet to pursue the research project I had in mind, it was necessary that I interview a range of jali. Thus my allegiance to a single teacher would be called into question as I moved about interviewing a number of jali. I also chose to live in a compound of people who were not jali. This decision had the advantage of providing a range of perspectives on the significance of jali as representatives of The Gambia by those not intimately tied to them as practitioners or patrons.

I was also struck during this second visit by what it meant to be a woman learning an instrument played exclusively by men. Although I assumed that gender would be an issue because men jali are associated with instruments and women jali with singing, I had not fully anticipated the degree to which gender played a part around issues of mobility, reputation, and access to performances. For instance, jali wives did not always attend the performances of their husbands. And while I initially thought that I might draw upon the "honorary male privilege" that many Western women researchers have reported as an advantage of their nonlocal status in non-Western settings, I did not want to assume this role throughout my fieldwork. Given my interest not only in music but also in the ways that performance entered the structure and dynamics of social life, it seemed inappropriate for me to spend hours in the company of men as I had done during the previous visit, following them to their performance events while at the same time rejecting the proper training given to women.

This decision led me to better understand the centrality of gender in creating the kinds of access to knowledge that made the difference between men and women researchers, as well as men and women jali. I listened to repeated stories about another woman researcher who had taken male privilege to learn an instrument. I found it disconcerting to hear the comments made about her.[8] Her notoriety was based reportedly on being pushy, aggressive, obnoxious, and acting inappropriately; some said she would do anything to reach her goal. Properly socialized local women, my informants' comments suggested, were not like that.

At the level of perceptions about what women should be doing, I felt that I had been warned about what people thought of women out of place. In addition, my research took place during a moment when foreign women were seen as having come to The Gambia in search of sexual partners. People constantly spoke to me of women travelers from the global North who, according to Gambian standards of respectability, had little sense of propriety and social decorum (see chapter 6). I soon decided that I could not present myself as a "male" apprentice; to keep a sense of my respect within the Gambian context, I would have to behave more like a "proper" woman. This limited my apprenticeship options. Women jali learn their trade from close family members, particularly mothers, aunts, and husbands. Yet these negotiations and decisions about my place while conducting the research not only provided certain restrictions but also allowed for other possibilities that would not have been available had I been perceived as attached to a single teacher.

Instead of learning about jali training from the "inside," I decided to work on jali interactions with others. I gave up the prospect of the "intimate" portraits I had first imagined (furthermore, a number of other researchers had meanwhile produced these kinds of portraits) to focus on the social practices and rhetoric through which jaliya operated. Jali are professional performers, and their job is also to make others perform. They move their patrons to action and urge them to perform their roles as patrons. Similarly, in relation to the tourist industry, many jali see their job as moving their audiences into an appreciation of African history and culture. And their audiences must also perform properly. The inter-caste and inter-group rhetoric of jaliya is thus a key aspect of its imagined effectiveness. In taking up this study, then, I did not abandon my interest in the making of social categories and processes; instead, I approached this issue from an angle that proved more informative in several ways.

First, in not being able to take gender and status for granted, my project required that I be self-conscious about my own performances of status even as I was being retrained by the jali with whom I interacted. Many of the "intimate" insider accounts of jaliya told by musicologists were told by men who could naturalize the travel, mobility, and relative flexibility generally accorded men. Portraying their jali informants mainly as talented performers, they erase the making of insider and outsider, that is, those with access to specialized jali knowledge and those who, instead, must be moved to appropriate action. Yet this is the central premise of jaliya.

Second, the conditions of my research pressed me to appreciate the blurred border between formal performance and the performance of everyday life. Reminded daily of the lines that divide age groups, men and women, social classes, jali and patron, Gambian and foreigner, I did not imagine a homogeneous community in which the performance of difference became irrelevant. Instead, I saw the ways in which jali as professional performers taught their interlocutors how to perform gender, status, ethnicity, and national difference. These lessons occurred not only in formal performances and ceremonies but also in commonplace, everyday interactions.

One of the most striking arenas for considering this issue turned out to be my interviews with jali (see chapter 5). Jali used interviews as performance spaces in which to tell not only of their professional talents but also of the gender and caste considerations that at least ideologically consign them to their social role as jali. Some jali prevailed upon me and my assistant, Ms. Jammeh, to treat them as proper patrons should, that is, with generosity and by creating opportunities. They made me self-conscious about my own performances as a researcher, and, indeed, about the performative nature of describing cultural difference. This then became a central theme of my research.

Gambians pressed me to reflect on race as well as gender, class, and caste status as performance. Among my small group of interlocutors in the compound where I lived, Gambians reenacted notions of who they thought African Americans were. Beyond my interactions with jali, I became the audience for a number of performances offered by my Gambian friends who reenacted images they had drawn from Hollywood films depicting African Americans. They had memorized lines and scripted gestures that portrayed African American men as tough gangsters always ready with a gun. Because of my immersion in reflexive anthropology, I had thought a great deal about Western stereotypes of Africans; I had thought much less, however, about African stereotypes of Americans: many of these images would come from the movies. Just as African Americans' sense of Africa is formed within powerful media-generated images, so, too, in The Gambia, African Americans are represented in media genres to which Gambians had access, and thus most often seen in negative ways.[9] Indeed, what was particularly striking was how my Gambian "performers" convincingly enacted the bodily gestures and voices of violent gun-slinging thugs and criminals.[10] In another representation, they mimicked pop music icons Michael and Janet Jackson and singer Neneh Cherry, performing their songs and copying their styles. Thus, performance was the medium through which cultural difference was assimilated and understood.

In writing about representations and performances of "Africa" that form the analytic frame of this ethnography, I look for the cultural interactions that characterize their mutual interruptions and I trace the histories that emerge from these cultural dynamics. I situate my work not only within anthropology but also within the interdisciplinary relationships among African studies, African American studies, cultural studies, and feminist studies. The commitment to both contribute to and at the same time interrupt different bodies of scholarship through an interdisciplinary approach is one of the most significant achievements of area studies and cultural studies.

I am in debt to the legacy that has made a path to this point. I have entitled this overture "Where and When I Enter," a twist of the title of an influential moment in the history of black women in the United States. The book *When and Where I Enter* by Paula Giddings (1981) was inspired by the work of Anna Julia Cooper, an African American feminist important during the first wave of feminism. I invoke the phrase here to mark the importance of this legacy for my work in its insistence on seeing the multiple influences and contingencies that make social histories and theories possible.

Acknowledgments

This project has developed in a number of important interactions. Recounting the list of institutions and names of individuals is a praise poem, for it is to each of these that I owe a great deal of gratitude. First, to Mr. B. K. Sidibe who took an interest in the project and suggested paths to follow when I began; this proved to be tremendously helpful. He was enormously generous in answering my often culturally bound queries as well as suggesting the names of jali who might contribute to the project. His appreciation of jali traditions made him an important ally in a project that sought to critically engage the work of jali. Mr. Sidibe also introduced me to my closest interlocutor, Ms. Mariama Jammeh, a research assistant with unfailing perseverance and enthusiasm for pursuing every lead. Ms. Jammeh and I approached the project with somewhat different aims. In the context of conducting interviews she and I negotiated these differences in a manner that allowed the two approaches to complement each other. But she and I also relied on the agreement of a number of jali, and it is to them—the jali interviewed here, who spent their time during the project reflecting on their profession—that I express my greatest appreciation. Without this engagement, the project could not have come into existence. I hope that my portrayals of jali bring to life the individual as well as collective personalities that make them compelling respondents.

To the jali who were particularly helpful I extend my sincere appreciation for their interest in the project: Jali Maudo Suso, Jali musaloo Funee Kuyateh, Jali musaloo Nano Sakiliba, Jali Papa Suso, Jali musaloo Aminata Suso, Jali Bunka Suso, Jali musaloo Sarjo Jobarteh, Jali Dembo Konte, Jali musaloo Kumba Suso, Jali Malimin Jobarteh, Jali Tata Dindining, Jaliba Kuyateh, Jali YanKuba Saho, Jali Nyama Suso, Kuyateh, Jali Sheriff Jobarteh.

A number of institutions have supported the research and related aspects associated with this project. These include the Wenner Gren Foundation, which provided the support for field research. In other capacities, Reed College, the Rockefeller Foundation, the African Humanities Center at Northwestern University, the Ford Foundation, and the Center for Cultural Studies at the University of California, Santa Cruz, by providing stimulating intellectual environments, allowed me to develop this project in more extensive ways. A summer seminar at the School of Criticism and Theory also contributed to my thinking. I also pursued this project during my fellowships at the Stanford Humanities Center and, more recently, the National Humanities Center, where colleagues fueled ideas that wonderfully exceeded the contours of my area of pursuit.

Each of these institutional settings introduced me to particular individuals who generated the kind of thoughtful engagement that, if we've chosen this life, we all hope to find. At the University of Massachusetts and Five Colleges in Amherst, Massachusetts: Ralph Faulkingham, Sandra, Morgen, John Cole, and Frank Holmquist. The Department of Cultural and Social Anthropology at Stanford University: Sylvia Yanagisako, Renato Rosaldo, Akhil Gupta, Carol Delaney, Miyako Inoue, Joan Fujimura, Purnima Mankekar, Ian Hodder, James Gibbs, George Collier, and Jane Collier, and, outside of the department: Harry Elam, John Rickford,

Kennell Jackson, Michael Shanks, Mary Pratt, Richard Roberts, Lucía de Sa, and Claire Fox. At African Humanities Center at Northwestern University: Ivan Karp, David William Cohen, Tejumola Olaniyan, Corinne Kratz, the late Kofi Agawu, and Adam Ashforth. Karen Hansen, Paul Berliner, Margaret Drewel, and Jane Guyer provided insightful comments during a subsequent visit. In and beyond UC Santa Cruz, James Clifford, Carolyn Martin-Shaw, Deborah Klein, and Hayden White have lent incredible support to my work. I am grateful to Gabrielle Hecht and Susan Cahn, whom I met at the Stanford Humanities Center. Finally, my colleagues at the National Humanities Center urged *Performing Africa* out the door and into the world: Bruce Grant, Kate Lowe, Deidre Lynch, and Thomas Keirstead.

Friends and colleagues have been there throughout the process of *Performing Africa*'s life: Margaret Cerullo, Kathryn Chetkovich, Marla Erlien, G. Jack Ferguson, Karen Gaul, Frank Holmquist, Mary Hoyer, Pamela Kangas, Ann Kingsolver, Donald S. Moore, Mary Orgel, Elizabeth Pollman, Lisa Rofel, Mitziko Sawada, Anna Tsing, Pat Vidal, E. Frances White, and Nano Sakiliba. Much appreciation, too, to the students in my undergraduate seminars at Reed College and Stanford, and to the graduate students in the Department of Cultural and Social Anthropology, the Program in Modern Thought and Literature, and the School of Education at Stanford.

My research associate, Ms. Mariama Jammeh, deserves a much lengthier expression of appreciation. Mariama Jammeh was essential in brokering and negotiating the interviews with jali; her enthusiasm and insight lent a great deal to the direction of my research. Furthermore, her sincere commitment to "wearing down jali until they offered the truth" was not easy.

I regret to say that it is no longer possible to consult Ms. Jammeh, for she died unexpectedly a few years following the research. The absence of Ms. Jammeh is a striking reminder of how difficult it is to capture the irony and sense of humor she maintained throughout the research project. Soon after our interview sessions began, Ms. Jammeh brought her own questions and concerns to the jali, for many of their activities were an enigma to her. She saw the interviews as both an opportunity to pose questions to jali and a way to open a world shrouded in mystery and intrigue. Throughout the process, she retained her sense of enchantment; even our worst frustrations did not wear her down. When certain interviewees were particularly difficult, she pushed on. She explained her role in a memo she wrote to me: "The interviewer should be the person who understands human nature, i.e., he or she can coax the jali to give them correct information on the topic being discussed. There is no need to force them but one can win them over through simple arguments like I used to do." As she posed particular questions persistently in search of an answer to adroit jali, I was reminded of the ways that knowledge and secrecy take on particular significance in West Africa (Bellman 1984). But Ms. Jammeh continued undaunted. When she felt frustrated, she often pushed herself harder: "I will get the truth out of these jali."

No longer here to participate in the actual process of the reconsideration of the materials we collected, Ms. Jammeh still speaks to me through her writings—critical reflections on her role as an interviewer and as a transcriber. Her short text notes, on occasions when she thought the literal translation missed the larger significance of the term, still bring alive her presence. Thus I hear her spirit in what she wrote to me about her learning about jaliya: "Indeed I gained a lot of experience from these interviews that I conducted with the jali because I now know most of their roles in society apart from the ceremonies they attended."

In a paradoxical reflection on the hazards of the job, she half jokingly reminded me of the meaning of the research to her. She wrote that the research "taught me my duties towards [jali], and I came to know a lot of them which is a big burden on my shoulders. I should always expect songs of praise when I meet up with them, which was due to my boss. Therefore I should always keep some money with me when going out because I am likely to meet up with them." Mariama was a most generous person before meeting jali, and now her resources would have to stretch to include a number of other people. All the praisesingers remarked on her generosity and kind spirit. I add my praises to theirs.

PERFORMING AFRICA

Performing Africa

Performance!—a ubiquitous term that currently is mapped onto disparate social worlds as if it were transcendent, its meaning immediately apparent. Yet the social life of performance as a concept is worth unraveling to track its significance in creating distinctive regions and different subjects. There is no better place to explore the contours of performance as an idea and as practice than in the context of *Africa*, which has been made into an object through a number of performative tropes. This work examines the ways performance becomes a frame of *enactment*, creating moments of "Africa" not just *in* Africa but, most significantly, in the performance *of* Africa for wide-ranging audiences. West African cultural aficionados, world music enthusiasts, policy makers, performers, social scientists, journalists, media spectators, and tourists all help form and contest notions of Africa through the idea of performance.

In this book, I use performance as a mode of inquiry on several different levels: first, in the analysis of formal events in which artists "perform" for audiences; second, in informal contexts in which one can observe the enactment of social categories; and third, as a way in which to analyze scholarly modes of inquiry. This last lens allows me to track the ways that notions about performance have framed Africa as an object, and to look at how ideas and categories surrounding performance produce particular effects. Throughout this book I ask how performance "works" to produce what one of my Gambian interlocutors humorously referred to as "The Africa," a term that collectivizes Africa and marks the importance of representations that fix the continent as a homogeneous object. The continent becomes an object of significance in various local and global contexts. Performance and the politics of culture-making come together to inform one another's ability to exist.

My analysis of the significance of the notion of performance with regard to Africa necessitates moving within but also beyond the customary referents of performance to analyze how performance itself becomes a relevant category for representing "Africa." To explore the implications of performance as social encounter and practice, as well as its significance as an ideological construct, I discuss these processes simultaneously. One can trace the contexts in which "performances," in the formal sense, occur. Yet I am also compelled to investigate the creation of the very categories that lend themselves in support of these imaginings of Africa. The focus on category making in the productive act of generating notions of "culture" allows one to observe how Africa becomes a significant site in the performance of place in a global context. Here, at the center of my discussion of Africa and performance, I focus my questions on a cluster of terms—representation, culture, modernity and development, and globalization—all of which are worth critical engagement in their travel itineraries as general concepts, and in the ways that they "capture" Africa in various discourses.

These terms have emerged in this study as categories initially inspired by the work of Edward Said in *Orientalism* (1978). Said critically engaged questions surrounding Western hegemony and the capability of *the West* to represent *the Other* through discourses of difference. His work turned the course of discussion about the significance of the non-West to the West toward the relationship of power to knowledge.[1] Similarly, V. Y. Mudimbe's *Invention of Africa* (1988) also became a critical work, particularly as it addressed the question of colonialism in Africa and the collaborative production of cultural knowledge by "natives" and administrators in sub-Saharan Africa.[2] These analyses of the interworkings of colonial culture deeply influence my thinking with regard to cultural formations and a cosmopolitan imagination. The project for an anthropologist, at least as I find myself, is one of combining a range of disciplinary procedures that are both philosophical—like these—yet also embedded in the encounters of fieldwork.

The Stage

Africa often enters a global imagination through news accounts of ethnic wars, famine, and unstable political regimes. Indeed, the image of "The Coming Anarchy," to invoke the title of Robert Kaplan's (1994) now-famous article on global unrest and nation-state conflict, fits a repetitive trope of media images that frame many of the stories told about African nations. Headlines announce, "Sierra Leonian Rebels Kidnap Peace Keepers and Children," "Rebel Leaders Take Hold of Ivory Coast," "AIDS in Africa Will Mount to Devastating Proportions in The Near Future." The repetitive refrain—signaling a cycle of destruction and unrest—encircles sub-Saharan Africa like a swarm of bad omens that, more often than not, fails to distinguish national differences or historical moment. Indeed, Africa is often portrayed as a timeless story of tribal rivalries, intended to invoke in the minds of its spectators the premodern. The noises from the media resonate in representations already part of an older legacy, a history that marks its place in the colonial era and the justifications of Western administrative regimes that see their way through to postcolonial dependencies. The discord draws us deeper into the present as it resounds with contemporary international anxiety about the New World Order.

The dystopic images of war, famine, and regional political strife in Africa may seem pervasive, and they do dominate at a significant level.[3] At the same time, counter-representations exist—images created by various communities, whose constituencies are also more often than not beyond the borders of the continent. Proponents of an alternative view often generate their imaginings through their enthusiasm for African culture. Africa, in this imagined geography, is expressive culture. Africa is evocative, disruptive. It is the noise of the outsider continent, the recalcitrant space, the resistant thorn that pricks the sides of the West in its refusal to embrace "the modern project." Proponents of this vision suggest that it is not that Africa cannot meet the challenge of modernity, but that it consciously resists the corrupting influences of the West. Africa becomes a countermove, a trickster, a hero figure that can combat the disaffected sentiments of the iron cage of modernity (an image so famously evoked by Weber). Where the first set of dystopic media images offers a deep sense of death, chaos, violence, and despair, the second set of representations attempts a recuperative spirit, with constituents seeking to reclaim "African" culture as a potent countervision to the hegemony of the West and its efforts to totalize its reach. In this vein, social scientists use Africa as a critique of modernity (Comaroff and Comaroff 1998; Hecht and Simone 1994). Cultural nationalists in the African diaspora as well as world culture enthusiasts adopt the continent for its ability to sustain their own oppositional version to the ill effects of "Western" culture (Asante 1987; Karenga 1982). Culturalists interested in embodied moments of experience join in this second instance, too, as proponents search for something beyond modern anomie—something that appears authentic and sensually alive (see, for example, Thompson 1983). These rather different projects, with somewhat divergent aims, share in an effort to generate a utopian vision meant to counter the despairing scenes of the mass media.

These global representations, whether made by cynical media imagers or sympathizers of the plight faced by most African countries, play a key role in keeping Africa on the global stage. Much of the rhetoric surrounding globalization as a success story cannot extend its reach to include the countries found in sub-Saharan Africa. Strikingly, stories of Africa, and the issues that continually plague national and regional governments, are generally left out of debates about globalization and transnationalization. For too many, Africa has not yet achieved the status that warrants consideration within most global discussions (Paolini 1997;

Piot 1999; Sawyer 1999). And still for others, Africa creates a different kind of transnational encounter, one that economic specialists rarely care to notice.

Africa's presence is strongly apparent in the cultural encounters formed by the African diaspora, ties created by the earlier traffic in people and goods of the Atlantic slave trade (Gilroy 1993). Post–slave trade African migrant histories are just emerging as part of the conversation; considerably less attention has been paid to the travels of contemporary Africans.[4] Those in the diaspora, along with other consumers of world cultural products, create two significant venues that enable the continent to enter international debates where both culture and economy are important issues—even as their interplay often goes unrecognized. For just as those interested in economic development ignore culture, so too its converse: those interested in the cultural links between the continent and its diaspora often neglect the place of economic disparities and national political differences that divide diasporic communities and most people in Africa.

This book focuses on the place of Africa in wide-ranging debates over the significance of the continent. To do so is to ask about the overlapping interests that have helped create "The Africa" as an object. The questions posed in each chapter are also intimately tied to debates within anthropology and social analysis. While historical conjunctures of political economy and social history helped create an object I refer to as "The Africa," I explicitly acknowledge the interface between the social sciences and the humanities, and between policy debates and aesthetics, by showing their overlapping moments and how performance is embedded within these moments. These connections have generated a number of confluences that I recognize and reflect upon to provide a stage for a dialogue between African area studies and social theory.

Theories frame—indeed, create—regions differently (Fardon 1985; Said 1983; Appadurai 1988). Theories give regions identities and make them into objects. But we are required to do more than identify regional stereotypes; we must also consider the translation of theory in its regional encounters. The discussion of traveling theory and its discontents has stimulated an important dialogue between cultural studies and area studies (e.g., Karp 1997; Wolff 1995). Traveling theories are transformed within particular regions; regions remake theories just as theories help configure regions. As critical social analysts we are pressed to combine ideology critique and ethnographic narrative. This requires tacking back and forth between groundedness and generalization (Comaroff and Comaroff 1992).

Sometimes fragmentary and unusual deployments of theory usefully disrupt conventional associations, illuminating both strengths and limitations of the encounter between region and theory. In the next section of this introduction, I try one such experiment with Africa and performance. What if we were to cross the abyss separating studies of development and the arts to ask how development is itself performative? In this spirit, I replay a meeting between staff members of the World Bank and government officials from an African country to show its performative nature. What has development got to do with aesthetics? In order to see how certain tropes have come to define Africa in global conversations we must engage the categories that have helped to constitute the continent. Africa, I argue, comes into existence through the multiply inscribed projects that together keep it as a subject of debate in international arenas.

Other African studies scholars have turned to performance as a way of tracking the response of Africans to the effects of international policy. Performance is thought to provide a sense of hope and the possibility for the powerless to speak back, indeed, to act out, in response to the West. Yet it is imperative, I argue, to see performance as more than a *response* to power; power is performative. Elites and bureaucrats are also performers, and the full stage includes high players as well as low. To see the performative nature of power is not to trivialize power but to see how it works. Power is effective when people are enrolled in the rhetorics, the stances, and the subject positions of its projects. Through these performances, subjects take up social statuses in the world.

Act I: Development Drama

In an early segment of the video *Our Friends at the Bank* (Chapell 1997), development experts discuss the fate of Africa's prospects for development aid given the relative lack of success of the World Bank and the International Monetary Fund (IMF) in shaping successful economic futures for many African countries. We learn, while listening to the solemn tone of the narrator's voice, that over a third of the Bank's projects in sub-Saharan Africa have failed. Now, with most countries suffering under enormous debt and extensive loans, the experts wonder what new course of action should be pursued. One of these experts, Jim Adams, remarks, "In a new changed world the Bank is looking for social programs." Yet, the bid for "social programs" is more than a straightforward proposal. Indeed, what constitutes a viable social program, from the point of view of national governments or from the point of view of international lenders, remains the subject of intense negotiation.

Shortly after this segment, a few people, seen emerging from an elevator, momentarily appear to search for direction: Conference Room 077. The video narrator introduces the Ugandan minister of finance, Mr.

Joshua Mayanja-Nkangi, who has arrived to meet with Bank representatives. Mr. Mayanja-Nkangi is prudently dressed in a dark suit and is joined by a few other serious looking colleagues. We are told that the delegation is there to ask for a loan of four hundred million dollars to rebuild Uganda's road system. Later, the critical issue at hand is explained in greater detail. Ugandan officials are faced with the problem of border encroachment by an enemy aggressor. The northern area of the country is threatened by rebel troops, putting the sovereignty of the nation at risk. Yet the Bank's donors seem to have little sympathy for this particular issue because the new agenda of the Bank strongly urges support of programs that will encourage democratization in a supposed effort to further the course of modernization.

Mr. Mayanja-Nkangi and his group walk through a long passageway between a row of office cubicles. For a moment we are given a glimpse of the hive-like nature and the enormous scale of a bureaucratic organization such as the World Bank. The members of the Ugandan team soon make their way to an open space where Bank representatives await their arrival. We are introduced to Jim Jacox, vice president of the Africa bureau and the person who controls the international development support for Africa that is channeled through the Bank. A tall and imposing figure, Jacox makes his way down the line of Ugandan representatives, shaking hands and offering welcoming comments: "Very good to see you . . . ." On the other side of the table, Jim Adams, head of the East Africa department, stands silently along with several other participants not yet identified. The foreign experts are in attentive presence.

After initial greetings, Jacox walks around the long table to reach his seat. In his hand he carries a stack of papers that he places on the table in front of him, symmetrically aligned with the documents displayed in front of each of the participants on either side of him. His team is ready; the bureaucratic regiment is in place. Jacox is positioned at the center of the table. He pulls out his chair. To Jacox's right sits Jim Adams, the right-hand man. In these opening moments we are introduced to the two sides of this encounter, two positions across several divides, teams that reenact familiar global divides: North/South; modern/developing; world lender/ Third World recipient; interrogator/defendant.

The team of Bank representatives sits poised with their typed papers in hand, all appearing to be neatly cued for the discussion that is about to begin. The Ugandan team, in contrast, is shown with fewer members; a stray coffee cup, pens, and blank yellow pads distinguish their team's appearance. The Ugandan team members are ready to take notes, to receive the edicts of the Bank representatives. A few moments pass with another exchange of cordial greetings that serves as a prelude to the formal discussion.

JIM JACOX: It's a pleasure to see you here in Washington.

MINISTER MAYANJA-NKANGI: Thank you so much for meeting with us. In Uganda . . . but we've had a long meeting with him [pointing to Adams, seated next to Jacox. Throughout the meeting Adams remains a silent observer] for about two hours, I think. So I thought he should brief you and then if anything you want to ask . . .

JIM JACOX: [interrupting] It's funny—you keep attracting these guys back to, ah, work on Uganda. [In the middle of the comment there is nervous laughter by the minister.]

[Move to formal discussion.]

JIM JACOX: [With a commanding presence of one who is in charge, he sits with his pen raised in his right hand and holds on to an upturned page with his left. His hand gestures throughout add important emphasis to the points conveyed.] Look, the way this has been reported to me is not so much that you all are pro-, you know, have a high priority for infrastructure. But that you have a negative priority for some of the other stuff that, uh, we've been involved with for a long time. For instance, primary schooling and basic health and that line. Is that correct?

MINISTER MAYANJA-NKANGI: [with a restrained manner and with deference in his voice] No sir, I think if one is forced—is it infrastructure now, roads, or primary schools, primary education, if it is either or—then we'd probably say at this juncture, we'd say let's have roads first.

JIM JACOX: It's not a question of primary school or secondary, tertiary, vocational. It's a question of the balance always [the minister remarks, "Okay."] and, uh, we need to discuss this because, you know, the ways we look at it the kids aren't getting educated. You've got a health problem in Uganda. It's very, very serious. [A single confirmation from Adams, "Right."] We got a, uh, the feeder roads are not being maintained. I mean if this were all happening. . . . [The minister is shown shaking his head.] It's a question of balance. But these are the sort of development issues.

MINISTER MAYANJA-NKANGI: [looks down and appears exasperated by the comments] Now [brief pause], you see, instead of pushing one area, possibly to the material neglect of the other, we should try and push them together. That's necessary, particularly from the point of view of potential growth in the economy. We've found, as a matter of experience now, that however number of schools, take primary schools, learning to read the Bible and local newspapers, that will not help us to take off. We can go on

growing coffee, but that won't help us really to move into the
secondary phase of, you know, of development.

JIM JACOX: [holding papers with both hands, giving a sense of the
importance of his role and his official status in this negotiation—
the man in charge] No, you can't go to the other side without a
base. I'm saying, if the people don't know how to read or count
and add and subtract, they're not going to be able to engage in
the modern age. That's all there is to it. That's my going in position. [The minister interjects, "I agree with you."] And I've got a
stack of evidence [showing the papers], and you're going to have
to overcome this evidence if you're going to win this argument.

This all-too-familiar script is typically associated with gatherings of this
kind. The meeting follows the protocol of a bureaucratic encounter well
known to the officials of many Third World countries. Its formal structure
and repetitive reenactment of official business raises the specter of a theatrical performance, a dramatic enactment of cultural practices, complete
with actors who restage the drama of development aid negotiations. The
position of powerful Northern countries shown in this formal meeting
with the African officials gives the illusory sense that the experts are
merely suggesting the terms to which the hopeful recipient country must
concede for it to secure development aid. The idea that the terms of these
negotiations are merely meant as suggestions, however, is telling; we are
left to wonder what form of aid the country might receive if they choose
not to go along with the "suggestion." The powerful Northern Bank representatives meet with the hopeful beneficiaries of these negotiations. Yet
the Southern representatives, virtually at the mercy of international donor
agencies, are well practiced in the performance of their subordinate differences, and have no doubt or uncertainty about what the international
plan might be; into what shape the country must work itself is the question they must contemplate.Meanwhile, the international experts must
also allow the whims of Southern elites if they want the North to have any
allies. I interpret these moments as well-rehearsed, performed positions.

The actors on both sides are part of a role-play that positions them
in complementary niches. The Northern Bank representatives, experts on
Africa, expect to be helpful, even if perceived as paternal advisors to "un-
developed" countries; they become the representatives of development, a
kind of extension of a social service–like industry. The clients are Southern
elites who become agents for their national constituency but must, at the
same time, be concerned with the question of how they can shore up their
own political positions. The Bank experts face the loss of their appoint-
ments if they cannot successfully interface with Southern political leaders.
The Southern political leaders lose their mandate and ministerial appoint-

ments if they do not obtain international development funds by working smoothly with the foreign experts. Both sides have everything to gain by recognizing each other with all the ritual formality and respect that their mutual survival requires.

This is a performance, then, because it is a self-conscious exercise in reproducing status distinctions by mutual ceremonial recognition. *Our Friends at the Bank* effectively reenacts the drama of global economic politics as Third World nation-states and international donor organizations interact—each represented by performance-honed specialists, who parlay about the needs of the developing world. The video provides an evocative moment of the theater of development negotiations, an opening that highlights the central themes and overlapping contours of my discussion: Africa as a site of performance in global debates about the significance of the continent, where culture and economy are partners.

The use of the idea of performance beyond the descriptive elements observed in the context of formal, recognizable performance (i.e., a concert or ceremony) is crucial. An analysis of the additional performative aspects of social interaction, as they script The Gambia in a global imagination, introduces the political economy of cultural difference.

Intermission

Since you're still getting oriented, the day is not particularly distinguished from other days. You wander down a road, in mid-afternoon in Serrekunda, a large town alive with market stalls and entrepreneurs working deals. This is an urban center just outside the capital, Banjul, in The Gambia. Amid the honk of car horns and roar of truck motors, you pass a compound where a number of elaborately dressed people are gathered. Given how the guests are dressed, you sense that this must be an extremely formal occasion. In the background of the social exchanges, you hear the melodic tones of some sort of stringed instrument. The sounds are not readily familiar, but still they register in your consciousness: What is this? Perhaps a harp, maybe even a lute. The melody is exotic to your untrained ear; the sound includes an unfamiliar scale, perhaps minor notes.[5] This tune could suggest a North African musical influence to the mind's ear.

As you observe from the entryway of the compound, your presence still undetected, you notice a man playing an instrument as strange in appearance as the sound. A large calabash forms the body of the instrument; a long pole is attached that has braided, thong-like, rawhide rings to which the many strings of the instrument are secured. The strings fan out in a parallel, yet slightly asymmetrical, sequence. The musician holds the weight of the instrument with the last two fingers of both hands; he plucks the strings, spread evenly on either side of the pole, with the thumb and the first two fingers of both hands.

To his side, another performer, a woman, stands striking a metal tube with a smaller, spike-like implement, keeping a rhythmic pattern, interrupting and urging along the progression of the song. The woman sings to the accompaniment of the stringed instrument and is joined by her male counterpart. Both performers are marvelously dressed in several meters of damask elaborately embroidered with intricate designs along the neck and cuffs. The music and the atmosphere conspire to make this a magical moment, even as you find yourself struggling over the full meaning of the performance. There must be more to this!

Act II: Performance and Representation

Imagine a debate on the contours of recent cultural criticism that catalyzes the anxieties of academic discussion over the past twenty years. Two issues would be included: representation and performance. My project requires that we read the literatures on representation and performance with and against each other. How do they complement and amplify each other? Where do they interrupt each other? And why are performance and representation so important to understanding contemporary Africa?

Since the precolonial era, Western observers have been fascinated by African performances, and, indeed, often they have looked to these performances for the *essence* of performativity that might even transcend the need to imagine context, history, or discourse.[6] A few performance theorists have even made clear the identification of Africa and performance by using African performance to demonstrate the transcendent analytic power of the term. Scholarship that uses African performance to show what is wrong with Western discursive traditions fits under this concern. The influential film *Reassemblages* (1992) by Trinh Minh-ha (discussed in chapter 1) is a case in point. The filmmaker deliberately refuses to learn the local language or work with a translator so as not to be contaminated by the use of words. Instead she offers a "raw" performative Africa of her desire: dust, rhythm, breasts, flies. In this literature, performance itself becomes a trope representing Africa for an international imagination. Why is it always Africa that dances to the drum's heartbeat? Reading this literature, I am referred back then to the discussion of representation.

The literature on representation reminds us that we have learned to imagine regions through repetitive tropes. "Performance" is one such trope for Africa, and African performance cannot be analyzed without attention to the geopolitical history through which performance has been made "African." Analysts who ignore this set of conventions only repeat its founding moves; within the barrage of sounds and rhythms, we learn only the repetitive idea "Africa." Yet because performance has so often been contrasted with discursive analysis, this observation fits awkwardly into scholarly discussions of representation. The Middle East and South Asia feature prominently in scholarship on representation in part because the written word is so central to how the two regions have been contrasted with the West. As prominent, non-Western, literate "civilizations," they have inspired a legacy of Western writing about non-Western writing. In contrast, to speak of performance as a trope of representation requires a back-and-forth engagement between discursive analysis and attention to performance itself. Performance is a mode through which representation is enacted and negotiated, and this is relevant whether one is studying written texts, oral traditions, or social interactions. Performance brings representation to life.

How can scholarship on performance and representation help us approach these issues? I backtrack here to introduce these fields.

Dilemmas of Representation

It is impossible to practice anthropology today without engaging issues of representation. Once the discipline's practitioners awoke to the ways our most innocent-seeming depictions of diverse cultures and societies followed conventions that stereotyped and exoticized peoples, forcing them into continuous narratives and allegories of difference from Western ideals, anthropology could never be the same. Most anthropologists have given at least some thought to this problem, which has been framed under the rubric "the crisis of representation" (Marcus and Fisher 1986). Yet issues of representation have rarely been brought to bear in the equally influential literature on performance, which also attends to the making of social and cultural "difference." To read across these theoretical fields, it is worth beginning with a brief review of the substance of each.

Representation became a concern as both humanists and social scientists began to ask how Western hegemony was built through normalizing depictions of non-Western people as exotic Others. Edward Said and V. Y. Mudimbe (referred to above) were pioneers in this conversation. Such literary scholars as Gayatri Spivak (1988) and Mary Louise Pratt (1992) asked how European colonialism in particular was propelled in part by depictions of colonized and soon-to-be colonized Others as essentially different from the West. This conversation soon entered anthropology, as scholars began to investigate anthropological conventions for depicting cultural difference.

Johannes Fabian, in what has now become a classic, *Time and the Other* (1983), noted that anthropologists tend to distance the people they study by placing them in a separate temporal schema. The influential volume *Writing Culture*, co-edited by James Clifford and George Marcus (1986), argued that anthropological "poetics" formed a political commentary by telling allegorical stories, positioned in the West, about those who were imagined as Others. Renato Rosaldo (1989) wrote of the useful reconfigurations of the field that followed from taking seriously the insights of the mid-1980s "crisis." Anthropologists now found it possible to position themselves self-consciously and also to experiment with new textual poetics (Tsing 1993).

The excitement of these insights transformed the field (James, Hockey, and Dawson 1997), creating a burst of attention toward the writing of ethnography. Meanwhile, and in addition, historians and historically oriented anthropologists began new readings of the colonial archives, showing the *writing* in the archives as an important feature of colonial administration (Stoler 1995; Dirks 1992; Cohn 1996). Postcolonial development programs were reanalyzed to understand how their categories and their rhetoric, often distinctly removed from the everyday realities around them, helped to create Third World dependency (Escobar 1994; Ferguson 1994). Even well-intentioned activists were open to scrutiny for the representations of difference through which they built their advocacy in the Third World. What are the implications, scholars asked (Schroeder 1999), of their categories? As attention to representation has joined other forms of ethnographic and historical analysis, then, its engagement has increasingly become an essential tool for all cultural and social analysis.

Scholarly attention to representation in cultural analysis naturally draws on the heritage through which it was developed: literary criticism. Its strongest insights involve the careful reading of written texts. The locus of Said's attention is on Orientalist texts. Clifford and Marcus inform us about *writing* in anthropology. Escobar and Ferguson read *documents* about development. These are critical attempts to interrogate the very field in which our research is conducted. Yet these analyses also suggest the exhausted ends to which studies of representation can lead us, as well as the gaps they leave unattended. First, the textual focus of the presentation of dilemmas of representation has sometimes limited it to an armchair management program for correcting texts rather than an analytic strategy for understanding culture. Here the recognition of crisis asks too much of scholars, forcing ethnography away from experience into a priori standards. Second, the dependence on written texts can ignore questions about the enactment of social life, pointing attention to the *reproduction* of social and political statuses without adequate regard for change, agency, and creativity.

Representation, scholars agree, is intertwined with power and can contribute to racism, conquest, and exploitation. As long as the written text is the model for this observation, however, it is also possible to imagine an actively lived social life that is free from the political curses of representation. Some interpreters assume, for example, that behind any representation there is the real or authentic object or experience that is masked by the representation. In this view, if we could only correct the representation, we could make social life transparent without causing political damage. And while this view may suit some reformers, it also invites criticism from those who imagine their representations free from political engagement. By ignoring the ubiquitous political field involved in symbolic process, it allows us to imagine a reformed practice of description that is neutral and objective—the very view that scholars of representation have decisively criticized. Yet such readings of the crisis of representation—positive and negative—have blossomed, in part because of the literary sophistication of many analyses of representation.

The popularity of a turn in the study of representation is augmented by the gaps that studies of representation leave for students of society. Studies of representation that restrict themselves to written texts can lead us to assume that vernacular and unwritten aspects of social life are unaffected by the history of representations. Furthermore, written texts gain a social life of their own in which only authors and conventions of writing influence other authors. The interplay between the written text and the social context of its writing falls outside the scope of analysis. And the cultural processes of the everyday, vernacular use of representations are completely ignored. The ordinary things people do to identify themselves and each other as members of particular social statuses—the very substance of representation—are lost to view.

Where do representations arise? How are they enacted? How do they change? How can they be manipulated, distorted, and transformed? These questions, at the heart of analytic concerns about representation, can only be asked if a dialogue is begun with a scholarly field that has had little contact with the study of representation: performance.

Expanding Performance

History as performance (Pollack 1998; Jackson 2000), performance archaeology (Pearson and Shanks 2001), science as drama (Hilgartner 2000), performance of the everyday (de Certeau 1984), performance of self and identity (Kondo 1997; Rahier 1999), performing gender (Butler

1989)! These are but a few invocations of the terms that attest to its wide-ranging circulation. This interdisciplinary interest in performance reveals that performance has become a fashionable idea of late. Yet performance also has a history in social theory. A consideration of one earlier moment—the late 1950s and 1960s—during which performance approaches blossomed in the United States, contributes to an appreciation of why it has captured the scholarly imagination today. In each case, performance has served as a way for scholars to pursue their concerns with agency in social interaction.

Consider the past use of performance approaches in U.S. anthropology. In the late 1950s and 1960s, analysts began to struggle against the restrictions of a structural functionalism best attuned to understanding the "skeleton" of society—and less well suited to understanding how individuals and groups made use of this skeleton in a flexible manner. This was the period during which social anthropologists turned to the study of social processes and the dynamic features of social organization. Meanwhile, social historians were beginning to draw attention to the role of ordinary people in making history. In this context, Victor Turner introduced an influential performance-based rhetoric for understanding ritual. Social groups enacted their organizational principles through performance. The dramatic enactment of social categories brought social worlds to life for people (Turner 1967, 1969). Turner was influenced in part by the interdisciplinary power of the writings of Erving Goffman, who used performance to illuminate the microdynamics of everyday life (1959): in "total institutions" (1961), in advertising (1976), and beyond. Goffman's work inspired a cohort of anthropologists to see performance in the making and remaking of everyday configurations of power. Fredrik Barth (1969), for example, used a performance approach for the study of ethnic boundaries: ethnic groups performed their ethnicity for each other.

The agency-focused approaches of this period were, in turn, superceded by a revival of structural approaches in U.S. anthropology, including Marxist approaches for the study of power. The Marxist anthropologists of the 1960s and 1970s belittled performance approaches as individualistic, microscopic in focus, and unable to see the forest of culture and power for too much attention to the individual motions of trees. They turned disciplinary attention back to the structural features of society, and particularly the articulation of local political economies and the world capitalist system. Yet this return to structure, in its own time, sparked a reaction. By the mid-1980s, analysts once again raised questions of agency and everyday practices.

It is in this context that performance approaches returned, including both the revival of Erving Goffman's work and the contributions of new theorists of agency. Michel de Certeau reinspired the appreciation of mundane activities or as he terms it, the "practice of everyday life." Social analysts began to investigate the performative aspects of ethnicity, class, and community. Similarly, linguists were drawn to questions of language performance and competency (Bauman 1992). Others turned toward specialized cultural producers, including musicians and theater troupes, who made community dilemmas appear particularly vivid in their performances (Drewal and Drewal 1983). Through their use of language and imagery, production of music, manipulation of materials, and management of audience participation, artists, storytellers, actors, and musicians create illuminating portraits and telling commentaries on both the taken-for-granted and the urgently pressing cultural categories that create the worlds around them.

The literatures on everyday performativity and ritualized performance come together in opening up the possibility of asking how social categories are vitalized in both informal and formal performative settings.[7] Yet scholars of performance too often focus their gaze too acutely on local details of self-presentation and cultural convention, ignoring the larger cultural and political contexts in which performance makes a difference (Drewal 1991). Just as an earlier generation of Marxists intimated, scholars of performance lose sight of larger questions of power, both in their ethnographic representations and in the world, in favor of attention to individual creativity. For example, ethnographers of traditional performance conventions in Africa become caught up in archiving tradition; thus, they have been likely to see performances only within debates about local cultural legacies. Studies of performance offer fine-drawn descriptions of particular performative traditions but not a discussion of how these performative traditions are dialogically formulated within multiple arenas including local, regional, and global politics and culture. Even the best new work, which asks about performance traditions in relation to class and ethnicity within modern nation-states, rarely steps out of the area studies' privileging of the nation to ask transnational questions about culture and power. It is in this context that I argue that attention to issues of representation could revitalize the literature on performance.

Indeed, several theorists may be helpful in mixing theories of performance and representation: those working on the making of power-laden social identities. Stuart Hall (1997) has argued that race as a category requires repetitive performative inscriptions. Race is not significant as a set of bodily traits except as these are mobilized performatively to signify difference. Similarly, Homi Bhabha (1983) argues that colonial difference must be repetitively enunciated. Enunciation is important because it transforms the authoritative text of colonial power, mimicking power with an edge of difference. In this process performance does not just enact power but also distorts and sometimes undermines it. Finally, Judith Butler

(1989) argues that gender is created through "citational practices," that is, the repetitive referencing of social ideas about gender. Gender, she argues, is not learned and then occupied as a social category but rather comes to life through enactment. Butler's work has been particularly provocative because so many people—including scholars—continue to imagine gender and sexuality as qualities of natural disposition. Butler upsets this naturalness, arguing that even the most material aspects of gender, such as that manifested in the difference between boys' and girls' bodies, are registered as "different" only because they are performed as such.

Each of these theorists extends the ways issues of performance and representation come together. Yet they do not allow their theories the nuance provided by an engagement with ethnography, in which theory must continually be reworked to speak to regional cultural and political dynamics. To bring theories of representation and performance to a particular time and place is more than a matter of application. The making of times and places itself poses a challenge to theories of representation and performance. In considering performance in Africa, I must return to the challenge of representations of Africa *as* performance. Because Africa is the geopolitical ur-site of performance from the perspective of the West, "African" performance and "Western" conventions of representation of the continent are always intertwined. The anthropological description of "African performance" is always both foreign and domestic. It is impossible to trace either "Western imposition" or "African cultural heritage" alone; the question of geopolitical positioning is central to the possibility of discussing performance at all. Abstract theories of performance require the term to be a transcultural operant that denaturalizes cultural categories of gender, race, or colonial authority. In contrast, the study of performance in Africa reveals that the theoretical apparatus itself is always geopolitically entangled.

In allowing the literatures on performance and representation to talk to each other, I am compelled to engage performance both as a method of analysis and as a subject of meta-analysis. It is this complex engagement that inspires this book, and my ideas have been made possible only because I have had a series of motivated and inspiring interlocutors, men and women who imagine themselves as both ambassadors of "Africa" and experts in local and international performance: Mandinka praisesingers, jali.

Act III: Praisesinging and the Mande World

Performance gains its life in this ethnography through the performance events created by and through the figure of the jali. As stated in the "Overture," a hereditary group of performers found in The Gambia and throughout the Mande diaspora, jali travel as symbolic figures important to the nation-state. They also offer a connection between Africa and its trans-Atlantic diaspora. In a geographic area that stretches to include the modern nations of Mali, Senegal, Gambia, Guinea-Bissau, Guinea, and Ivory Coast, jali, in their capacity as praisesingers, highlight the performance of status—their own and those of whom they sing. In Senegambia, jali serve several functions intimately related to performance. In the literal sense, the status to which jali are born brings them into the realm of everyday enactments of status and social positioning. Jali confirm and yet can also tamper with social positionings in their attempts to negotiate the social order. It is the jali's role, in part, to enact and inspire social roles of distinction that position the jali in a markedly different relationship to their patrons of noble and elite status. Most practicing jali continue to offer traditional performances—that is, many perform in naming ceremonies and weddings, and at community and political events. The recent popularity of jali music, particularly among international audiences, does not signal its presence as a new invention.

Yet a relatively recent event propelled jali into a transnational arena. Jali came to fame in Alex Haley's *Roots* (1976).[8] In Haley's mythic story, a jali traced Haley's family connections from the United States to The Gambia. This geneaology established Haley's personal "roots" and grounded a dream of a link between the African diaspora and West Africa. Indeed, Haley used a figure that already had significance to some African Americans as a kind of idealized folk icon, but in the process he spread the fame of jali. The appeal of the jali's ability to remember and retain the history of a people through mnemonic abilities was an important inspiration, particularly for those who were taken as slaves; memory was all they had left. Haley's story made the jali's skills concrete and personal. The global circuation of *Roots* significantly popularized jali. Here the medium of film helped to generate a kind of imagined community of those in debt to common "roots"—African or otherwise (Anderson 1992).

Jali, trained in historical recitation, recall and recount genealogical narratives. In the Senegambian region, these oral traditionalists connect the precolonial past with the nation-state to offer the past as a way to inform the present. The past is said to provide a guide to contemporary social relations. Men jali in particular are seen as authoritative narrators in building a sense of nationhood through creating genealogical continuity between the contemporary nation and the ancient empire. The recent promotion of several women jali performers as part of the world music circuit has greatly increased the presence of women jali in an international arena. Meanwhile their roles in the national context are said to offer a complement to the role of men, but without the authority of masculine privilege.

In connecting precolonial empires to contemporary politics, jali also reaffirm the power and vulnerability of speech. Present day jali praise poems tell of the rise of the thirteenth-century Mande kingdom and their own importance to political figures. Jali are said to have inspired many contemporary political figures in national politics in their moves toward greatness. An important aspect of what helps to constitute power, in hegemonic terms, is that noble men of status speak through the mediation of jali. The words of patrons are conveyed to the public at large through the jali in a kind of ventriloquized fashion. This act of circumventing public displays of power as embodied in the speaker through the medium of a jali contrasts with Western assumptions that conflate the ability to speak and authority itself; here, there is a fundamental difference. Jali are those given speech, those able to display their competencies through verbal performances. Jali strength and authority is created through words, but precisely because of this, jali hold less powerful positions than those for and of whom they speak, their patrons.[9] Speech confirms status differences between jali and their patrons but in a hierarchy in which speech is topped by the patron's silence. The patron needs only whisper to his jali.

Jaliya is the practice of jali arts and politics. Jaliya includes the duties of the ritual and ceremonial specialist as well as the political go-between. Jaliya is not just an archaic form, although jali are proud of their deep historical roots. Jaliya brings to life the Gambian nation-state as a political culture with a heritage of authority rooted in the Mande diaspora. Thus, jaliya also moves beyond national borders. The reach of this political culture informs regional ethnic movements that attempt to destabilize the boundaries of the current nation-states, which follow colonial claims. Jaliya calls up the geopolitical imagination of the historic Mande kingdom, which crosses several contemporary nation-states.

A few jali are exceptionally competent entrepreneurs in transnational events, particularly in the world music scene. Some are able to move away from the image of traditionalist or folk artist to open up performance opportunities. Others are able to turn the notion of traditionalist to advantage in some of those same transnational circuits of culture. Some Gambian jali effectively combine their talents as professional musicians and professional mediators, which makes it possible for them to negotiate some of the terms of their activities as they position their "traditional" skills in Western late-capitalist consumer culture. Thus, the multiply authored nature of that "Africa" presented in international jali performances is particularly evident. Their performances bring attention to a variety of facets of the Western imagination of Africa. Jali music—despite its sharp divergence from the "primal beat" of Western fantasies of Africa—cannot escape European and North American evaluations within a discursive framework in which the spirit of Africa is music. As oral historians, the jali's art figures into certain European and North American ideas of authentic "tradition." Western notions of tradition have been particularly important in placing Mandinka praisesingers at the center of that music production from the continent that has made its way into world music scenes.

The chapters of this book trace some of the ways that the past, tradition, and regional culture are drawn into contemporary performances through the efforts of jali. I explore the ways that jaliya is significant in a variety of projects. The projects of jali are disjunctive and at times invisible to each other in their multiplicity and differing patronage agendas. I show how the framework of performance allows one to notice divergent projects. Performance allows us to think about the divergent agendas of those in The Gambia, the West African region, the African diaspora, the music and tourist industries, and more. Performance guides us to the "circuits of culture" that tie the production and the reception of jaliya in various venues.[10]

This study finds that jali performances are an exceptionally rich and multilayered site of cultural negotiation. As jali perform in a wide variety of contexts, from ceremonial events to political rallies, national radio and television programs, or tourist shows, the range of performance venues expands. In each context, they reinterpret and reposition their stories and skills, recreating an "African" past for varied visions of the present and future. Audiences' awareness that they are witnessing only one of many contexts in which jali perform further layers the significance of the ways jali performances traverse different types of scenes. Peasants are awed by jali world travelers just as tourists hope to catch a glimpse of once-and-future village performers. World music producers see the potential of these musicians in building a global village of the arts. Development experts leap at the possibility that culture can be made into a commodity. This is an auspicious time to gather up these accumulated events and engage the question of the significance of jaliya in national and transnational debates over the meaning of Africa.

Act IV: Africa in International Debates about Culture and Economy

Consider another meaning of performance: "Africa's dismal economic performance over the past 20 years has given rise to attempts to explain and understand the causes of such performance" (Mkandawire and Soludo 1999, 1; see also Bayart 1993). This notion of economic performance is frequently used when discussing worker output and management efficiency, an arena not generally thought of as theatrical. It would be possible to study the drama of industrial production, though the critical lack of this type of production in The Gambia would immediately become apparent. Although that is not my purpose here, I do want to argue for the link between economic performance and aesthetic production, particularly in relation to the economic importance of self-consciously cultural activities. How has the art of jaliya become an object of economic *and* aesthetic value during the post-independence era in The Gambia? To answer this, I need, once again, to look at representations as well as performances. I turn to the debates about economic and cultural development as they first emerged in relation to modernization plans and then to structural adjustment policies. Why have scholars had difficulty studying *both* culture and political economy? And why has this become urgent in an era of privatization and international tourism?

A set of developments that took place at the end of the Second World War are of critical importance to this discussion. At this time, African nation-states, as did many other post-independence nations, came under the gaze of a new international ideology: modernization, a plan generated to offer alternatives to colonialism and communism as political and social systems for these new emergent states (Latham 2000). Modernization was widely viewed by proponents as the road to national development. As discourse and ideology steeped in the notion of universal progress, modernization refuted the most notorious frameworks of colonial rule, which under certain colonial regimes had separated "native culture" from "European history" and in which all associations with dynamism were attributed to the latter. In contrast, the promise of modernization was to offer the same advantage to all nations.

In their effort to present modernization as a universal idea, proponents of modernization theory found the idea of culture problematic. Ignoring the fact that modernization itself was a cultural vision, modernization theorists viewed African cultures, like cultures across the Third World, as an impediment to progress. Development programs facilitated by emergent nation-states, under the guidance of international expertise, would bring Africans beyond culture, into the modern world. At the same time, of course, development programs would tie these new nations to international guidance, creating their political and economic dependence on the metropolitan centers that needed them as sources of raw materials, inexpensive labor, and emerging markets.

With the emergence of African nations into the world of development dreams and expertise came the production of new kinds of knowledges about Africa. Development experts generated the "facts" and statistics of underdevelopment. At the same time, critical voices emerged. One ardent set of critics were Marxist-inspired political economists, whose approaches were particularly effective in transforming neo-colonial studies of Africa. In contrast to the gathering of development facts to support modernization interventions, these scholars of Africa asked critical questions about what "modernization" meant. Rather than taking modernization and its benefits for granted, they studied how African societies were being ushered into global political and economic histories. For example, Africanists showed the transformation of rural society; both land and labor were made through colonial and postcolonial policies into commodities that linked the resources of Africa to metropolitan projects and profits, in effect creating "the development of underdevelopment." In the process, they also criticized scholarship about Africa produced during the colonial era. This scholarship, particularly under the theoretical regimes of functionalism and structuralism, they argued, created the static and closed native "cultures" of the colonial imagination. Colonial administrators were most fascinated by native custom; this knowledge, critics argued, enabled administrators to control African people more effectively. Scholars helped codify and describe custom within this mandate. In the process, colonial scholars had cordoned African "cultures"— as they imagined them—away from history. Cultures were portrayed as closed, completed traditions, without the dynamism attributed to European history.

Scholarship on African societies generated by Marxist critiques of development and modernization influenced the formation of a new "area studies" approach to understanding Africa. In contrast to those earlier "colonial" moments in the scholarship on Africa, African societies now had history and were shown in their dynamism, both internally with African neighbors, and externally with Europeans and others. As scholars showed the importance of changing patterns of land tenure, crop production, gender, customary law, and political authority, they produced a complexly political vision of rural society (see, for example, Berry 1984 and Guyer 1984).[10] For example, they traced how European mercantilism and then capitalism expanded into Africa through forced specialization in particular cash crops, together with requirements for taxes in money, which forced people into wage labor (see, for example, Wallerstein 1979, Curtin 1975, Wolf 1982, E. F. White 1987, Saul and Arrighi 1973, and Roberts 1996). In the 1970s, economic histories on a global scale were in vogue, influenced by Braudelian history, and Africa had a significant place in these world histories. In this scholarship, "culture" was rarely important as an object of study in itself, although African cultures were portrayed as creating standards of land tenure and labor recruitment, or, alternatively, as forming an ideological justification for colonial impositions (see, for example, Goody 1976 and Meillassoux 1981; Hart 1985 reviews such work). The study of culture was coded as a colonial exercise from which Africans were gratified to be liberated.

Ironically, culture has recently returned to the agenda. In some regions, African nation-states are peddling "traditional culture" as their most important economic product. Scholars have been forced to take note. But what is the course of this reversal?

In the 1980s, international development expertise took a new turn as development agencies withdrew support from African nations that failed to meet the agencies' expectations about economic development. International polices shifted toward favoring the privatization of the economy as a means to elevate the nation-state above state corruption, criminal activities, and inefficient state practices, qualities commonly associated with many African states. International development agents began to promote "structural adjustment." Under structural adjustment programs, ushered in under Reagan- and Thatcher-era economic policies, African states were encouraged to seek privatized support through international investment schemes. Privatization required a withdrawal of resources from domestic programs.

States lost funding for their modernization projects and suddenly the tenets of modernization began to loosen. Under the old regime, modernization had come to refer to state-subsidized commoditification of land and labor; without the state, small-scale agriculture was not always a profitable enterprise. Under the new regime, new products were required. In the context of the burgeoning leisure industries of Northern metropoles, the marketing of "traditional culture" as an revenue-generating commodity seemed appealing, and tourism was promoted as the industry of the future. African states acted quickly to invite foreign developers to build hotels, offering the land that once had been targeted for agricultural development. "The creation of jobs" suddenly meant the development of a service industry of waiters, informal tour guides, maids, and souvenir hawkers.

Furthermore, after the official end of the Cold War, international developers declared the triumph of the free market and the necessity for everyone to become an entrepreneur. African states and nongovernmental organizations struggled to promote entrepreneurship of any kind. For those without abundant natural resources (such as gold and oil, as in the case of Ghana and Nigeria, respectively) to sell on the world market, selling traditional culture has been one of the most available avenues for generating national revenue.

Ironically, the traditional culture being sold by African entrepreneurs is often closely related to that codified and collected by colonial-era scholars. Yet the approaches of colonial-era scholarship are not sufficient to understand how this "culture" is being produced and used. Also inadequate are the area studies approaches of social scientists of the 1970s and 1980s, in which "culture" was often scorned, and thought of as a useless, outdated category. Yet these approaches can inform a new understanding of "culture" within and not opposed to the international political economy.

At one level of analysis, "culture" is that set of goods and practices now being fashioned into a commodity for international consumers. I use the term to refer to performances, stories, art objects, clothing, folklore, and traditional knowledge that draw from a long local heritage at the same time that these artifacts are fashioned anew for the market. At another level, "culture" remains useful as an analytic lens to focus on the specific characteristics of the process of fashioning and refashioning these ideas, material objects, social relations, and practices.

To appreciate how the transformations are made requires a "cultural" analysis of the making of "culture" as commodity. In this kind of analysis, then, culture is neither static nor closed. Culture is intimately tied to political and economic processes that involve both Africans and the geopolitical configurations. "Representation" refers to the conventions through which Africa comes into being as a recognized cultural object in the world. Because the emergence of the continent as a unified object has been the key strategy for selling the superimposed variety of African culture, the representation of Africa is a central problem in the entrepreneurial era. Representations emerge not only through historic conventions but also through performances. Thus performance, representation, and the commodification of culture are linked in my analysis of the present moment of African political economy.

Curtain Call

This book confronts a challenge posed to anthropological analysis, one that urges ethnographies to offer a global perspective and, at the same time, to produce a study that is locally informed. Throughout the book, I consider the methodological questions generated in the debates that have framed cultural anthropology in the last fifteen years. The chapters are designed to address these moments of "rethinking the field." In this regard, the chapters engage and overlap with one another. The first and second chapters, "Music" and "Performance," work together to address the question of how African music and performance frame Africa in a global imagination. Chapter 1, "Music," begins with the premise that music is one of the dominant ways that Africa comes to the minds of many. My central concern is to inquire about how stories of cultural difference get told through discussions of music. I am interested in how notions of "African" music are configured for a popular imagination. I argue that notions of rhythm and community, often seen in popular studies on

African music, have found a compelling resonance with wide-ranging audiences, who use them to appreciate Africa.

But the counterpart to many popular ideas of African music, Western "art" music or classical music, is considered here as well. In contrast to African music, Western art music is more often than not represented as socially detached, aesthetically transcendent, and performatively individuated. In this contrast, we can see how *difference* is made. My approach in this chapter is to link Africa and Europe in search of the social history of this difference; I do this by putting the literatures of ethnomusicology and musicology in dialogue. This bicontinental history becomes necessary when engaging questions about cultural value in a global context. To see the global significance of "African music," it becomes necessary to see African musical systems within the reach of European standards. Contingencies of value thus emerge in dialogue. My analysis plays with stereotypes and their histories, as these provide windows into how Africa is storied through music.

Consider, however, the limits of textual analysis. A necessary complement to the first chapter's focus on texts is a study of responses to performances. How do performances of African music, and their reception, take us beyond a textually based interpretation? In chapter 2, "Performances," the interactive role of audiences and performers, and the sedimented histories that help people interpret their "experience" of African and jali music, are brought to the center of the discussion.

In chapter 2, formal performance events held in various locations— Boston and Lee, Massachusetts, and Banjul and Georgetown, The Gambia, as well as Sedhiou, Senegal, and Santa Cruz, California—form the basis of a comparative analysis of audience expectation and reception. My discussion provides a disruptive moment in the study of performance and audience reception by arguing for the making of "experience" before an event as well as at the particular moment of reception.

The chapter provides a critical engagement with the previous chapter's privileging of stereotypes by arguing that the effects of music are not totally determined by earlier representations of "African" music. The critique also moves in the other direction to propose that audience studies cannot rest at the level of experience while neglecting to address the question of how sensibilities and predispositions are cultivated before the event. As an enactment of difference, performance becomes a moment of *negotiation* of notions of Africa. Thus, a "third space" is necessary: a space of analysis where a range of changing and mutually challenging audience responses are formed, both with and against the histories of geopolitical difference that make "The Africa" an object. The first two chapters exemplify the central analytic frames for the book: performance and representation.

The next three chapters form a second set of linked stories in which I move from the level of "The Africa" as the unit of discussion to look more specifically at Gambian political culture in the context of its global framing. These chapters attend to the question of what happens to place or location in global analyses. Scholars of Africa are often distressed to find the continent absent in analyses of globalization. They call for a re-engagement with the specificity of place (Paolini 1997; Piot 1999). I engage with this dialogue by focusing on Gambian cultural politics, particularly at the national level, as I continue to trace global interconnections through depicting situated moments within transnational encounters.

In chapter 3, "Curators of Tradition," I analyze a postcolonial history-making project in which Western-trained academic historians, Gambian nationalists, commercial record producers, and jali join together to circulate varied, overlapping, but sometimes contradictory histories of the Mande kingdom. At issue here is the question, What is history? The players compete over how Mande, and Gambian, history is understood. In this process, too, jali "tradition" has developed in dialogue with the nation-state. "Curators of Tradition" examines key institutional forces that shape jali traditions in conjunction with the dilemmas of building a postcolonial nation. I show how a government supported office, the Gambian Oral History and Antiquities Division, under the auspices of the vice president's office, creates both itself and its jali allies as "curators." In the process, they form dialogues with Western historians, other African nations, and the global culture industry.

The engagement with the question of history is followed by a discussion, in chapter 4, of the "Personalistic Economy." This discussion focuses on the social and entrepreneurial practices of jali, particularly as their specificity is highlighted in transnational encounters. I analyze the habitus of jaliya. By the term "personalistic economy," I refer to economic relationships based on a continuous performance of social status and dependence. For jali, making a living occurs within a performative tradition, which is sometimes referred to by detractors as "begging," in order to establish relations of patronage. The entrepreneurial skills employed by jali become useful in negotiating the international business encounters in which some Gambian jali find themselves. Rather than being a peculiar artifact of a small place in the world, this detail animates a larger discussion about the ways charisma and the negotiation of personal ties are necessary in many entrepreneurial activities around the world. The discussion allows us to consider how the personalistic economy operates even in social systems—such as that in the United States—committed to denying its presence in celebrations of rational and even-handed efficiency.

The chapter that follows, "Interview Encounters: The Performance of Profession," studies the microdynamics of the interview. In dialogue with chapter 4, chapter 5 allows jali to speak back—in effect, to enact jaliya—in the face of the preceding structural account of their social roles. Chapter 5 sheds light on the processes of interviewing. By allowing that interviews are, for jali, occasions for the performance of their arts, I also discuss what jali find important to convey about their lives in the context of transnational conversation. Just as "Personalistic Economy" highlights structuring principles of jaliya, "Interview Encounters" focuses on jali agency. Performance is discussed here simultaneously as an analytic lens and as a key aspect of jali self-making.

To note the performative elements found in interview encounters may appear to undermine the authority of the information being conveyed. Yet, I argue, the interview is itself a key site for the transnational negotiations of jaliya that make it significant for academics, tourists, national politicians, patrons, and, of course, jali. The interview is, then, a cultural encounter in which Gambian culture and politics is remade in transnational perspective. Attention to such cultural encounters and negotiations within their Gambian location is important for showing the multilayered aspects of the production of culture. Gambian culture is not produced autonomously, in situ; instead, it grows from the confluence of varied communal, ethnic, national, religious, regional, and transnational perspectives.

The third part of the book moves beyond the direct presence of jali and their performances to return to the "Africa" that jali help to produce through their performances, particularly as it is significant to international audiences. International aid programs and national officials, together with jali, promote tourism as an economic development strategy. These dreams come to life, in part, in the travels of two groups: Europeans on holiday trying to escape cold Northern winters, and African diasporic "homeland" visitors who are looking to Africa as cultural heritage. These chapters retain a focus on the interplay of performance and representation through attention to nonprofessional performers, in this case, travelers. Their performances as tourists complement the professionals who serve them in negotiating the meaning of Africa.

Chapter 6, "Travel Stories," examines the travel adventure narratives of European women tourists on holiday in The Gambia, as well as those of young Gambian men who seek travel plans of their own through their associations with these women. One aim of the chapter is to engage recent insights of feminist theory that move beyond essentialized categories of gender through analyses of the shifting and contradictory aspects of social location. The chapter dwells particularly on stories told by Gambian men about their masculinity as they understood it in the context of the transnational limitations and possibilities that their identification with "Africa" offered them. The stories are analyzed for their allegorical significance in relation to the performance of geopolitical identities as a gendered form. The men's stories show their anxieties about the vulnerability of the Gambian nation-state as well as their sense of opportunity within the very cultural frameworks that make them vulnerable. The stories astound in their portrayals of what one might call an international sexual "traffic in men" at the same time as they establish that gendered difference is never a universal but rather a regionally shifting construction within unequal global power dynamics.

In chapter 7, "Tourists as Pilgrims," I analyze a journey of African Americans to West Africa, understood as a pilgrimage of "return." In 1994, McDonald's sponsored a homeland tour that took eighty-nine African Americans to Senegal and The Gambia in the shadow of the story created by Alex Haley. I traveled with the tour, which primarily included contest winners of McDonald's African history month promotion, as well as a few others, myself included. A heterogeneous group of people, brought together to revisit an imagined African "home," they found themselves guided by earnest Senegalese tour guides who hoped to mold this diverse group into a temporary community.

Readers of the chapter are encouraged to travel along as tour participants to experience the significance of a return journey to several sacred sites. Here history is scripted as a "rites of passage" journey modeled along a set of rituals of an initiation ceremony. This performance of place and self produced a rich exchange in which to see the production of Africa through the practices of tour guides, corporate sponsors, tourists, and local entrepreneurs. In what they refer to as a "pilgrimage and not a safari," tour guides attempted to carve out a distinctive niche in the itineraries of international travelers. Here the sacred and the commercial shadow each other. My discussion of this process allows me to return to analyze how identities increasingly are formed and sponsored by corporate interests. Again, I rework the guiding themes of the study: performance and representation, culture as an aspect of development, and the world created through their mutual existence.

A concluding Coda reengages the dominant themes of the chapters to ask about the possibilities of anthropological analysis in transnational arenas of culture making. This discussion also allows me to reflect upon the self-consciously heterogeneous methodological approach taken throughout the book, which can be better appreciated, I believe, at its end. The Coda rearticulates the global question in relationship to anthropological practice, including the practice of writing.

PART ONE

Representations / Performances

Cultural theorist Homi Bhabha has suggested that there is something in the nature of stereotypes that makes them easy to utter repetitively (1983). For Bhabha, this repetition can be attributed to the role of stereotypes in the making of the psyche. Yet it is also possible that speakers are caught up in repetitive modes, that is, narrative conventions that encourage them to repeat stereotypes, which allow them to remain in the conversation. Conversations, then, as well as psyches, are constituted in repetitions of their foundational frameworks. These ideas provide a context in which to discuss my interpretative lens for understanding music and Africa.

Historian of colonial Africa Luise White (1994, 33) uses the term "sites of speech" to refer to semi-autonomous modes of discussion in which speakers repetitively comment on the conditions of their rights to narrate. White (2000) describes how people in colonial East Africa, in speaking of social hygiene and disease control, were drawn again and again to talk of blood sucking and cannibalism. She argues, provocatively, that these idioms are not in any easy sense *African* responses to colonialism; these are not African "voices." Rather, White asks that we begin with the conversations themselves. To the extent that discussions of hygiene and disease control created categories of "African" and "European" in colonial juxtaposition, anyone who embarked upon these discussions, "African" or otherwise, necessarily repeated the categories of difference to which blood sucking spoke so well. Thus, White argues, discussion of blood sucking crossed genres of oral and written history and involved people of various ethnic, political, and professional identifications, African and European.

Similarly, in the discourse surrounding witchcraft in rural France, described by ethnographer Jeanne Favret-Saada (1980), speakers were "caught" in the framework of the conversation. Either one was inside and spoke within the established narrative conventions, or one was outside and had no understanding of what was going on. This idea is further extended by anthropologist Susan Harding (2000) as she stresses, in analyzing Christianity in the United States, that this is not so much a matter of "belief"—or the sociology of believers—as of the power of the narrative conventions themselves. Harding suggests that one can disagree and have doubts as a Christian, that is, within the narrative frames of Christian storytelling. Similarly, White also argues that skeptical retellings of blood sucking stories by Europeans in East Africa were themselves part of the repetition that constituted the genre.

Perhaps these comments appear tendentious as an introduction to "Music" and "Performance." Yet I submit in chapter 1 that contemporary discussions of African music form one such site of speech, in which differences between "Africa" and "the West" are repetitively rehearsed. It is possible to get some distance into a narration about performance events or traditions in some place that happens to be in Africa without entering this site, yet all that is required is a momentary detour into that place in which "Africa" and "music" create each other so forcefully, and the narrator finds himself, or herself, "caught" in the repetition of familiar tropes. Even well-intended efforts to turn around the valences of "Africa" and "the West" or to question the sophistication of this contrast still tend to repeat the framework.

This set of conventions is not a Western "voice." It can be enunciated by Africans, Asians, or North Americans. It crosses oral and written genres and stretches to include popular opinions and serious scholarship, naive listeners and professional musicians. I find myself frustrated by its reach and its power, and I struggle unsuccessfully to extricate myself. Yet I can draw our attention to this framework as I acknowledge the conventions within which we must narrate.

This is not easy ground to travel. Some ethnomusicologists may worry that my attempts to explore the prism that "African music" creates undermines their best efforts to teach us about the variety and intricacy of African music. Indeed, I am casting my analytic net at a simplification—the repetition of "Africa" through its articulation with "music"—and, to do so, I too must simplify. Rather than telling a history of studies of African music, which would certainly bring attention to struggles and achievements as well as disagreements and internal stakes among musicologists, I ask how we are drawn again and again to identify "Africa" through music. I focus on simple, popular texts, deliberately turning our attention to the habits of mind that tie music and Africa. I reduce even these texts to search for core repetitions.

This analysis leaves aside numerous more complicated studies of African music. At the same time, I am deeply indebted to those scholars whose work on performance in Africa has made it possible to think beyond any monolithic story of "African music." Such scholars as Christopher Waterman (1990), David Copland (1985), and Paul Berliner (1978) have shown the importance of music in making distinctions of class and ethnicity and in building modern national public cultures. Each of their works asks about the relationship between particular social formations and the production and consumption of musical forms, musical trainings, and performances. Their accounts refuse generalizations about "African music"—and make it possible to pose questions about the power of this category.

Equally significant is the work of scholars of West African griots—including the Mande tradition of which the jali I studied are a part—including Thomas Hale (1998) and Roderick Knight (1973). Especially exciting is Eric Charry's (2000) recent book, *Mande Music*, which offers a comprehensive account of the regional world in which Mande jali participate. These works offer us richly detailed descriptions of the role of musicians, their repertoire, training, aesthetic conventions, and performance goals, making it possible for me to assume a savvy readership. Because of these authors, I am able to ask questions that are simultaneously too large and yet too small for the demanding task of introducing a musical tradition; for this I refer my readers to these sources without hesitation. Meanwhile, these same sources inspire me to consider unanswered questions: Why is there still such a category as "African music"?

In chapter 1, I attempt to answer this question by examining how the relationship between Western art music and African music frames discussion. I rely on popular but also scholarly texts that stress the contrast between Africa and the West, as these show us the play in what Arjun Appadurai (1996) has called an "ideoscape," a formulation of global geopolitics available to general audiences and specialized scholars alike. My analysis of these texts searches for the framing dichotomies that make the articulation between "Africa" and "music" such a magnetic site of speech.

In chapter 2, I continue to look for frames, but in performances instead of textual narrations. Performances enact and encode popular ideas of "African music" and bring the practical knowledges of both audiences and performances into action. Yet here I interrupt the simplifications of chapter 1 to stress the dynamism and flexibility of performance frameworks. Each jali negotiates the expectations of diverse audiences, mediating and transforming ideas of Africa. Audiences also bring diverse repertoires for enacting Africa in music performances; they interact with one another as well as with the musicians in creating local moments of "African music." The performance is thus both a site of speech for the repetition of "African music" and a site for creative play. Texts, of course, also could be analyzed in this way. Readers consider them, discuss them, and bring new meanings into them.

Taken together, the two chapters argue for the importance of studying representation *and* performance. "Africa" comes to life through performance, and thus is repetitively framed. Performance disperses and disarticulates "Africa," but only because of this repetition. The tension between representation and performance is essential to the process of making and remaking all that we can imagine as African.

CHAPTER ONE

Music: Europe and Africa

> The idea that Europe is an idea is one whose time has come.
> But to reach back to the point of its origin is not an easy
> task. A more feasible project is to observe Europe in the act
> of reaching back or out toward an idea of what Europe is
> not: the "primitive," the "Orient," "Africa."
> —Christopher Miller, *Blank Darkness*

Upon mere mention of the phrase "African music," a list of features readily comes to the fore. A sampling of comments: "African music is all drumming"; "It's rhythm"; "It is the heartbeat that just makes you want to get up"; "It is noise and not music"; "African music is so primal." This brief list of common refrains in no way gives one a sense that informants agree about the value of African music. Yet attentiveness to the ideas behind some of these statements helps illuminate the sedimented logics that hold in place Europe and one of its Others, Africa. Ideas are always formed in dialogue; thus, in teasing out overlapping conversations about music we are immediately drawn to the ways particular mythic stories form allegorical narratives that reinscribe geographical difference.

A focus on stories and their mythic qualities offers one way into a discussion that attempts to get at popular assumptions that surround music and that become "everyday" knowledge. Stories help shape and negotiate reality.[1] Edward Said (1999, xiii) suggests that "stories are at the heart of what explorers and novelists say about strange regions of the world." Similarly, musicologist Kofi Agawu (1992, 247) suggests that early stories generated by North African and European explorers, travelers, and geographers formulated stereotypes of the distinctive and exotic features of African music. An example: "Dancing and beating time are engrained in their nature. They say: were the negro to fall from heaven to the earth he would beat time in falling" (attributed to Ibn Botlan, died ca. 1068, by Mez 1937, 61). Contemporary stories, I suggest as well, are at the heart of the ways we imagine different musical and cultural geographic regions.

Two key terms are discussed in this chapter to illustrate how regional distinctions between Africa and Europe are configured. The first is *rhythmic repetition*, most often viewed as the salient feature of African music;

it becomes a repeatedly told aspect of African music's difference. The second is *community feeling*: African music is said to create a communal experience. While these features may indeed be associated with a great deal of music in Africa, their repetitiveness and communal coercion constrain the range of possibilities found in musics across the continent.

What compels my discussion here is the way certain features attributed to African music become facts not just about "music" but about "Africa." These generalized features are transferred from a discussion of music onto the geopolitical landscape by both popular and scholarly audiences. How often do we hear about the communal, polyrhythmic qualities of African music, to then move to an idealized generalization of all of Africa's social relations, rooted in tradition? Whenever commentators try to eschew the other stereotype—Africa in ruins, the coming anarchy—why do they retreat into an idyllic unstratified Africa, the Africa of "African music"?

In contrast to the communal and rhythmic "Africa," the West, both as music and as a conceptual region, emerges as individuated, distinctive, and complex. While these "facts" tend to be challenged by area specialists, and the terrain of image-making is fraught with overlapping and competing ideas, such grand generalizations continue to assert themselves in the popular imagination. I suggest that the conviction with which these truisms appear as real attributes has something to do with the status of music itself and the complicated legacies that cordon music off from the nuances of scholarship on ideas, texts, and images. Unlike other areas of the humanities, including literature and art history, discussions about music often seem above rigorous debate.

Music still occupies a distinctive place in discussions of Western high arts. Among the arts, music is often viewed as beyond representation, as evoking feelings first rather than stimulating thought. Music, for some, becomes the sensual side of the "reason versus emotion" dichotomy. These distinctions are sustained when musical "traditions" are presented as autonomous, ahistorical, self-perpetuating entities—bounded moral systems—thereby obscuring how ideas of particular musics were formed within and against other musics. Here lies the critical difference, for even as aesthetic value and hierarchies of difference between popular and "art" music erode, cultural values attributed to differences rooted in place of origin persist. How African music and Western art musics come to be understood as such is key to this persistence.

Defining African Music

Another feature that is common to all types of music in
black Africa is rhythm. . . . Some people regard it as a purely
mechanical thing—the periodic repetition of downbeats and

upbeats that mark given musical phrases. Others believe it is
a kind of magic that is exclusive to Negroes who employ it
in order to render their music "bewitching" or "satanic."
The truth lies somewhere between these two viewpoints.
Rhythm is an invisible covering that envelops each note.
—Francis Bebey, *African Music*

Is there such a thing as African music? How does the idea of African
music get sustained and maintained? It is a mistake to answer these questions with generalizations about musical phrasings or musical sociologies.
Instead, our ability to imagine "Africa" and "music" as fitting together
depends on intertwined histories of category-making in which a whole
continent has been located as a place that might best be characterized
through a nonverbal aesthetic. In other words, we have had to work hard
to create notions of "Africa" and notions of "music" that might fit together. As one might argue from Bebey's quotation, cited immediately
above, African music is that Other sensibility that is always "somewhere
between" mechanical and neutral-seeming technologies of reality-making
on the one hand, and the magics of European bewitchment and satanic
fears on the other. As the repeated remembrance of that in-betweenness,
with its "periodic repetition of downbeats and upbeats" of dispassionate
recording and exoticization, African music is always rhythm, the "invisible covering" that envelops each meaning-making gesture in difference.[2]

African music as a category is constructed in a variety of texts and
contexts: popular and scholarly, improvised and official, musical and
tone-deaf. African drumming classes in Boston and world beat concerts
in Melbourne take their place beside up-country naming ceremonies in
The Gambia, addresses by the Nigerian ministry of culture at the United
Nations, and the latest ethnomusicological texts in the university library.
I begin a discussion of the ways "African music" is made by turning to
one of the influential accounts that helped pave the way for scholarly
discussion of the then emergent field.

Francis Bebey's *African Music: A People's Art* (1975) is now considered a classic, foundational text.[3] It helped establish the legitimacy of African music as a field of study. Its production was supported by UNESCO,
and it remains, along with Nketia's (1974) *Music in Africa*, an important
examination of African music. Without Bebey's book, which presents a
broad survey of Africa through music, it would be difficult for scholars
to talk about something called African music.[4] Bebey argues for the integrity and unique features of African music, which he places in self-conscious dialogue with Western standards. As Bebey argues, African music
was generally thought of as noise in the West; to counter this image, his
aim is to offer a complex African aesthetic.

To postulate something known as genuine African music, Bebey must frame it as an object sustained through the repeated production of a dichotomy between the distinct and separate musical traditions of Africa and Europe. In this formulation, Bebey is clear about the development of a parallel but different "African" civilization—a civilization whose accomplishments are equal to, though opposite from, those of Europe. This task requires the reification of "European music" as a single entity that can produce Africa. Thus, for example, Bebey constructs Western art music as autonomous, independent of social life. This then delimits its African opposite. "African music is fundamentally a collective art" (1975, vi). Moreover this collective spirit, distinct from European universalism, turns out to be the true universalism, surpassing even Europe itself. Music, Bebey continues, "is communal property whose spiritual qualities are shared and experienced by all; in short, it is an art form that can and must communicate with people of all races and cultures" (Bebey 1975, vi).

Similarly, Bebey draws his picture of the role of the musician in African society in contrast to the image he conjures of the West, again in stereotypic form: the West produces musicians as individuals, while Africa produces collective participatory activity. His comparison depends on a notion that Western art music is produced by an individual genius transcendent of collective representations. In contrast, he is able to argue, African music is an integral part of every aspect of social life, an expression of that life. Through this contrast, both Europe and Africa are reduced to static repositories of tradition. Only European music, as a unified phenomenon, can produce and preserve "authentic" and "traditional" African music. And only a cultural broker, trained in both civilizations and musical in both ways, can explain the beauty of each side.

In the role of cultural broker between Africa and the West, Bebey can create a classificatory system for African music paralleling that of European music. His typology of African instruments and musical styles lends a scholarly legitimacy to the former. One must read a text for its appeal as well as for its information; its ability to attract a following draws on many aesthetic levels. Thus, Bebey illustrates his text with stunning photographs and ends the book with a long discography. The visual images illuminate for readers the idea that African music is a thing of both difference and beauty; the discography—which suggests the archival depth of a "civilized" music collection—leads us to listen to this music with respect. In this process, Africa itself comes to be identified with music. "No other art is quite so specifically African," Bebey writes (1975, 122). The unity of Africa is the unity of its music. And the unity of its music is the rhythm of the repetition of difference.

Bebey's strategy has been effective in that the field he helped introduce has flourished. Two features of its success come to mind. First, those who appreciate the arts of Africa have found African music a powerful rubric not only to valorize the beauty of the aesthetic they know but also to defiantly criticize imperialisms of the West. Second, those who study European music have busily gone about the process of codifying Western music as if it were a homogeneous and transcendent thing against which other musics can at best form oppositional parallels. The ongoing strength of the story of "Western culture" as an autonomous, special object deserving reverence has necessarily reproduced narratives of difference like the one Bebey tells. Thus it would be disingenuous to single out Bebey's discussion of music as problematic without acknowledging the limitations of the hegemonic constructions of music and value that preceded his book. His work is a product of a particular time, but it also continues to capture the attention of general audiences interested in Africa and African music. Before discussing the literatures that have followed the trajectory of Bebey's "African music," that is, those that have grown up within the domain of African ethnomusicology, I turn to the realm around which all ethnologies revolve, the domain of high culture in the West.

Music and the "Western" Experience

In certain societies where sounds have become letters with
sharps and flats, those unfortunate enough not to fit into this
schema are tossed out of the system and qualified as unmusi-
cal and their sounds are called noises. It is known that one
of the primary tasks of ethnomusicologists is to study what
traditional societies consider music and what they reject as
non-music. A music bound up with movement, dance, and
speech, one in which the listener becomes a co-performer,
one that has no overall form except a continually recurring
sequence of notes and rhythms, one that plays endlessly—for
nobody has enough of life—has been called elementary or ru-
dimentary.
—Trinh Minh-Ha, *Framer Framed*

Western art music is continually placed in a hallowed space in the conversations of both popular and scholarly audiences, evoked as *the* representative form of Western music even as it is thought to be dying among Westerners. (Or, at least, this is the rumor regularly spread by recording companies in the United States.) Without reflexively acknowledging the historical conditions in which the category of Western art music was created, one can produce a list of the features that are thought to make Western music distinctive from Other musics, including the disinterestedness

and aesthetic autonomy of both musicians and audience. Here the meaning of a particular musical performance is thought to be derived from
something beyond social context. The cult of the artist as an individual
and inspired creator reminds us of music's historical tie to its sacred past;
inspiration is at heart divine. Furthermore, critics as well as musicians
hope to be inspired. Unlike literature and art, where more attention to
the social production of aesthetic forms now appears more commonplace,
music is often still portrayed as being above discourse and representation
and—in this way—beyond ideology.

Challenges to the notion that music is transcendent historicize the
processes through which classical music becomes a reified category. The
lack of critical attention to the social production of music is central to its
seductive power as a privileged discourse in Western society. Precisely
because music appears to be above ideology, discourses on music are free
to reproduce dominant social relations.

Recent histories of the development of Western music draw us into
the cultural legacies that have shaped different musical traditions. In
Music and Society (1987), cultural critic Janet Wolff explores the development of the notion of aesthetic autonomy and the possible explanations
for its persistence. She traces the emergence, during the late Renaissance,
of a growing distinction between artists and craftspersons. Artists were
no longer dependent upon guilds and therefore had a greater degree of
autonomy. The artist became the originator of the work, and genius was
attributed to the creator. Later, the Enlightenment further developed these
trends. Wolff shows how many of the ideas that gave Western music its
prestige in the late twentieth century are inherited from the Enlightenment, though it is important to note that Enlightenment ideas are themselves heterogeneous and often sites of contest. Here, too, she traces ideas
that art music is apolitical and nonrepresentational.

Central to the endurance of Enlightenment thought has been its ability to categorize the non-Western world, that is, to put it in its place in
relation to the West. As Mary Pratt (1992) points out, eighteenth-century
travel narratives of explorers served as the basis of knowledge about the
Other, testifying to Western Europe's growing interest in the non-Western
world. In many of these narratives we see the codification of cultural traits
that were imagined as real distinctions between the West and the Other.
These travelers' and explorers' reports also served as a framework of assumptions about music for armchair philosophers (Agawu 1992), and
also stimulated attention to music as a measure of both universality and
difference as key features of humanity. Line Grenier (1989) has demonstrated that concern about the non-Western world included an interest in
exotic music, an interest assuming its universal origin. At the same time,
non-Western musics were judged by the standards of Western music, in-

cluding, as Grenier points out, norms for composition and performance (1989, 27). Western art music became the pinnacle from which standards of judgment could be made. "Judgment" is a key term; Enlightenment thinkers believed that they could develop rational standards by which to judge both Western music of various classes and non-Western music. Kant's *Critique of Judgment* (1951 [1790]) stands as one of the most important philosophical underpinnings for these formative ideas.

When non-Western music, especially African music, was cited in critical conversations about music, it was often invoked as antithetical to Western art music. African music was viewed as primitive, not-quite-music, noise. Even relativist understandings of non-Western "difference" helped to bolster the universalism of Western (transcendent) art music. Everyone could learn art music; this was the process of civilization. This civilizational gradient was closely linked with the emerging bourgeoisie, who increased distinctions between arts and crafts, and between amateurs and professionals. By the nineteenth century, a growing number of emerging institutions—critics, publishers, and agents—sustained the notion that only high art transcended the social. Finally, and ironically, the idea of aesthetic autonomy was further developed by academic institutionalization and support of art history, literary criticism, and aesthetics itself.

The rise of art music as a prestige system is linked not only to the rise of the bourgeoisie to hegemony in the West but also to Western Europe's dominance on the world stage. The connection between classical music and the modern world system is not a simple one, however. Elite music does not only represent the desires of the hegemonic classes; its categories of meaning are shaped and contested, and its history itself is continually reinterpreted.[5]

Edward Said's *Musical Elaborations* (1991) provides insight into music as a cultural field and how its global figurings create powerful social distinctions. Said's discussion of music opens debates about the elements that constitute Western music—specifically, performance, reception, and the effects of commodification—that help situate Western music within complicated social histories. Yet Said is willing to study Western art music on its own terms, that is, as a self-developing tradition of performance innovation. In contrast to Said's other works, best known for highlighting the ways the West imagines its Others and how those representations form powerful narratives of difference, his work on music avoids an analysis of the interactive relationship between Western art music and imperialism. The text on music offers only a little information on global interconnections. Where *Orientalism* (1978) and *Culture and Imperialism* (1993) point to the ways that power is infused in relationships between Europe and the non-West, *Musical Elaborations* offers a guided tour through Said's experiences as a student *inside* Western classical music.

This difference is perhaps explained through the distinction Said sees between literature and music (cf. Sher 1992). "Music, like literature, is practiced in a social and cultural setting, but it is also an art whose existence is premised undeniably on individual performance, reception or production" (Said 1991, xviii). By ignoring the ways "music" comes into being, socially and historically, Said eschews the question of how the West and its classical music are inscribed in global history. He fails to disrupt Western art music as a coherent, locally configured object.

Said does, however, call our attention to the transgressive elements of music: how performance, reception, and production are ambiguously attached to social formations. Said's work reminds us of the problems that music presents as a system of abstract signs of indeterminate meaning. Exploring how these ambiguous elements are transculturally configured might be useful. Cultures are fashioned in global dialogues and contact zones, as V. Y. Mudimbe reminds us in the *Invention of Africa* (1988) and as Mary Pratt argues in *Imperial Eyes* (1992).

Is music so ambiguous as to refuse all structural analysis? Perhaps it had to be made so; thus social histories and ideologies still figure in its elucidation. Cultural analyst Georgina Born points to one approach. She suggests that musicologists have played a major role in building an image of Western art music as nonrepresentational, and, indeed, music does have a core that is nonrepresentational. Born suggests that

> unlike other media, musical sound itself is algogenic, completely un-
> related to language, non-artifact, having no physical existence, and
> non-representational, referring in the first place to nothing other
> than the specific musical system or genre to which it is related. . . .
> And it is this non-representational core of musical sound that
> makes it especially resistant to decoding and ideology. (1991, 166)

Born's project, however, is to develop a theory of musical signification that moves beyond reducing music to a single meaning. She argues that we should see music as inherently mediational and intertextual. Music can be analyzed textually because it is of course much more than isolated sound. As an intertextual medium, it takes on its meaning in relationship to other texts, imagery, and discourses. We experience connotations of music as inherent or immanent when in reality we have projected those cultural connotations onto it.

> It is in this process of projection that music achieves the naturaliz-
> ing effect: The connotations appear to be natural and universal
> where they are historical. It is the forms of talk, text and theory
> around music—the metaphors and rhetoric explaining and con-
> structing it—that may be liable to analysis as ideology. (Born 1991,
> 167)

Born shows that ideas about music have been in part shaped around Other musics; notions about African music have played a significant part in formulating distinctions within a global meaning-system. The configuration of the scholarly field confirms this difference. The many subdivisions within the study of Western "art music"—from studies of philosophy and aesthetics to biographies of artists and histories of classical periods—serve to inscribe the importance of that music. Yet the territory carved out for the study of all other musics is a relatively undifferentiated "ethnomusicology," which—churning together philosophy, biography, and history—relies on the practices and techniques of participant observation.

(Re)-Imagining Africa through Music

African music does not require a theoretical representation
or an explicitly interpretive understanding.
—John Chernoff, *African Rhythm and African Sensibility*

We are often led to understand Western music through its relationship to philosophical debates in Western theory. In contrast, knowledge about "African music" often results from practice-based apprenticeships that help generate an understanding of "local" ways of being. African music is thought to be the domain for immersion into experience, not theory. Yet, as I have been arguing, African music itself is a category based on a philosophical argument about the status of the West. Why, then, is there an aversion to theory in understanding it?

A body of thought has developed in which African music stands in for a critique of the theory-bound, over-intellectual West. African music has been proposed as not-Europe, where "Europe" refers to a tradition of compilation and exclusion in which a few men are honored as geniuses and the rest of us must only receive their wisdom. As a learning tradition, this imagined Europe requires most of us to become the uninitiated adoring audience at the feet of a few geniuses. In contrast, African music can be imagined as a realm of participation and collective embodiment.

In this section, I turn to John Chernoff's discussion of African aesthetics in *African Rhythm and African Sensibility* (1979). The enduring popularity of Chernoff's book testifies to its importance to students of African ethnomusicology. I then move to an equally powerful (if less specifically musicological) set of texts: Trinh Minh-Ha's cinematic portrayal of West Africa in two of her works, *Reassemblage* (1982) and *Naked Spaces* (1985). Trinh is well known as a critic of Eurocentric cultural representations. Yet as a musicologist challenged by the presence of Africa, her critique of Western stereotypes of Africa lies side-by-side with her endorsement of African sensuality. Together they create an artistic moment of perhaps-transcendent and perhaps-critical repetition; thus we return, by another route, to African rhythm and African sensibilities. Both Chernoff and Trinh, I argue, use music to conceptualize "Africa" and to restate its repetitive difference from the West.

I have deliberately chosen to center my discussion around texts that are not the most specialized but are broad-reaching attempts to capture audiences both within and beyond academic settings. These texts link Africa with music in an effort to show how the study of African music can disturb conventional Western ways of knowing the world. I do not see these texts as representative or even of primary importance to the specialized field of African ethnomusicology. I do find, however, that their basic assumptions about an *experience* of African music have informed the field of African ethnomusicology, and more importantly, consumers of African music. I understand that many ethnomusicologists, including ones cited here, have worked hard to dissolve some of the very images of African music that I discuss, yet I believe the field would not hold such power and appeal without those images.

African Rhythm and African Sensibilities

Probably because I enjoyed music more than scholarship, I
was interested in finding a place for myself within a musical
context rather than finding a place for my involvement with
music within a scholarly context.
—John Chernoff, *African Rhythm and African Sensibility*

John Chernoff thoughtfully discloses a sense of his experiences learning Ewe drumming, and perhaps this accounts for his book's long-standing popularity, especially among college students, for whom the book has achieved an almost cult status. Readers are invited to experience African culture with him as he moves with increasing sophistication into an appreciation of drumming and the world he finds around it. Chernoff writes of his field experience, which began in 1971 with an apprenticeship to an Ewe drummer; the relationship continued for ten years. Although Chernoff had trained and was committed to being a social scientist, his interest in learning to play drums shaped and transformed his research goals. Chernoff both immerses himself in Ewe music and, more generally, finds it a critical link to African cultural traditions. Chernoff hopes that his writing about Ewe music will challenge Western biases and allow us to explore the values and aesthetics that help him understand the music he is learning. Moving beyond the structural descriptions of some ethnomusicologists, his book emphasizes what music means to the Africans he met. Chernoff's account of learning to play drums thus brings his readers into a world of Ghanaian culture often lacking in more distanced, "objective" ethnographies.

Like Bebey, Chernoff imagines himself teaching a naive Western readership, unfamiliar with African music. And in the early years of attempting to establish an object called African music, those who knew much about it, beyond specialists, were few. Unlike Bebey, Chernoff's goal is not to catalog African music but to immerse readers in a continental aesthetics. To accomplish this goal, however, he finds himself in the heart of the repetitive binary that produced Bebey's catalog: the difference, and, again, the difference between the West and its African Other. Chernoff is self-conscious about this. He writes, "Discussing 'African' music, therefore, we must recognize that, academically, we are examining music as potential evidence for a conception of Africa." "This is necessary," he continues, "to sense the significance of the variety of specific details we may experience" (1979, 30). Any generalization requires adherence to a category. This much said, Chernoff still does not explore why the category "Africa" in particular becomes the most useful one for generalization. Yet his choice of "Africa" produces his experience of music, as much as the other way around.

Rhythm is the distinctive characteristic of Chernoff's "Africa." African music, he reiterates, is defined by rhythm. He assumes that every scholar or naive participant knows this; it need not be demonstrated or historicized. Chernoff's effort instead moves toward explaining the complexity of the rhythms of Africa. First, they are multiple and overlaid. "Only through the combined rhythms does the music emerge, and the only way to hear the music properly, to find the beat, and to develop and exercise 'metronome sense', *is to listen to at least two rhythms at once*" (1979, 51, emphasis in original). Second, the rhythms are in a constant state of flux. "It is the duration of time that a drummer plays a particular rhythm, *the amount of repetition and the way the rhythms change*, to which the drummers pay attention" (1979, 100, emphasis in original). Third, the audience and the musicians are equally engaged in the production of rhythm, music, sensibility, and Africa. "In African music, it is the listener or dancer who has to supply the beat: the listener must be *actively engaged* in making sense of the music" (1979, 50, emphasis in original).

As I have tried to demonstrate with the quotations I have chosen, Chernoff's prose privileges rhythm; in these passages, he alternates roman and italic type to create a beat of emphasis and explanation, which overlays and crisscrosses, back and back again, a rhythm of difference between the West and Africa. The implied counterphrases—that is, the audience-supplied polyrhythms suggested by the quotations above—are Western monorhythms, predictable Western phrasings, and Western audience-artist separations. It is this distinction between the West and Africa that prioritizes rhythm, and in turn rhythm repeats the difference. Africa is singular and unified because its difference is that which can be repeated in the form of rhythm.

For Chernoff, the experience of Africa is also the experience of community. He sees African music as a unifying force in African communities, integrating individuals into the larger community. Indeed, African music is not abstract and distanced like Western music but is instead an important form through which African people organize their lives. In an article, Chernoff sums up the communal nature of both music and Africa as a formal aesthetic principle.

> The predominant participatory mode of African music can be said to constitute a formal characteristic that takes precedence over other elements of musical organization. In this regard, therefore, aesthetic issues can be contextualized by functional concerns of communal cohesion. The aesthetic principles that make African music work reflect the manner in which the music has been institutionalized to provide frameworks for participation. The music is important to communal objectives of bringing quality to social and cultural occasions. (1991, 1094)

Community is clearly important in Chernoff's understanding of African music, and he repeats this theme many times. Thus, for example, "the aesthetic principles of African music are to an extent dependent on how music can become socially relevant" (1979, 35). "The fact that most people in Africa do not conceive of music apart from its community setting and cultural context means that the aesthetics of music, the way it works to establish a framework for communal integrity, offers a superb approach to understanding African attitudes about what their relationship to each other should be" (1979, 37).

What is surprising about these reiterations is their similarly abstract quality. Chernoff's book, despite its experiential basis, has few stories of the social relations that united and divided the people he knew. His teachers are presented as mentors, not as social actors involved in complex communities. Further, Chernoff presents himself as a teacher about community rather than a full participant in one. I suggest that this abstract quality of community is what makes it possible to understand it as a continental sensibility. Only dreamed-for, wistfully glimpsed, and lectured-about communities are quite so unifying and aesthetic. If Africa, as Christopher Miller argues, is imagined as a "blank darkness," (1985) then the blankness, the unreadability and darkness of an abstract community aesthetic that need not be lived out in historical time, reaffirms the continent. Together with the repetitions of rhythm, the blankness of community makes the unity and persistence of Africa possible. Repeating the communal, we find—once again—Africa.

Reassemblage

In the film [*Naked Spaces*], the way women bodily relate to
each other while working is very rhythmic and musical. In
other words, daily interactions among the people are
music. . . . The way an old woman spins cotton; the way a
daughter and her mother move in syncopation while they
pound or beat the grain together; the way a group of women
chant and dance while plastering the floor of the front court
in a house; these are the everyday rhythms and music of life.
In such an environment one realizes how much modern society is based on compartmentalization—the mentality colonialism has brought in with its spread.
—Trinh Minh-Ha, *Framer Framed*

Filmmaker and cultural critic Trinh T. Minh-Ha began her professional career as a musicologist teaching at the Institut National des Arts in Dakar, Senegal. Her experience of everyday life in Africa as a musicologist led her to make two films, *Reassemblage* (1982) and *Naked Spaces: Living Is Round* (1985). Music pervades her filmmaking and her films. She organizes the tempo and arranges sounds and images to capture a viewer's attention in self-consciously musical ways. She writes of *Reassemblage*: "Looking at this film is like listening to a piece of contemporary music" (1992, 215). Furthermore, as she suggests in the epigraph with which I began this section, the films record the music of African life. Both films introduce us to the integration of everyday styles, syncopations, and harmonies on the one hand, and everyday living spaces on the other. The pounding of grain is "the collective background sound" with which she evokes African village life (1992, 126). Trinh is also particularly concerned to tell her audiences about the musical quality of African languages. She avoids translating the words of the African villagers whose voices she records; to translate, she argues, overemphasizes and colonizes the meaning of their words. Instead, she would have us listen to African voices as pure music: rhythm, inflection, and melody. Here the artist's lack of linguistic comprehension becomes, she argues, a privileged vantage point.

When I travel across African countries, it is precisely by the inflection of the voices, by the music of people's utterances that I am able
to tell where I am and with whom, whether I've crossed a territorial
boundary or not. This is what I would like to bring out in the film
[*Reassemblage*]: language as musical communication and information. . . . [Cutting up and repeating fragments of untranslated con-
versations] is one way of bringing out the music in the language
and challenging the tendency to consume language exclusively as
meaning. (1992, 226–27)

In presenting African languages and cultures as music, Trinh's intention is to critique the knowledge regime of Western stereotypes. Rather
than situating herself within the history of ethnographic descriptions of
Africa, she imagines herself positioned against them. In particular, she
opposes authoritarian interpretations of a culture, such as those she associates with anthropology. Her filming techniques—with their erratic
movements, plurality of views of the same subject, repetition, and abrupt
cuts—self-consciously draw attention to "the limits of the looker and the
camera" (1992, 115). *Naked Spaces* alternates three voices, intended to
represent the villagers, the Western authorities, and her own personal sentiments, respectively. "My approach is one which avoids any sureness of
signification," she writes (1992, 228). *Reassemblage* criticizes Western
specialists on African culture who, Trinh believes, are always commenting
on Africans, turning them into objects of Eurocentric difference. In contrast to "[t]he habit of imposing / Every single sign," she proposes to
"copy reality meticulously" through unexplained visuals, music, and un-
aligned commentary (1992, 103). In *Naked Spaces*, she deliberately pulls
music and visual imagery out of their local context, mixing sounds from
one area with images of another. To break the rules in this way, she suggests, works against ethnic stereotyping by giving culture a "transgressive
fluidity," like that of music (1992, 125).

Trinh's commitment to presenting Africa as music is obviously quite
different from that of John Chernoff, or indeed, of most ethnomusicologists. One important divergence is that Trinh has no particular stake in
arguing that such a thing as "African music" exists. Her effort to make
her films musical bridges aesthetic goals and principles among modern
Western music, daily life in African villages, and traditional African
music. She makes no attempt to sort these out as particular "kinds" of
music. Yet, precisely at this point of maximum divergence from the ethnomusicological project, her work can be seen to circle around to join it.
Where Chernoff goes to Africa to get away from transcendent art, to join
ranks with the people's expression, and to teach us a new kind of art,

Trinh pulls her imagined Africa into the world of transcendent art—where it is asked to expand art in the same familiar way. "Africa may be restless," she writes, "but for me it is full of wisdom, a wisdom that always reminds us of this global village in which we all live" (1992, 220).

For Trinh, the wisdom of Africa expands contemporary and experimental notions of art and communication, for example, by tying the daily rhythms of village life to metropolitan artistic experiments in repetition and syncopation. Rhythm and repetition are "generated by the material" (1992, 114)—that is, by African languages, musics, and daily patterns— as tools of contemporary critical filmmaking. As in the epigraph with which I began this section, Africa is the principle of difference from "modern society" even as it is drawn into the making of modern art. Indeed, African houses and languages and rhythms seem not much different here than other "natural" raw materials that Trinh could have chosen—sand dunes or birds in flight, perhaps.

What Chernoff and Trinh have in common is that despite the respective forms of self-consciousness about the notions of "Africa" that they generate, it never occurs to either to ask any Africans to join them in their ruminations on the problem of how to generalize about Africa. Chernoff stresses the difference of African music while Trinh builds Africa into the avant-garde, but both address themselves entirely to the problems and concerns of non-African audiences, or so we are to conclude from the absence of attention to how the "local" people with whom Chernoff and Trinh interacted might think about "the problem of Africa."

Indeed, Trinh seems less excusable in this regard given her critical stance. While condemning ethnographic research and local language learning, she glorifies her own authority as an artist to speak against Eurocentric stereotypes. Yet to make a productive difference in the regime of stereotyping, she might have to speak to and with the people who are experiencing these stereotypes, not just, as she carefully designs, to "speak near by" (1992: 105). Clearly, Trinh has made considered choices about how to present her African villagers: she doesn't present them with trucks because they are "remote" villages, but she does show their plastic dolls and cups to show the villages "as they are" (1992, 129). She avoids "exotic" ceremonies to present the everyday. Yet for all this self-consciousness she appears never to try to engage the villagers in thinking with her about the very problems she addresses: the relation between signification and colonialism in the production of Africa. Without this engagement, her reflections and deflections of colonial discourse only reverberate with themselves in an endless regime of repetition: more difference, more of the same, more difference, and once again, Africa.

Mediating Rational Translations
through Sensually Embodied Ethnography

As anthropology has undergone its most recent period of self-critique, experimentation, and expansion—as a result of which ethnographic description can no longer be considered objective, neutral, and omniscient—we are urged to see ethnographic accounts as always partial and positioned, not only by the status of the ethnographer but also by the techniques of research and writing (Clifford 1986, Marcus and Fisher 1986, Marcus and Cushman 1982, Barz and Cooley 1997). Discussions of the senses have also recently attracted the attention of ethnographers, for an expanded notion of the senses intervenes to critique the empirical reality described in many "realist" ethnographies (Stoller 1989). Within this critical trajectory, one important move has been to reemphasize the immediacy of fieldwork experience, including the full range of possible sensual involvement with which ethnographers can approach their work as a way into "local knowledges."

With this emerging critique, new attention to the senses has seemed relevant and important. One of the most impassioned pleas for this approach has come from Paul Stoller. Much of the corpus of Stoller's work focuses on Songhay systems of knowledge and healing. In *The Taste of Ethnographic Things*, Stoller invites readers into his sensually heightened initial encounter with Africa during his first days as a Peace Corps volunteer. "At first Africa assailed my senses. I smelled and tasted ethnographic things and was both repelled by and attracted to a new spectrum of odors, flavors, sights and sounds" (1989, 4).

After spending some time in Africa, Stoller, like Chernoff, speaks of his senses becoming dulled as he became more familiar with his surroundings. Stoller, however, considers long-term immersion in the field useful as a way of "tuning [his] senses to the frequencies of Songhay sensibilities" and as a way of countering the methodological constraints of ethnographic realism. This critique of anthropology is important, but it is not without its own limitations as well. First is the distinction between the West and Niger—one alienated from sensuality and the other embedded or filled with sensibility. In assuming the dichotomized features that have so inscribed Africa and the West, Stoller reaffirms the Cartesian divide between mind and body. Is there any question that Africa is "full up" with sensuality, while the West is locked in its own alternate positioning, unable to free itself from rationality. Here again we see neither an undermining of constructed geographies of difference nor greater attentiveness to the range of distinction within each context.

These texts then raise a conundrum that haunts most anthropological analysis that seeks to understand cultural difference and to frame it for multiple audiences. How does one discuss the features that configure differences between the West and Africa while one conveys Africa's levels of complexity? To move beyond these binaries, we may have to raise some questions about some of our most cherished methodologies. Two of the most important tools of the new reflexive anthropology have been the notions of *experience* and the *everyday*.

"Experience" has authorized a subjective mode of writing ethnography, challenging earlier disciplinary demands that knowledge must present itself as neutral and objective, and allowing accounts of fieldwork that show the social and historical particularities of what ethnographers learn, sometimes reaching beyond the too-much-assumed white male gaze. Similarly, the notion of the everyday has been intellectually enlivening, expanding ideas of history to encompass the activities of ordinary people. Yet scholarship on Africa has relied perhaps *too* heavily, and too non-reflexively, on these empowering methodologies: they have come to constitute the essential African. As Chandra Mohanty (1984) argues, criticizing well-meaning but essentialized portrayals of Third World women, we need to be careful of tools that themselves inscribe difference by homogenizing those we are trying to describe.

In this light, consider Trinh Minh-Ha's celebration of the role of music among African villagers.

> Every illness is a musical problem. Music has a magical energizing and creative power. The mere shaking of a cow bell is enough to make people drift into a state of excitement. It is then said that "strength has entered them." Elders who can hardly move in daily situations without a cane would emit war cries and dance frantically to the sound of music. Farmers who feel tired and lack enthusiasm will be fired with desire to work in the fields upon hearing the drum beats or the chants of the masks. "Even if you have eaten and are full," a man says, "you have no sustaining strength to plough the land vigorously and endure the hard work if no music flows in you. (1992, 7)

This description is a celebration of music and its full appreciation in African life. It tugs at our recognition of "experience" and the "everyday," bringing us into another world. Yet it also essentializes Africa, allowing no divisions or debates. We are back with the people without history—and even without gender, class, ethnicity, or the state. The use of these methodologies can naturalize our field encounters as timeless and homogeneous realities.

In a parallel interrogation of experience as a central framing device, historian Joan Scott (1994) puzzles over the use of experience as an authoritative and legitimating kind of evidence in social history as she traces the ways that experience entered into the constructions of counterhegemonic narratives of history. As the histories of the missing, the marginalized, and the less powerful were seized upon, and as the possibility of creating one's "own" history came into vogue, a narrative space was created for those hidden or obscured by normative notions of history. To illustrate the point, she cites E. P. Thompson's *The Making of the English Working Class* (1966), which charted a narrative depicting the experiences of working-class people during early industrialization. Yet Scott carries further Thompson's effort to include only underrepresented subjects by asking how the *categories* of those experiences were formulated. Rather than naturalizing experience, Scott wants to further probe the ways that the very notion of experience is constituted; she thus challenges the homogenization and reduction of history to presentist formulations.

> When experience is taken as the origin of knowledge, the vision of the individual subject (the person who had the experience or the historian who recounts it) becomes the bedrock of evidence on which explanation is built. Questions about the constructed nature of experience, about how subjects are constituted as different in the first place, about how one's vision is structured—about language (or discourse) and history—are left aside. The evidence of experience then becomes evidence for the fact of difference, rather than a way of exploring how difference is established, how it operates, how and in what ways it constitutes subjects who see and act in the world. (Scott 1994, 367)

Scott argues that the problem of experience in social histories is reproduced by using the same strategies and tools of representation as "hegemonic" histories. Indeed, while counterhistories offer a challenge to other histories, such additive approaches fundamentally accept the frameworks of conventional history.

The Critical Difference: Beyond the Rubble of Exploding Categories

In recent years cultural critics have critiqued the essentialized subject, and analysts have challenged the notion that identity is a stable object, unmediated by time, space, social difference, and rank. Many scholars interested in the study of Africa have played a key role in these debates, exploding the idea that there is something that can be unproblematically thought of as an African personality, an African philosophy, or an African way of life. Instead they suggest that the conjuring of an essential African identity is nothing more than a tactical invocation that should be seen as part of various powerful discourses, including—among others—varied forms of cultural nationalisms (Mudimbe 1988, White 1991, Appiah 1992).

Yet nowhere is a reductive notion of Africanness more persistently invoked than in discussions of African music, with its features often constructed in contradistinction to those of Europe. "African" music becomes a critical marking device inscribing the features of a cultural continental divide. Music and Africa come together to form a distinctive niche in the global trafficking of culture as commodity. In the contemporary version of the world-as-exhibition, African musicians travel international performance circuits, offering "traditional" culture and authentic identities for consumers who crave the resources of an imagined homogeneous traditional society.

In this global circulation of "African" culture, "local" distinctions are merged to form a uniform continental identity, and in this formation the unity of African music is created in opposition to its Other, an imagined West. As I have suggested here, two contrasting meanings figure distinctions between the West and Africa: the immediacy of African music (thought to be the embodiment of rhythms) and its role in forming a community of feeling (a communal aesthetic formation).

I have suggested that certain key musicological texts have played a major role in negotiating the meaning of non-Western musics and cultural contexts. Also crucial to this discussion is anthropology's role in developing field methods used by musicologists of non-Western music. I have suggested that it is necessary to go beyond experiential accounts to explore the intellectual categories that we inherit and thus write into as well as against, which constitute a history that often naturalizes "facts" without questioning how they became facts to begin with.

The alternative, I argue, is not to abandon ethnomusicology but to pay more attention to the construction of our categories. One important text that suggests possibilities for doing just that is Paul Berliner's (1994) exciting exploration of the notion of improvisation in relationship to jazz. An important reaction to Adorno's negative impressions about jazz, Berliner's study critically intervenes in the commonly accepted wisdom on narratives of jazz performers. Combining interviews and textual analysis with a look at the process of becoming a musician, Berliner's work allows readers to see how the category of improvisation emerged. He asks, What is improvisation and how is the mystique surrounding improvisation maintained? He writes,

In this regard, the popular definitions of improvisation that emphasize only its spontaneous, intuitive nature—characterizing it as the
"making of something out of nothing"—are astonishingly incom-
plete. This simplistic understanding of improvisation belies the discipline and experience in which improvisers depend, and it obscures
the actual practices and processes that engage them. Improvisation
depends, in fact, on thinkers having absorbed a broad base of musical knowledge, including myriad conventions that contribute to formulating the ideas logically, cogently, and expressively. (1994, 492)

One critical aspect that differentiates Berliner's work from that of the
others discussed here is that he does not expect all "truth" to reside among
the people with whom he is speaking; he points to how social actors are
caught up in the ideologies and practices of musicianship just as one might
expect audiences to be. Berliner argues that because musicians appear to
perform spontaneously and intuitively, and because of the absence of written music, people—including musicians themselves—act as if music just
happens. Through his early work as a musicologist studying the Shona
music of Zimbabwe, Berliner retains a sense of the rigors of composing
music in performance (1994, 2).

Berliner clearly delineates the process of conducting his research,
which adds another step to contextualize and deepen the study. He writes,
"I approached this jazz project with the conviction that there is far more
to improvisation than meets the ear" (1994, 2). The same could be said
of African music. There is much more to understanding music than we
sometimes gain in generalized accounts of African music. Reading the
intertextual narratives that surround this music reveals its even deeper
meaning.

To dispute the importance of experience-based research in anthropology and ethnomusicology is not my goal. Rather, the question remains
how to move beyond the enclosure, both methodological and conceptual,
that sometimes characterizes ethnographic description. Thus I have argued here that the study of global cultural phenomena requires a method
of analysis that can attend to global links rooted in histories that precede
the field encounter. Tracing these histories allows us to see how particular
regions get formed and how the categories through which we think of
culture and cultures "catch" us despite our most empirical motives. In
exploring narratives about "Western" and "African" music, we come to
understand how social narratives of global significance help constitute
both Africa and Europe.

Performances

One evening at Jacob's Pillow, an exclusive dance theatre in the Berkshires hills of western Massachusetts, a musical concert offered an interlude in the summer's regular lineup of performances. On stage, in a space normally reserved for the dance, renowned musician Jali Foday Musa Suso appeared along with a North American flutist. Together they offered a concert of Mandinka music. The assembled audience that evening had little familiarity with the type of music performed, but they sat and listened attentively. Perhaps a few had heard of Suso because of his musical collaborations with contemporary musicians/composers Phillip Glass and Herbie Hancock. Jali Foday Musa Suso also had his own musical ensemble, the Mandingo Griot Society, a group that offered variations of Mande-inspired music along with other popular forms of music primarily aimed at international audiences. At the time of the concert, Suso had resided in the United States for a number of years.

A quick survey of the gathering suggested that most of the audience members were regular concertgoers, many of whom most likely ritually bought season tickets to theater and performance events held at Jacob's Pillow or nearby Tanglewood. A few others in attendance, including the members of the small party that I had managed to convince to come along with me, had come for the single day's event. The price for a ticket seemed costly to those unaccustomed to the scene. The event was held on the elegant grounds of what had once been a working farm, with its old buildings now converted into a ticket area, a gift shop, restaurant, and coffee shop, which together helped enhance the sense of distinction. My arrival in advance of the concert provided some free time to reflect on differences in performance contexts and audience composition that distinguished this event from other formal performances I had attended.

Beyond the areas designated as the preperformance spaces, the formal setting for the event was a barn, the site that Jacob's Pillow developed in the 1940s for dance performances.[1] Within the rustic frame, this New England–style barn was distinguished by its understated attention to details allowing its austerity to complement its high cultural status. The seating arrangement confirmed the sense that this was a refined space, acoustically and visually equipped in a far more sophisticated way than any farm structure would offer. Patrons were ushered to their seats by students in residence at the summer dance school; we sat waiting for the performance to begin.

Just before the start of the performance, the front walls of the barn were pulled back, and the stage was transformed into a different environment. The side walls, pulled away, opened out to a view of a woodland background; the scenery helped give an expansive sense of wonder. It was easy to imagine the ways this "natural" setting would lend itself well to the concert we were about to enjoy. The forest grove, densely filled with the deep green leaves of summer foliage amid tall conifers, provided a magnificent environment.

After the evening was opened with speeches and words of appreciation to the contributors for their generous financial support of the Pillow, Jali Foday Musa Suso entered the stage with his kora. The melodic strings of this instrument held the audience in its sway. A cultured crowd, well-socialized to respond favorably to diverse cultural events, the audience sat with attentive appreciation although they didn't understand the significance of the words Jali Foday Musa Suso sang along with the tunes. The Gambian-born musician stood at attention in a stance I would soon become familiar with within the context of performances I observed in the early 1990s. Jali performances in many North American contexts caused many performers to adopt a stiff stage presence. In part, their activities were hampered because many of the performances were conducted in a language other than that of the audience. The performers sang songs in Mandinka; the audience, uncomprehending, showed barely a trace of awareness of the ways this music might have been performed and received in The Gambia.

At Jacob's Pillow, the response of the audience drew on their ideas about how one is supposed to appreciate high art; they expected that they were indeed listening to a performance of classical music and they responded accordingly. Several elements helped create this atmosphere of discipline and high regard: patronage support, the history of the place itself and the kinds of audiences it tended to attract, and the history of previous performances for which this place had become known.

I open the chapter with the performance at Jacob's Pillow to strike a different chord from chapter 1. Perhaps you immediately became aware through my description of the context of this event of the contrast between this type of performance and the ideas about African music I discussed in chapter 1. How can it be that an object that was configured as "noise," as I suggested African music is sometimes thought of, can now be considered high art music? This atypical performance introduces the focus of this chapter: the importance of performance venues in structuring differences in the production and reception of "African music." The discussion is meant to further engage, and at the same time critique, the limits of the interpretative frame provided in the last chapter's consideration of music's relevance in the context of postcolonial critical discourse.

In looking at a number of diverse performance events, I tease out throughout this chapter the structuring elements that help frame performance and help condition the experience of performance. It would be a mistake, I caution, to see the chapter 1's *representations* of music as the invariant structural framework for making "African music" while this chapter's *performance* is creative improvisation. Performance too easily evokes the notion of agency. Yet performances are also structured and structuring. Here I explore diverse performances to consider the contours of making one kind of "African music" in interactions between performers and audiences—as this both makes and challenges stereotypes of "Africa" and "music." Thus, while I have moved away from the world of written texts, I have not abandoned issues of representation.

Performance venues structure the performance context and therefore inform the reception of the performance. These considerations, however, in no way determine the response to and reception of African music in a rigid way. Performer and audience roles are framed but not fully determined. The performance of performance both constitutes subjects—musicians and listeners—and makes it possible for them to engage in creative deformations and reformations of their situation.

To develop my argument I rely on Pierre Bourdieu's (1990) theory of practice, as presented in his work *The Logic of Practice*. In particular, Bourdieu's discussion of the Kabyle house nicely lends itself to a discussion of the architecture that helps create subjective encounters with the materiality of experience. His discussion raises a number of important questions about the uses of time and space—whether in a house or in the performance venues in which Mande music is played. Bourdieu points to the significance of the material aspects of space and time, and to their creation in the use of artifacts and the following of routines. Understandings of space and time are embodied—they are inhabited—and in this way they could be said to be performed.

Bourdieu's concept of habitus offers a means for understanding both the reproduction of social process and its everyday transformations. The concept allows us to look at how subjects are formed as part of a social milieu, which orients them and predisposes them towards certain actions. Subjects are made through the habitus. They share common cultural constraints through embracing certain practices; they also gain their agency as subjects through these practices. Even as they reproduce their cultural frameworks through their everyday enactments, they do so with the uncertainty and slippage of agential action.

Bourdieu's description of the Kabyle house is a compelling example of this theory of practical enactment. He describes the spatial arrangeient of a house to show how physical structures help frame the way people are oriented toward the world and come to occupy and domesticate space. The design of the house makes subjects who use their bodies in space in particular ways. The house produces an "architecture" in both a literal and a metaphorical sense. The house inspires a performance that is both structured and creative. In much the same way, performance venues provide the frame for musicians and audiences by offering a literal and metaphorical stage for the enactment of subject positions. They reproduce the "difference" that constitutes Africa, but they reproduce it unstably and with room for maneuver.

The contexts described here are formal performance events and, although different in location and purpose, they share elements that place them in privileged arenas. They are set apart from ordinary everyday events, while at the same time they draw on everyday expectations to inform the experience of the performance. A number of elements create the "architecture" through which the expectations of both performer and audience are formed. In describing the concert at Jacob's Pillow, I mentioned the structure of funding and patronage, the spatial and physical arrangement of the venue, the events that preceded the performance that create a history through which audience members receive and interpret the event, and representations that help inform what the performance comes to mean. These multiple elements, to which others could be added, create a stage for enactment of the experience of African music.

In what follows, I track back and forth between concerts in the United States and concerts in The Gambia and Senegal. As in chapter 1, I am looking for the making of cultural frames and practices in transcontinental dialogues. As I look for the conversations provoked by the performances of African music, in this case with an emphasis on music performed by Gambian jali, the chapter also addresses questions of interpretation and translation: how do audience participants at performance events interact with Gambian jali in both Senegambian and transnational contexts? A consideration of how both producers and engaged audience members frame Africa within the performance event rests at the center of the discussion. While many aspects in transnational performance events confirm the expectations that audience participants arrive with, it is also possible to observe unexpected transformations.

One of my goals here is to introduce the diversity of concert arenas in which Gambian jali perform, which include urban and village events, national political and local community events, and international cultural festivals, including "world music" events as well as performances billed as "traditional African music" concerts. What sorts of cultural assumptions do audience members arrive with in each of these venues? What sorts of mediations take place during the performance event?

The Ethnographer at Home?

Late in October, 1990, in a small New England town on the outskirts of Boston, musicians from The Gambia, together with American musicians, presented a concert. The group had formed a temporary alliance to offer performances as they toured the U.S. east coast. Billed as a "world music" event, and part of a series of intercultural events scheduled at the center throughout the year, the concert attracted an audience interested in what was more broadly defined as "world beat" music. The concert was sponsored by a local "New Age" center. Having only recently returned "home" from fieldwork in The Gambia, I was acutely aware that the protocol for this U.S.-based event, as at Jacob's Pillow, offered a striking contrast to the performances I had observed while I was in The Gambia. The entrance to the event offered an initial sign. Those in attendance at this event, including myself and perhaps fifty others, paid the admission price and entered a large dimly lit auditorium reminiscent of a public school hall. The atmosphere in the hall as the people entered was certainly subdued, at least compared to many Gambian concerts. The stage was already arranged with instruments and amplification equipment.

When the musicians appeared, the audience members took their seats, gazing ahead, waiting patiently for the performance to begin. The performers conformed to a familiar image associated with many world music groups. They picked up electrified instruments to combine with each other in what was clearly a nationally diverse group. The music produced by this group was an explicitly "fusion" sound of jazz attached to Mandinka praisesongs. The kora was one of the instruments positioned closest to us and was the least familiar of the instruments to most of the audience. Its twenty-one strings filled the front of the stage with a resonant sound.

During the early songs, most members of the audience continued to sit sedately. But soon enough, a few young white people got up and started to dance in the aisles, throwing their bodies around with an abandonment that suggested they were listening to a different melody or set of tunes than those of us who remained in our seats. The kora does not produce a strong rhythmic dance beat of the sort their dancing implied; its rhythms are more subtle and layered. Yet the dancers re-imagined it within their hearing of "African music." Such dancers had been affectionately referred to by a colleague of mine as "the organic dancers" when we watched a similar event.[2] The audience performers were not an unfamiliar sight; they often appear at world music events, dressed with a fashion sense most immediately derived from the 1960s. As they danced, their bodies in motion appeared to be controlled by alien spirits. But perhaps these entertainers were moved to respond in contradistinction to the reserved performance code displayed by most of the audience participants, generally people who appeared to be older than the organic dancers. The dancers appeared to seek a release from the restraints of everyday life. Moreover, their display seemed part of an already prepared script. Their response to the music reminded me of the popular ideas about African music discussed in chapter 1: It is rhythm; it transcends reason to touch the spirit. Their response, although awkward in relation to the music, resonated with broader configurations of "The Africa."

The musicians offered their own awkwardness. They followed conventions sometimes found in the United States where some performers appear rather aloof, ignoring the audience in a studied detachment. Here the performers appeared to presuppose that the audience simply was made of mass consumers with little appreciation of the sounds they were producing. This particular event suggested that for the most part the audience members had not sought out Mandinka music or known what a jali might be. The performers from West Africa were presented as generic "African" musicians, and distinctive associations to Mande jali music were not apparent. Both the dancing and the seated audience's uninspired reception further suggested that this was just another exotic cultural attraction, a world music performance staged under the tent of the global cultural marketplace.

In contrast to the overwhelmingly distanced response of most of the audience participants, the organic dancers seemed to find an eclectic blend of sounds that generated impulsive reactions. This music offered a different version of being in the world than their everyday lives in the West; it offered a sense that African music overcomes the numbness of the Western body and mind. In their mind's ear they heard—behind the kora riffs and jazz tunes—the beat of African drums, audio-scripts made decades ago by premiere artists like Nigerian drummer Olatunji. Yet in their effusive response to "The Africa," few of the organic dancers seemed to notice that the melodious sound of the kora created its own distinctive sound and rhythmic patterns. The kora's sound was overcome by the spectacle of dancers pounding out a rhythm to a different beat.

A closer look at the audience revealed that the spectators consisted mostly of white Americans. Their numbers had swelled to about seventy-five people. At the other extreme of behavior from the organic dancers were the small group of African Americans whom I had invited to hear one of the musicians, a superb kora player with whom I had studied in The Gambia. The seven African Americans were reverent spectators, often glancing at the white dancers with their own stiff embarrassment. We sat sedately, showing our respectful attention to "African music" as if it were a symphony—a music to be revered. Most of us knew a little something of Gambian praisesingers. Gambian musicians were not just another cultural product in the world supermarket, but something central to our sense of connection with Africa: the griots wondrous., ___ nected to our imagined past, creating the fictive kinship ties to our African relatives.

Certainly our ideas about proper responses to the music were formed by the conventions of classical European concerts, as much as—undoubtedly more than—by our limited notion of what "African" standards might be. It became irrelevant that the form of the music might have called for a more active response, although not necessarily the response of the expressive organic dancers. In showing respect, we were constructing an "African" culture just as old and valuable as European civilization. African culture should be respected; the appropriate response is learning and reverence. Toward the end of the concert, a few of the African Americans rose to move to the music. They did so, however, with a keen awareness that dance steps are learned and not just the random responses to what one feels. Indeed, even these steps toward active engagement were cautious rejoinders.

Not to be forgotten here are other elements that help create a performance, including the dress for the occasion. One version of "The Africa"—a sense of distance and awe for something out of time—was created and sustained by the attire of a few of the musicians. Seeing their long flowing robes, massive amounts of cloth covered with elaborate embroidery, while listening to the intricate and unfamiliar melodies of Mande-inspired music, the Gambian musicians helped create a unique moment, a moment of exotica. For some spectators, the "costumes" confirmed Africa as a place of timeless tradition, a view helped along by references to Mali.

The strength of this version of an imagined Africa became especially clear to me at a moment of disillusionment and confusion after the concert. As I went to introduce one of my friends backstage to my Gambian teacher, she was startled by his appearance. During the concert she had been impressed by the refinement of his classic, authentic, African dress. When the musician emerged from his dressing room in Levis and a plaid shirt, however, looking more Western cowboy than Gambian jali, she was shocked. Kiddingly, she scolded me, "You didn't tell me he was a dude!" Could the familiar figure in Levis represent the authentic Africa for which she longed? This "authentic African" musician looked like any African American man.

But the jali was not exactly a familiar "dude." The musician had his own distinctive projects and agendas in traveling and performing jaliya not just in The Gambia and the United States but worldwide. He was more cosmopolitan than the traditional outfit indicated to her; jali are cosmopolitan travelers by profession. Furthermore, he had no investment in being seen as a village elder; he was an entrepreneur, attempting to bridge the gap between Africa and the West. He was gaining a reputation that would help him spread his circle of influence and jaliya communication beyond The Gambia. His interest in expanding ways of marketing his talents into a viable income was crucial. The jali performances, though limited by the institutions and conventions of the U.S. culture industry, were negotiated by performers and sponsors of the event.

The disjunctive reactions of audience members heightened my awareness of the basic cultural frames that "staged" the performance. I had to think about aspects of performance that Western audiences generally take for granted when attending a concert, particularly, although not exclusively, a concert of classical music. The audience members generally turn to face a stage that spatially separates audience and performers. The performance is scheduled for a particular time. The higher the event's status, the more likely the concert will start on time—with only a fifteen-minute grace period—and with little notable attention to the arrival of patrons. The money is transacted either through prepaid credit card arrangements or at the concert hall door. The more prestigious the event, the more likely that appreciation is expressed by distant attentiveness, quiet appreciation of the music with clapping, and perhaps a bit of pleased sound and a standing ovation at the end of the performance. In popular concert events, there is a lot more noise and action, but many of the conventions separating performers and audiences are similar. The distinctions among audience members are played out in the lobby of the concert hall—upon the arrival of audience members and during intermission—but generally these distinctions are less actively noticed by the musicians during the concert.

The concert in Massachusetts, which followed this format, offered a sharp contrast to performances given by Gambian musicians in other settings. First, in comparison to the familiar routine for jali performing in Africa, at this concert the musicians could neither call out particular members of the audience to praise them, nor, in offering praises, expect the audience/patrons to give money above the admission fee as a way to express appreciation for the music. Second, the musicians neither differentiated among audience members to refigure status distinctions, nor thereby acted as provocateurs for the steady stream of people trying to be seen by other audience members. One could only look out and see what appeared to be—with the exception of the organic dancers—a relatively homogeneous mass of calm faces.

During the concert one musician appeared amused by the audience's reaction to the music. As he gazed out at the collective mass with relative disinterest, he had achieved one feature of Western classical music: distance, recreating the hierarchy that often exists between audience and performer. He was forced to play within a frame in which his music produced an Africa appreciatively consumed by the audience and movingly expressive to them. There was no way out of the construction of audience as homogeneous mass, thus configured as the West.

To see how Gambian jali negotiate "The Africa" within a different set of conventions and audience expectations, consider the conventions of a concert setting in The Gambia. While performances in the United States vary, they often fall within the formal concert setting of world music or traditional African music frames; performance events are much more diverse in The Gambia, where jali figure prominently in many scenes. Strikingly, "tradition" is not a category of constraint in The Gambia; it does not cordon off musicians to repeat only "authentic African" performances. Jali historically have been positioned as important cultural brokers with a keen sense of performing tradition to enact a past usable for the present. Patrons aware of this fact work within the borders of jali's rhetorical power and ability to create history relevant to their own agendas.

Patronage systems that support the activities of jali in The Gambia are varied; concerts are sometimes sponsored by the government for political causes, such as literacy and national development programs as well as the installations of new political figures in national office. Jali also perform for foreign tourists as well as community groups and kin networks. Because Gambian jali perform what is self-consciously constructed as Mandinka tradition, within their performance agendas they make a statement about Mandinka ethnic pride and history within a multiethnic nation. And in contrast to the performances in the United States they do not construct their audiences as a homogeneous Other; instead, they make status distinctions within their audiences central to the performance.

Unlike audiences in the United States, Mandinka and other Gambian audience members—sometimes including members from other ethnic groups, such as Wolof, Fula, Serer, and Jola—often understand the words and the meaning of the songs. Furthermore, they have a sense of the meaning of the words in context. For example, as jali sing songs as "Kelepha Ba," which narrates the life story of a great Mande warrior of centuries ago, some hear the history of a once-powerful kingdom. Yet songs about past kings and warriors always also apply to current political relations; the songs of praise draw in contemporary heroes and politicians and make them known to audiences. Jali songs are genealogies even when they are not directly about kinship; they tell the history of the past for the glory of the present. As particular audience members are honored, they—and members of their social network—approach the stage to give money to the musicians. The performance thus distinguishes not just the jali but also the families and friends of those being praised.

I turn to three more performances to focus on the kinds of differences that create certain meanings of African music, and I analyze how audience response and expectations differ in each case. Central to each event described are the social configurations and dynamics that operate in these contexts and how they become sites for understanding lines of difference as well as convergence.

The Ethnographer Abroad?

Santa Cruz, California, is a town renowned for attracting international cultural producers of various traditions, among whom are shamans, herbalists, and alternative healers as well as international musicians and performers, notably Gamelan orchestras and African drummers. The following incident conveys a sense of the town. Early in 1996, a local controversy in Santa Cruz focused around the rights of drummers who had been given a curfew restricting the number of hours and times of day that drumming was permitted. This curfew issue was fiercely debated, which offers some sense of the intense enthusiasm among the small gathering of patrons at a performance of Guinean musicians in a small night club. The eclectic nature of this California town was evident on a Saturday evening in the spring of 1996.

The performance began with a brief introduction by an African American drummer and instructor, who would later participate in playing drums with the performers from Guinea. The musicians entered with percussion instruments—drums and balaphons—and were accompanied by a woman who danced and sang. The concert followed the usual convention of audiences in a coffee house setting. For the most part, people remained in their seats drinking tea and eating desserts while they waited for the performance. The tables and chairs left little room to move about—or so it seemed at first. A few people swayed behind the rows of seats that filled the space. But rather than simply being a performance for tourists that reproduced binary distinctions between the West and Africa, this performance realized more flexibility and allowed for the display of the cultural knowledge of audience members. In this small café space, audience members lined the back of the room and filled every available seat. Many of those left standing were thus well positioned to start the familiar organic dance once the performance began, and, indeed, within seconds the erratic swaying and convulsive behavior started, carrying audience performers on their journey to "The Africa." This was a performance dominated by percussive instruments, thus confirming many of the stereotypes of African music as consisting of a repetitive rhythmic beat—a beat that soon allowed some participants to appear to enter a trance state, as a less enthusiastic participant suggested to me.

Yet I was in for a surprise. After a tense segment that featured the adroit talents of one of the drummers in the group, a few women in the audience slowly made their way to the stage to place dollar bills on the forehead of the lead drummer. Obviously, these audience members knew something about West African aesthetic conventions. As the musicians reached the end of the concert, the lead drummer for the evening invited audience participation more directly, first by encouraging people to clap along and then by inviting people up to the stage to dance alongside the other musicians. One of the women who had earlier expressed appreciation of the drummer's performance reappeared on the stage to participate in the dancing. Yet she did so in distinct contrast to the early dancers (some of whom appeared quite drained after an evening of full participation). The woman's movement suggested that she had studied dance somewhere in West Africa or even Santa Cruz, and understood dance as a studied practice and not as the wild movements that captured the bodies of the organic dancers.

For those of us who remained in our seats, this mix of stage presentation by members of the audience and the performers culminated as an effective way of viewing the enactment of various "Africas"—from organic dancers to people who just wanted to move around to those who appeared to have studied dance with the African American drummer to the teacher himself, who rejoined the drummers—all disrupting distinctions that seemed so entrenched in the world music performance in Massachusetts. This mingling of audience and performers disassembled, if only momentarily, "The Africa" and the "West" as homogeneous entities. Perhaps the exposure of the United States to African music in the 1990s was having a significant effect in creating new American audiences with African talents.

In The Gambia

I now turn to a performance I observed in The Gambia featuring a very popular performer, Jaliba Kuyateh, to offer a sense of one set of performance conventions and audience expectations in The Gambia. Jaliba is one of the most popular jali in The Gambia and outlying regions, especially among young audiences, for his music addresses the concerns of many Gambian youth, in addition to a range of other themes. An elderly patron explained to me that he and people of his generation also liked Jaliba's music. The patron mainly highlighted the musician's personal charisma but admitted that Jaliba was also considered an innovative performer. Meanwhile, teenagers with whom I attended one of Jaliba's concerts saw him as a rock star; as one explained to me, the feeling just can't be articulated in words. In contrast to the more conventional setting of a jali family performing with balaphon or kora, at times Jaliba performed with a nine-member band. He incorporates a great variety of instruments, some of them amplified.

The concert described here occurred when Jaliba's group offered the entertainment at a fund-raising event for a village community association. The performance began late, but the time preceding the music was critical. The concert was held in a public meeting space in a town just outside of Banjul. A modest admission price was collected at the door. The door was a center of attention not because of ticket-taking but because of the expected appearance of notable guests. As audience members sat and waited, each time an important patron arrived, jali women stood up and sang, offering extended praises of their patrons. Each of the patrons was expected to offer a token of appreciation for the elaborate praises bestowed upon them; only then did the praising simmer down gradually as the next patron's entrance drew some of the attention of the jali. The former patron was escorted to the seating area reserved for special dignitaries, and jali women would soon be off to greet the other arriving celebrities. This welcome before the musical performance gave the appearance of a Hollywood gala affair where the stars are ushered in before the concert.

As the entering guests were praised, the preconcert performance provided enough entertainment for those waiting. We waited over an hour beyond the concert's scheduled beginning time. The delay, however, was not a surprise; it was just a fact of life. This is not to say that the audience members, at least the ones around the place where I was sitting, were not put out by the excessive delay. Everyone familiar with the scene knew that an important official had not yet arrived, and only when the official walked in and was appropriately praised could the formal stage become the center of attention.

The patrons' work had only begun. Political dignitaries made speeches from the stage, displaying their elevated status by speaking through their jali. In a form of communication found in many parts of West Africa, a political official or dignitary will stand in front of the crowd (sometimes even in front of a microphone) where the audience can clearly hear what is being said, and the message will be repeated in a kind of relay system of patron to jali and then jali to the audience. In addition, other jali throughout the audience shouted enthusiastic approval from the floor as statements were made; in so doing, they offered honor to the speaker and also kept the audience engaged.

But the beginning of Jaliba's music did not stop the play of interaction between performers and audiences; distinctions between patrons and clients were enacted throughout the evening. The patrons, their families and friends, and audience members wove their way back and forth between the stage and their seats, offering money to the members of the band as well as to the jali women who had only recently attached themselves to the performance. The parade to the stage and back to the seats gave people an opportunity to publicly exhibit their distinction, showing off their fine clothes as they greeted appropriate members of the audience. The women jali danced—and not the wild spectacle of organic dancing. Jali women, whose fame is enhanced, many explained to me during our interviews, by being bold and daring, danced with expressive movements that exhibited both their skill and their less-than-noble origins. (The mark of a powerful individual is public restraint in speaking as well as dancing.) While members of the audience paraded back and forth, the women's village organization that had sponsored the event displayed their social power and solidarity by appearing in matching dresses and head wraps. They also danced on stage along with Jaliba's band.

As suggested in this account, the performance site was not restricted to what was formally happening on stage; rather, the stage extended to include audience members as well. The performance generated a variety of distinctions. Performers differed in status from their patrons; jali marked their distinction in manner, speech, and dress. The play of praises, donations, and self-presentations contrasted rank, individual power, and prestige. Social networks were displayed when associates of an honored guest made public donations to further praise the important person, and by extension, his jali. Gender distinctions within the performance event further framed personal displays of control, sometimes at the borders of appropriate self-display and restraint. Gender lines were affirmed and manipulated as elite men displayed their status by gathering jali praises, as wives showed off their finery and honored their husbands by donations to the jali who praised them, or as unmarried elite girls displayed their modesty and coy reserve.

That evening seemed akin to a call-and-response concert. Praising one's patrons generated audience approval in the form of an endless circuit of contributions to the jali during the performance. I could not stand outside this display of distinctions. (If given the choice, I would have acted in a more sedate U.S. concert-going fashion, I'm sure!) Jaliba played one song especially to honor me, though in a case of mistaken identity he started playing a song he had composed about the struggle in South Africa. South Africa and apartheid had become more than a BBC news story for Gambians because, as I mentioned earlier, many Namibians were offered refuge in The Gambia for a period of time. It took me some time to figure out why, when walking down the street in Banjul, people would occasionally raise a fist to me and sing the South African anthem, but clearly Jaliba also thought that that was my national origin. The song touched on issues of much concern to The Gambian public, while bringing me into the status dynamics of the performance. I made my way as modestly and appropriately as I could to the stage to deposit my donation, embarrassed at being called out in spite of my evident shy resolve to stay in my chair unnoticed.

Jaliba's Gambian performances generally try to incorporate such outsiders as tourists and researchers. Tourism, as one of the biggest sources of immediate cash flow income for The Gambia, offers some jali an additional performance outlet; the reputations of jali in international circuits make them one of the main cultural attractions for the tourist industry in The Gambia.

One jali told me of how he made a practice of greeting arriving tourists in The Gambia with his balaphon, and welcomed them with some praisesinging. Of course, the tourists neither understood nor fully appreciated his attempts at generating an income or getting new patronage. The tourists probably assumed they were just viewing another "native custom" from the Third World living museum without realizing how they were expected to respond.

Indeed, in jali concerts in The Gambia, many tourists sat gazing with a detached stare while other adventurous participants tried to dance, often to their own rhythms with little attention to the studied distinctions of the moves of Mandinka women and men around them. In a concert I attended, held for Peace Corps volunteers, a jali played the "Battle Hymn of the Republic" to welcome the American volunteers. It was a song no doubt of immediate familiarity to the Americans, although perhaps this was not the missionary spirit with which they wished to be associated. The jali saw this as an effort to honor his U.S. audience; the audience was pleased, but instead of offering money to express their enjoyment, they clapped politely. Other conversational ploys were missed as well, including status distinctions of age, rank, and gender among the musicians. How surprised one guest was when I explained that senior men controlled the activities of junior male musicians and had to give permission for the junior musicians to perform.

These examples of misrecognition across a divide of aesthetic conventions give insight into how audience and performance conventions are learned and not just absorbed through the music. The transcultural incorporation and misunderstandings that I witnessed in The Gambia form part of a common, though varied, conversation about "The Africa" in which jali, patrons, tourists, researchers, and Peace Corps volunteers all take part. Another node for this awkward dialogue forms around distinctions created by dancing to jali music. Most European and American audiences not familiar with African dance and performance conventions cannot distinguish the degrees of modesty and skill that differentiate status in Mandinka audience dancing. For those of us not terribly familiar with the conventions of forms, the musicians and dancers blur together to create a homogeneous African mass. Most tourist audiences want to test this, to taste it, as they mimic an imagined Africa in their own dancing. And representations of Africa beyond the immediate event call up an Africa that can fill in where information does not.

Meanwhile, Gambian audience members, including members of various ethnic groups, look on with expressions of bewilderment or disgust at the revealing clothes and wild dancing of many tourists. At the heart of this disdain is their stereotype of the behavior of Western women. Especially for many older people, the West becomes the homogeneous, eroticized mass of wild dancers. Elderly Mandinka women remember their modesty and contrast themselves as Not-European. Gambians often imagine the Western woman as a dangerous erotic Other, just as tourists assign that position to African men, who, after all, produce the music they associate with unbridled sensuality. In this eroticized global space framed by various attractions and repulsions, members of the Gambian audience insist on status distinctions of modesty, community, and prestige, while Euro-Americans disregarded such distinctions. Gambians stared at tourist participants, particularly women, as if they really had crossed some boundary. At the same time, note that Gambians were appreciative of what they considered honest efforts to learn traditional arts.

I have suggested that audience reaction is an important site for understanding varied meanings of Africa as they are played out in performances of African music. The ways people make meanings, however, should be understood within the histories that shape them and that serve as a lens through which interpretations are filtered. What is exciting about performance as an ethnographic lens, when combined with discursive construction of Africa, is that we understand some of how audiences create new meanings that might ultimately help transform the boundaries that would otherwise only confine. Performance space reconfigures understandings of Africa, even within the apparatus that makes performance happen.

Beyond The Gambia—and the West

This next description of a performance event's complexities and contestations illustrates competing visions and agendas observed during an extended cultural heritage festival held in Sedhiou, a predominantly Mandinka town in southern Senegal. Art and politics came together and, in contradistinction to ideas that music unifies, formed deep divisions.

The festival was organized by the Senegalese cultural ministry in conjunction with officials from The Gambia, Guinea Conakry, and Mali. On the surface, the festival innocently brought together musicians and dancers from a broad region to celebrate their respective traditions, but it also provided an opportunity for divergent agendas to emerge. To some organizers, the festival provided an opportunity to bring together Mande peoples across national borders to express an ethnic-political unity. Held in a region of Senegal known for its animosity towards northern Senegal, some thought ethnic mobilization of a pan-Mande celebration in Sedhiou might help support villagers in the region. This vision, however, was not shared or even apparent to all who attended the concert. In facilitating the festival, officials from northern Senegal diplomatically hoped to keep control over a tense situation by appeasing local Mandinka leaders as well as making peace with Mandinka-dominated neighboring nations. But the political balance that would emerge through the festival was clearly in question.

The festival at Sedhiou further staged an antagonism between two competing political visions of "Africa." On the one hand, for some Mandinka officials the festival would potentially display the force of Mande history and culture, a call for postcolonial regional organization. Mande is an ethnic category that includes Mandinka as well as related groups, such as Bambara. Some imagined that Mande culture could be an alternative to European colonial culture and thus form the basis of a new regional political orientation. If performance traditions could provide a common focus, they could also lead to a sense of shared political values—at least this was the desired effect for which some of the organizers had hoped. Here the invocation of tradition played a dual role: first, reinscribing a vision of old hierarchies and rightful rulerships as once found under a precolonial regime; and, second, addressing contemporary imbalances between northern and southern Senegal.

On the other hand, other leaders and officials fought for a "modern" state order, continuing the political orientation inherited from Europe, which was imagined as overseeing a "pluralistic" Africa based on nationalism in which every group had its own performance heritage but not an overarching political culture. This contrasted with a different nationalist longing for an imagined community that preceded the carving up of territory that took place under various colonial regimes.

Participants in the festival at Sedhiou were caught up in a variety of ways, drawn into the debates among varied versions of culture; yet many participants were not aware of all the dynamics. Those in attendance at the festival included state officials from a number of countries, representatives from several ethnic traditions (although with a major emphasis on the performance of Mande music), community dance groups, local towns-people, stray tourists, and visitors from other countries in Africa.

Some of the visitors who were not invited national guests but who came from other African countries did not catch on initially to the "Mande world" theme; three visitors from Sierra Leone, for example, expressed their disappointment that they had not sent their own dance troupes. To them, the pluralistic heritage festival model was self-evident and drew on other models of music performance used to unify Africa, such as Festac.[3] To these observers, the intense debates that shadowed the festival were not visible. In contrast, some of the Gambian officials who accompanied the Gambian jali assumed that the entire event would be a celebration of Mande culture; some refused to accept until the very end the possibility of other agendas. Other Gambian officials were being courted to view things from a different angle by Senegalese officials. As for the Gambian jali, many wanted their moment in the spotlight; they had practiced a long time for this event. With an awareness of the tension between models, perhaps they might be able to finesse all sides.

During the festival, I was caught up in the tension of the event, though in a different way. I was hastily recruited for my ability to document the event. As the official recorder of the event for The Gambia, a position sprung on me without training or prior consent, my duty was, at the request of the director of the Oral History and Antiquities Division (OHAD), to tape record the events. This position offered a particular challenge as it was not exactly clear which perspective I was supposed to record. In contrast to the concert I described earlier in which I was placed in the position of a patron, here I was rather like a jali, a cultural worker dependent on the political sponsorship of competing patrons and officials. In this position, I was particularly aware of the battles being waged in even minor performance arrangements. Over the next seventy-two hours, participants used control over time, language differences, and scheduling difficulties as means of political maneuvering. Within performances, the relationship between jali and patron further revealed the interdependence of performance and politics.

On the first night of the festival, officials from each of the represented countries set the tone by ceremoniously arriving late and speaking in European languages. They established their power over the cultural event, making who was in charge clear to the audience. The festival could not go on without the sponsorship of the politicians. At the same time, the officials could not establish the control they might have envisioned. The praisesinging that greeted the entrance of each politician reminded the audience of the dependence of political leaders on the performance work and cultural frameworks of jali.

A case in point involved the arrival of an important official from The Gambia. He arrived late, although he had been nearby for hours, and he spoke in French, to the great irritation of his fellow countrymen, who saw his speech as an attempt to display his closeness to the French-speaking Senegalese elite. Even if he were too snobbish to speak Mandinka, one person I spoke with reasoned, he could at least have spoken in English, the language of Gambian colonial rule. Yet his speech was marked by one of the most extended praisesinging episodes of the evening. Certainly, the jali's extended praises spoke not just of his power but of the power of jaliya and the united Mande culture for which it had become an advocate. The French speech and the Mandinka praise were thus not reconstituted in *their* dialogue.

In some ways, the official's lateness alone instituted the pluralistic model of African heritage. Village-based groups had also practiced extensively to present local performance traditions at the festival not just to display their dances, costumes, and music but also to highlight the power of their social networks and political idioms. Because of the lateness of the hour, the groups jammed together as if it were a parade lineup, each group passing across the stage in front of the special dignitaries' box of seats within only a few minutes of the performance, one troupe after the other. The timing itself created a procession-like spectacle of what appeared to be insignificantly different local customs, each powerless to assert its hegemony even in taking over the stage. Yet the other major event of the first night created the opposite effect. The popular Gambian jali, Jaliba, whose music I discussed earlier, provided appealing dance music and rekindled the sense that the festival was a celebration of Mande cultural power and youthful exuberance. It was late, however, when he appeared—the hour when one would expect to see the young and not their parents, who had long ago retreated.

On the second day, tensions rose again. The audience had to wait for late-arriving officials, this time for more than three hours. At 11 P.M. the lateness of the hour condensed the performance time to a bare minimum. Performers had to struggle for an even more limited time on the stage than they had the night before. By the end of the third and climactic final night, tempers were short, and dissatisfaction was voiced from many quarters. The Gambian jali had expected to offer a major performance that night; they had practiced for months for this event. First, they were disappointed to hear that jali from other countries and performance groups had been scheduled ahead of them in the program. There was considerable grumbling about the ineffectiveness of Gambian politicians, who should have pushed for a more prestigious slot. Second, the officials were once again hours late, and when they arrived, the sound system malfunctioned. When at 11 P.M. the first jali began to play, spectators, who once more had been waiting for hours after the expected time, were frustrated. Yet perhaps the jali would still carry the evening.

After the first jali group performed, however, a Senegalese theater troupe presented a play about wife abuse, a theme far from the thoughts of those organizing a Mande cultural event that would inspire regional reconstruction. The group was ushered onto the stage and interrupted the sequence planned by the jali performers. The theatre troupe's notion of an issue of concern clashed with the heroic stories of the Mande kingdom. The play, however, was well received, at least given the lateness of the hour.

The consequence of these scheduling issues was that the Gambian jali were not able to take the stage until 3 A.M. Many in the audience stayed, but as time went on, the audience began to change from a mixed age crowd to a younger group, anxiously awaiting the dance band's appearance. By the time the Gambian jali finally came on to perform traditional songs, the performers were forced to limit themselves to three short songs, performed in about fifteen minutes. Under such constraints, the competition to get even a moment as lead player became intense. The Gambian contingent left the festival for the evening a few hours later as a dispirited group. Even more than the jali, some of the patrons were disappointed that the Mande world they had imagined had not emerged by the end of the event.

In the festival, as in other jali performances, distinctions of rank, social network, and gender were manipulated, displayed, and confirmed. Yet the debate over visions of "The Africa" made both performers and audiences aware of the fragility of these distinctions and their dependence on institutional support for particular conditions of performance. The possibilities of performing these distinctions rests on a framework of political culture that even the most powerful Gambian patrons cannot unconditionally guarantee. Yet as the Massachusetts performance I discussed above suggests, jali have long been flexible in adapting their skills to address and reconstruct varied expectations about "The Africa."

Even in their disappointment, jali are flexible; so are audiences. In the United States, jali have been used by various groups, including folk heritage organizations in the United States such as the Smithsonian, World Music, Inc., New Age groups, and African American cultural nationalists, to create their own distinctions among audience members. Members of the Gambian diaspora in cities around the world are also constituents who continue to rely on the services of jali; they add their own distinctions. Representations of Africa are contested and negotiated in relation to multiple social histories: class, race and ethnicity, gender, age, status, and national origin. Audiences participate, then, in cultural production.

They create social and political commentary about tradition, the Mande world, and the place of Africa in a global cultural economy.

In this chapter I have argued that performance practices are unstable, shifting in the histories, debates, and contingencies of enactment. Performance contexts provide an important arena in which to observe how multiple claims about culture and difference are staged and negotiated. Performance is a way to gain access to the meaning of Africa for audiences and performers of jali music. I have shown the play of different kinds of distinctions, ranging from local social distinctions of status, gender, caste, and ethnicity, to regional, national, and international geopolitical discourses. Cultural formation is a process in which meaning is various, contested, and emergent; "The Africa" exists in negotiation and flux. At the same time, its meaning is reproduced through the institutional practices of performance events.

Professional Dreams

> The history of nations . . . is always already presented to us
> in the form of a narrative that attributes to these entities the
> continuity of a subject. The formation of the nation thus ap-
> pears as the fulfillment of a "project" stretching over centu-
> ries, in which there are different stages and moments of com-
> ing to Self-awareness, which the prejudices of historians will
> portray as more or less decisive.
> —Etienne Balibar, *Race, Nation, Class*

H istory projects attempt to make a past that answers the challenge of nation-building and political identity. Yet the elements
required to generate a sense of national identity and political
culture are not clear. The chapters in this part discuss the negotiation of
Gambian political culture in the postcolonial era up to the early 1990s,
before the shift in political leadership in 1994. I examine the divergent
political and cultural projects of those who imagine themselves as its
makers: professional historians, government bureaucrats, national
elites, and jali. I discuss the social context and cultural frameworks in
which these official forays have been made.

Most of those who aim to create history in The Gambia take on the
work of creating narratives from the memories and informal histories of
a range of elites and ordinary people. But just what should count as political agency in these narratives? What should be valorized as national
culture? The next chapter explores the "professional dreams" of those,
including jali and their patrons, who have a stake in setting the terms of
national history. The following chapters then extend to investigate the
cultural politics and political culture in which these professional negotiations take place.

Yet it is difficult for a reader to dive into these negotiations with little knowledge of the Gambian nation. The following sketch offers an

orientation to The Gambia as a place to begin. It also juxtaposes particular styles of telling history, thus introducing the very problems of negotiation of history, as well as political culture, in and beyond the nation.

The Gambia is a one of the smallest nations on the continent of Africa,
surrounded by Senegal on every side but the west, which looks to the
sea. Its awkward positioning in relationship to Senegal easily recalls the
arbitrary histories of all national boundaries established in this part of
the world. In contrast to Senegal, established as a French colony with a
French settler presence, The Gambia was ruled by Britain through indirect rule. Local chiefs, and particularly Mandinka chiefs, had considerable authority throughout the colonial period; the nation's continuing
emphasis on Mandinka culture as national culture dates from this administrative situation. English is the official language.
    The British formally claimed The Gambia in the 1880s, but the Brit-
ish presence was much older. The mouth of the River Gambia was a
major port for the British sector of the Atlantic slave trade. The British
dealt particularly with Mandinka nobles who traced their ancestry to
the spread of the Mali empire in the thirteenth century. This spread created what scholars call "the Mande world," which includes cultural
groups in contemporary Mali, Senegal, Guinea, Guinea-Bissau, Sierra
Leone, Liberia, and the Ivory Coast, as well as The Gambia. The Gambian location can thus be imagined as a narrow spot in which the British imperial heritage and the Mande imperial heritage have intensely
touched and wound around each other amid the political asymmetry
and cultural confusion of the growing capitalist world system. Mandinka were also shipped out as slaves from the mouth of the River Gambia; "Mandingo" became a term for "slave" in the United States even as
it brought to mind a heritage of kings in West Africa. The linkages and
confusions of African Americans and Gambians have long played a
small role in the construction of the Gambian "contact zone." (The
term is Pratt's [1992].)
    Jali have their own stories of this past. As the Malian empire colo-
nized westward along the Gambian River in the thirteenth century, jali
spread with their noble patrons. The history of this expansion is recorded in jali songs; it is also the history of the political categories from
which nobles derive their dependents, and jali their professional skills.
Several small Mandinka kingdoms, such as Wuli, Niumi, and Baddibu,
grew during the Malian expansion and assisted in the exchange of
coastal salt for Malian textiles (Quinn 1972). These kingdoms usurped
an already established trade in salt for kola nuts from the forest region
to the south (Brooks 1980), and they vied for dominance in a social context of many languages and forms of political and cultural heritage. In

the process, certain common political understandings developed. For example, Wolof, Serer, and Mandinka all recognized divisions among endogamous groups of slaves, freeborn commoners, and nobles, as well as an even more clearly marked artisan caste (Barry 1981). It became more acceptable to marry across ethnic boundaries than across caste divisions (Curtin 1975). Yet this history of ethnic relations, whether terrible or benign, is not the jali version. The jali version tells of the greatness of Mandinka rule and the inevitability of its spread.

By the late fifteenth century, new developments in the region placed jali in a political role opposite Islam. The Senegambian area found itself part of the African-European trade, and was increasingly incorporated into the world market. The Malian empire declined. Trade in gold, gum arabic, and slaves made the coastal area an important entrepot for European traders. Throughout this period, jali attached themselves to a ruling class that lived off this trade but that was often antagonistic toward the growing numbers of Muslims who also participated in the trade. Indeed, Muslim scholars and clerics viewed jali as people who hampered the spread of Islam (Colvin 1981). Islamic revolts against the Mandinka rulers in the eighteenth and nineteenth centuries disrupted Senegambian society; jali were attached to the nobles overthrown by these jihads. The jali resisted Islamization into the colonial period of the twentieth century. Some scholars have found that jali sometimes still put themselves in tension with Islam today (Robinson 1985) when 90 percent of the country is Muslim (Wiseman 1990). Such tensions increase the number of versions of "history" locally available to Gambians. Most contemporary jali, however, are involved in complex positive relations with Islamic beliefs, and many narrate the history of jaliya as, from the start, the history of Islam.

The Gambia was central to the Atlantic slave trade because of its strategic location along the Atlantic coast. Initially, Africans were supplied through a long established internal slave system involving people captured during raids and wars. As the market in slaves developed in the New World, the rules that once governed the internal system were abandoned and slaves were rounded up everywhere. In the 1880s The Gambia became a colony of Great Britain but was administered mainly through indirect rule. Formal colonial rule further institutionalized the ethnic dominance of the Mandinka in the Gambian area, which was also occupied by Wolof, Fuulbe, Jola, and Sereer groups. (In contrast, the Wolof became the politically dominant ethnic group in surrounding Senegal.) The political dominance of Mandinka continued during the postcolonial period in the Gambian nation. The importance of Mandinka jali in representing Gambian culture as well as Mandinka culture both nationally and internationally stems in part from Mandinka dominance over other groups in The Gambia.

After the abolition of slavery, The Gambia had little to sell. Groundnut (peanut) production brought in a little export revenue and continues to do so today. This is a small country that experiences periodic droughts. Most people combine a variety of part-time economic activities. Smuggling is one way of generating more income (Gamble 1988). Industry is not even a remote possibility; although 85 percent of the people are engaged in agricultural activities, especially rice cultivation, this in no way supplies all of the needs of the country's citizens.

Under the administration of Sir Dawada Jawara, first prime minister and then president of the Gambia from 1965 (the end of colonial rule) until 1994, The Gambia attracted a great deal of foreign investment in support of various development strategies because of its relatively stable political system (Wiseman 1990). President Jawara's success at gaining foreign aid is attributed to his stance on democracy, human rights, and anti-Communism. The Gambia gained other sources of support though ties with the oil-rich Persian Gulf states and, at various periods, Taiwan and the People's Republic of China. In 1981 a failed coup attempt brought The Gambia and Senegal into an alliance as Senegalese troops lent support to put down the coup. Out of this alliance, the Senegambian Confederation was formed, a relationship that lasted until 1989. One of the constant political fears in The Gambia was that the nation would lose its sovereignty to Senegal, which created a lasting tension between the two nations.

In July 1994 a coup changed the government, installing to power Lieutenant Yahya Jammeh, head of the Armed Forces Provisional Ruling Council. Yahya became president and remained after an election in 1996. This shift in regime has had consequences for the external support of the country. Initially, many Western foreign investors withdrew their support because of fears that the military government would remain. President Jammeh sought support from African countries, particularly Senegal, Ghana, and Nigeria. Soon he approached other donors. The World Bank and IMF began to provide loans again in 1998, and although The Gambia has managed to regain the trust of foreign investors, the effort to maintain that support is constant (Saine 2000).[1] In addition to foreign fundraising the country depends on tourism, which has been one major source of revenue since the end of the colonial period. Although a relatively low percentage of the gross domestic product is generated directly from tourism (Wiseman 1990), tourism provides the necessary foreign cash flow for a country heavily dependent upon imported goods for its existence. The Gambia attracts a large number of tourists from Scandinavian countries and the United Kingdom, as well as an increasing number from the United States. Tourists from the United States are mainly African Americans on "roots" journeys, or world music enthusiasts in search of Africa through music. The jali play an important role in both of these instances.

Indeed, jali are among the most successful groups of people making a living within tourism and the trafficking of "authentic national cultural products." These benefits, however, accrue differently among the jali. Not all jali perform; not all extend their activities beyond the local roles that inform, empower, and entertain neighbors and village patrons. Status differences in age, gender, professional networks, and patronage are influential factors in how a jali fares. Still, a major demand for their services has developed both nationally and internationally—directly, as they find themselves performing, and indirectly, as they become tourist attractions. Urban jali may well have more access to cash and consumer goods than many of their rural patrons. Some are able to generate an income that surpasses even their elite patrons' salaries. Jali play in popular dance bands and give music lessons—to tourists and anthropologists among others. They can use the money they gain to open other businesses. Some jali are members of a national troupe, which offers a stable income but closes down opportunities for other, more lucrative kinds of entrepreneurship because of performance demands generated by rehearsals and formal events.

In an economy in which almost everyone depends, directly or indirectly, on some kind of independent commodity production, jali have done relatively well. In the process their cultural production has been transformed by the demands of tourists and international audiences, yet they are not passive recipients of this transformation process; they have an active and entrepreneurial role in creating "African culture."

Jali, as I mentioned, have their own stakes in telling the past. I can think of no better way to introduce these stakes than to offer a little of their famous, foundational epic of Sunjata, the founder of the Malian empire. While giving a sense of the political struggles involved in the founding of Mali, the story also highlights the importance of jali and particularly the responsibilities of patrons toward their clients, and clients toward patrons. Many versions of this story exist, and it is told over a number of hours with a great deal of flair and detail. I sketch it here to provide just a bit of introduction and to refer you to the wonderful range of sources that retell and interpret the epic in much richer detail.

The literature on Sunjata is written for varied audiences; it variously captures the imagination of scholars, readers of fiction, and even children. For sources that provide the narrative of Sunjata as a praise poem, see Suso and Kanute (1999). For a narrative effort, see Niane

(1965). Other sources interpret the narrative's historical and literary qualities (see, for example, Miller 1990; Austin 1999). Novelist Camara Laye has written an original literary version (1980). Sidibe (1980) offers a schoolbook on the tale. For a full discussion of sources before 1990 see Dusan Bulman (1990).

Sunjata was a prince who had a rather difficult beginning. He could neither walk nor talk. The story of how he gained his heroic manhood is one of the more exciting episodes of the epic. When his father, the king, asked his advisors who should succeed him upon his death, they recommended Sunjata. This, however, did not sit well with the king's first wife, who thought her own son should be the rightful heir. Little at the time signaled Sunjata's extraordinary abilities. Indeed, his mother regularly endured the taunts and ridicule of her cowife. But the king accepted the advice of his counselors, and upon his death the first wife was relentless in the promotion of her son.

The king bequeathed to Sunjata his most skilled jali. And, indeed, Sunjata's first words were whispered to his jali: "You are my jali." Sunjata's wordlessness was in this revealed as a sign of power, not weakness! Now his jali would speak for him.

Yet Sunjata still could not walk. As a result, Sunjata's mother could not depend on her son to do a man's work. She asked the cowife for help, symbolized in her request for baobab leaves, but the cowife scoffed and threw the leaves at her, leaving Sunjata's mother to cry in shame. She turned to Sunjata to express her grief, and he was moved to action. He spoke to his jali, asking him for a rod. The blacksmiths forged him an iron rod so heavy that it took several men to carry it. Yet Sunjata lifted it and rose to his feet for the first time. Again, his imagined weakness was revealed as strength. When he walked, he was more powerful than any other man. Instead of picking leaves, he pulled up a great tree to offer his mother baobab leaves. He was a hero.

Still the first wife pursued her interest in promoting her son. Sunjata and his family eventually left the area to get away from the cowife's many evil acts. The story of his exile tells of both privation and heroism. Sunjata had to provide for his dependents, including his jali, as well as himself, yet he had no home. It is told that once when he had nothing else to offer, he cut off a piece of the flesh of his leg to nourish his jali—so highly did he treasure this advisor and spokesperson. Thus the relationship between jali and patron is extremely close, each needing the other to succeed in life.

They arrived in another area where, the king welcomed them and treated Sunjata like a son. Eventually, Sunjata thought it was time to return and fight for what was rightfully his. His mother died after giving him her blessing. Thus women aid, but do not themselves shine. What followed was a climactic series of battles in which Sunjata was able to reclaim his throne. The subtle knowledge of the jali—as well as the seductive power of Sunjata's sister—were required to outwit the usurper, who was a great sorcerer. Sunjata prevailed. He became the most respected founder and leader of the Malian Empire. He instituted the heroic social order that still inspires West Africans today.

All of that other history—of jihads, colonial conquest, ethnic strife, and national modernization—only reworks those heroic times, for better or for worse, allowing great men to make their names in action and requiring of bards that they make the great line of history into a song.

CHAPTER THREE

Curators of Tradition

On February 18, 1965, amid the cautions of many anxious observers, The Gambia raised its flag as an independent nation. The tiny country in transition, so obviously a colonial port of call, with its thin strip of riverside territory, could not present the mass of a former empire or the solidity of an ethnic homeland. Some, no doubt, felt that the country would fold into the encompassing nation of Senegal. A place so small and with so few resources, they reasoned, would by necessity require the protection of a more substantial nation-state. As people wondered about the feasibility of this unlikely place, others took a leap of faith.

To even imagine The Gambia as a nation, and one that was independent from its colonial attachments, took some faith, given the number of obstacles that had to be overcome. First the improbability of national territory that existed only as the north and south banks of a river, the ferries in between, and nothing else. The Gambia owed its existence as a separate territory to squabbles between Britain and France over colonial control of West Africa. Without British colonial pretensions, many wondered why this territory should continue to be separate. Second, the lack of vital national resources contributed much to this ambivalence, for how could a nation-state survive off a small number of peanut farms, traders, rice, and fish? From the seventeenth to the nineteenth century, the River Gambia was a key trading post from which a reasonable income could be made through the control of commercial activities. But by the twentieth century, commercial activity had long moved to more promising locations, leaving the question of how one could build state institutions that were self-sustaining without British assistance. No robust preexisting infrastructure afforded this nation-building project an easy passage into existence.

This chapter examines one particular aspect of nation building: creating a national history in postindependence Gambia. National history mobilizes the nation imaginatively, and provides a sense of a past and thus a future. The Gambia's search for national history developed in parallel to that of other postcolonial nations. National history also formed part of an international expectation about what was involved in creating a nation. Yet the challenges of the Gambia's developing nationhood were distinctive and in some ways more starkly outlined and extreme than those of other postcolonial nations. Compared to many other nations, The Gambia has been domestically peaceful and internationally unassertive; it has not had wars or violent ethnic conflicts that have determined the outlines of nation making. Instead, national concerns have focused on the symbolic and discursive challenges of forming a nation.

I became most aware of the challenges of crafting national history as I followed the evolution of a specialized agency under the sponsorship of the Gambian government that had been developed for the task of creating a history of the country. In 1970, the vice president's office was expanded to support the Oral History and Antiquities Division (OHAD) of the Gambian government. A National Archive was also developed for colonial and postcolonial political documents. The National Archive had an easier task than its counterpart: to collect written documents and to make sure The Gambia had some of this internationally recognized history. OHAD had the more difficult task of creating a national history from the recollections, skills, material artifacts, and narrative traditions of people who were neither international politicians, colonial administrators, nor professional historians. The national history that remained to be built at OHAD had to be crafted from the bottom up both in the sense of drawing raw materials from a wide range of people and of making those "raw" materials into something new and different to enable efforts to mobilize the nation.

Several major ethnic groups reside in the national borders of The Gambia: Mandinka, Wolof, Fula, Jola, Serer, and Aku. The question for postcolonial officials remained how these diverse ethnic identities and cultural linguistic communities could be brought together as an imagined nation. How could those within its borders be made to feel that they shared a common national history? The charge of OHAD was to devise a set of activities and ways of thinking that would transform a variety of stories and traditions into something that would build the nation. This task could only be accomplished by addressing not only local conceptions of past and present, community and identity, politics and custom, but also international standards for what might count as history and national culture. In this way, the challenges that faced OHAD were common dilemmas concerning the contours of postcolonial national history and culture. These dilemmas raise theoretical questions about how history and culture are defined, and offer the opportunity to follow how history and culture are built within institutional mandates and resources as well as the overlapping and contradictory expectations of local, foreign, and newly "national" historians.

When considering questions about history and nationhood, a number of general issues cannot be avoided. First, does Africa have a history? While it might be commonplace in the early postindependence moment to assert that of course Africa has a history, Europeans had learned to imagine an Africa that was outside the narratives of progress that constituted historical time. Africa was easy to picture as colonized space to the extent that the continent had no history. Thus all postcolonial African nations had to work to transform this understanding of Africa to make history possible at all (for further discussion, see Mudimbe and Jwesiewicki 1990, 1993).

Second, how can we know that a particular account of the past is history? The kinds of history that OHAD—like other institutions of social history—planned to collect and present to the nation were oral histories. They were performative histories, caught in conventions of representing mythical time, personal biography, or rank-oriented hierarchy. The challenge confronting Gambian historians was how these kinds of histories could be made to legitimately enter the world defined by libraries of written records and classic texts. And yet it was also not clear that archives alone could mobilize the nation without the traditions and histories better known by the citizens. In this chapter, I show that the challenge of creating national history in The Gambia was always a challenge of properly mediating performance and text: textualizing performance to give it historical legitimacy; performing text to make it live for the nation.

Third, who defines history? Historians of Europe have always defined what counts as history, and no history of The Gambia could succeed without taking into account European standards. European standards of history, however, entered Gambian conversations particularly by way of European-based historians of Africa, who cared as much as Gambian historians about crafting histories of the region. Thus the project of working out the contours of history could only be accomplished in dialogue with European-based historians who have had as many—although different—challenges in crafting historical narratives for the region. European-based versions of African history also mediate performance and text, but differently than those who imagine the nation through these mediations. National historians must construct a dialogue with these foreign international versions of African history, and in this they cannot avoid negotiating issues of "myth," "bias," and "truth."

Fourth, how should varied regional cultures and varied ethnic identities be incorporated into the story of the nation? A national history must be an expansive, inclusive story, and, ironically, it cannot be large enough if it is pluralistic and embracing of every ethnic tradition within the national territory. Only the colonial state can imagine and contain the pluralist coexistence of separate, autonomous cultures; the nation requires a rather different cultural frame. A national culture must be vast; it has to grow to fit the territory, and it must accumulate knowledge and experience to meet the circumstances. In short, a national culture must be a spreading, flourishing civilization, in contrast to a community bound by colonial custom. This transformation can only be accomplished by abandoning the pluralistic frame to hear and develop the imperial stirrings of a dominant cultural tradition fit to define national greatness.

Fifth, what practical activities should be initiated for making history? What are the implications of these technical choices for the meaning of history? Experienced elders and learned women and men must be interviewed. Representative and exotic objects should be collected. Textbooks, training guides, and funding proposals must be written. Conferences, training workshops, and educational programs can be staged. Museum space will be arranged. All of these, furthermore, require political negotiations to keep the institutional infrastructure of making history in place. In this crossroads of seemingly mundane activity, important decisions about what will count as history and culture are made.

Finally, how might national history speak to the goals and challenges of international development? No nation-making activities after World War II could avoid the international expectation of development goals. Luckily for those who would design a national history for The Gambia, the international development apparatus included funding and support for activities that build national cultures, and national history projects could receive assistance and protection within this frame. Yet the frame of development also presents a challenge: How can it best be used within the Gambian context? And what are its demands?

This chapter recounts the debates and contests over the making of national history in The Gambia, particularly through the auspices of OHAD.

From Tradition to History

OHAD owes much of its institutional shape and commitment to the initial direction of Mr. Bakary Sidibe, who was appointed founding conservator in 1970. Sidibe explains the development of OHAD as a special concern of the nation's first president, Sir Dawada Kairiba Jawara, who approached him while Sidibe was attending a scholarly seminar in London. The president requested that Sidibe direct a national project of collecting oral histories. According to Sidibe, speaking during an interview I conducted with him, President Jawara was particularly concerned about cultural preservation and development as an aspect of nation building. The president felt that conserving oral traditions was a priority, for he had observed that these traditions were rapidly disappearing. The resources for the national cultural archive, the president imagined, lay in the memories of elders and such traditional specialists as jali, craftsmen, and Koranic scholars. Sidibe agreed to accept the position of collecting, compiling, and preserving cultural history from the raw materials of performance and memory, folk story and traditional artifact, as a counterbalance to the administrative records that had been the main source of information on The Gambia in the National Archives.

From the first, then, OHAD was a key participant in postcolonial nation making, and Sidibe's active leadership kept history and culture alive in national discussions. Before accepting the position of director of OHAD, Sidibe had been headmaster of a Gambian high school. He also worked with various foreign scholars in translating and rendering Mandinka history into written texts.[1] Few Gambians of his generation had obtained a Western education beyond high school; thus he was a figure of respect. Furthermore, his genealogical ties to noble status placed him in the center of contemporary Gambian political and social life in the sense of having a critical investment in a history that could recount the past of the Malian empire and its important constituents. Sidibe's goal was to create a national repository from which Gambians might know their past and their future. The first task was to salvage traditional knowledge and to reformulate it into a usable "history."

The staff at OHAD, which included Gambian participants as well the regular presence of foreign researchers, began collecting or "salvaging" oral traditions from a range of informants, including village elders, marabouts (Islamic religious authorities), and jali. They recorded myths, legends, folk tales, epic poems, genealogies, and village histories, as well as traditional forms of singing and the music of a variety of instruments. They also collected *tarikas*, traditional histories that combine written or memorized outlines and oral embellishments. Soon the office had acquired an overwhelming abundance of tapes that lay awaiting transcription, creating an enormous backlog of collected oral material, as yet unusable, for future consideration as national history. The most pressing problem facing OHAD was the lack of adequate staff to process the material being recorded and amassed. Moreover, this was not the only difficulty. Many of the early documents the office circulated, such as progress reports and appeals for international aid, chronicle the office's dilemmas involving the gathering and processing of materials. Indeed, it was not until 1977 that OHAD received a predetermined budget (OHAD publication 1984).

While considerations of staffing and budget raised critical issues around the infrastructure necessary to maintain such an institution as OHAD, a number of substantive intellectual issues were also of pressing concern. The beginning of the collection process raised a number of problems characteristic to oral testimony, such as the role of everyday oral histories and their relationship to the histories of jali (the relationship of untrained storytellers to professional orators). The issue colored every decision. What kind of remuneration should be offered to the participants in the project? While village elders might tell their stories with little expectation of compensation, jali, who considered themselves professional orators, were often less willing to offer any information to the archive without adequate reimbursement for their time and information; this was, after all, their livelihood.

OHAD could never have the resources to satisfy jali desires. Worse yet, OHAD competed with other institutions whose standards of compensation left it out of the circuit of competition. Radio Gambia, for example, also worked with jali as performers and had funding available to pay jali; OHAD could rarely match these offers. The staff at OHAD often felt themselves locked into a struggle with some jali in which the jali, negotiating for more funds and opportunities, teased them with snippets and fragments of the national heritage that OHAD hoped to preserve for all.

By 1984 OHAD had collected roughly four thousand tape-recordings, primarily of village elders. They also had plans to record prominent jali in greater depth, and they were seeking external funding for this project. In particular, the director and his assistants hoped to tap the knowledge of "master" jali, those between the ages of fifty and seventy, before age and death deprived the nation of the insights of these important historians. Meanwhile, the staff at OHAD had begun to write village histories that could be used as high-school history texts. OHAD attracted Gambian as well as foreign researchers to work on these projects. Most notably, in the formative years of the institution, Winifred Galloway, an historian from the United States, had initially come to The Gambia to conduct her dissertation research. She stayed far beyond the original project to work with Sidibe and the OHAD history project (Galloway 1978, 1980). Gordon Innes, a British scholar, also worked with Sidibe before the official beginning of OHAD, translating jali's epic tales of village history and of the founder of the Malian empire (Innes 1976, 1974). These collaborations combined both literary and historical interests in an intertwined project that helped constitute two influential strands of Mande cultural history.

These collaborations produced a number of publications. Those that circulated in the Gambia ranged from school textbooks to occasional papers (some published in the Gambia Museum Bulletin) on topics including traditional wrestling, tie-dyeing and batik, masks, marabouts, and jujus, to edited versions of family genealogies and famous epics as related by jali. Yet, with the small staff of the director, one U.S.-born historian, one U.S. Peace Corps volunteer, and a secretary, OHAD regularly appealed for funding for the training of field researchers, transcribers, translators, and typists.

OHAD staff spent much of their time in the early years attempting to generate financial support from international agencies including the

Ford Foundation and UNESCO. Development agencies from a few affluent countries of the North sometimes sent personnel to participate in the project. The German government helped supplement the salary of a German researcher. The U.S. Peace Corps also supported various projects by offering occasional workers. But the OHAD always had to perform its tasks on an extremely modest budget that had to provide not only for training researchers but also for transcribers, translators, and secretaries.

The difficulties in making a "lasting record" from the oral materials collected within The Gambia's postindependence constraints became strikingly apparent to me when the director, while giving me a tour of the collection, illustrated the problem of preservation by showing me one of the places where OHAD stored tapes of oral testimony. Limited resources precluded highly sophisticated methods of storage for tapes and documents, yet this is a place where tropical weather conditions quickly take their toll. Most of the written documents were stored in a metal cabinet that was open to dust, humidity, and insects.

Much of the material on tape in 1989 awaited transcription, but it was not left alone. The tapes were undergoing a metamorphosis of a different sort; and not the desired kind. Upon opening the drawer of a wooden storage unit, I was struck with horror by the sight of the determined efforts of termites who had gnawed away the plastic cases of the tapes as if they were breadsticks. This moment immediately brought a keen awareness of the difficulties of making a written archival history in The Gambia. The tropical environment undermined the sanctity of the permanent record while preserving only its symbolic authority. Nationhood requires records. But what if the termites continue to eat them?

The preoccupation of OHAD staff with the ordinary logistics of negotiations for interviews, funding, and the preservation of records is not to suggest that the staff was unconcerned with more abstract questions about the definition of culture and history. On the contrary, they discussed these questions and decided on answers precisely in the midst of, and through, their work with the details of history-making in The Gambia. The everyday problems of the OHAD staff were also the template for making national history. Consider, for example, their resonance with other postcolonial histories. Certainly, the meager budget and the endless rounds of funding proposals at OHAD cannot but remind one of how postcolonial history always stands behind and runs to catch up with European standards (Chakrabarthy 2000). Consider, too, the problem of the authority of recorded knowledge. Homi Bhabha (1990) argues that the circulation of European-based forms of knowledge in the colonies led to distortions and reappropriations; the legitimacy of "the English book" was retained even as it was deployed for local purposes. In this sense, one might read the crumbling of Gambian oral history tapes as a reaffirmation

of the legitimacy of archival records even as it confirms the effervescence
of performance, thus satisfying both national historians and their sometimes reluctant informants.

The most distinctive theoretical problem facing OHAD, however,
may have concerned their negotiations with the traditional experts whose
knowledge they were determined to preserve. Mandinka jali always
formed the key group whose expertise OHAD had pursued as the basis
of national cultural knowledge and history. But in what sense should
Mandinka jali represent the nation? After all, the Mandinka were only
one of several Gambian ethnic groups, and the jali were only one group
of many potentially knowledgeable individuals. Furthermore, many
scholars, particularly from North America, argued that jali are unreliable
precisely because they are performers and canny negotiators, holding out
for their own interests.

Other demands on jali knowledge and performance ranged from
events at tourist venues to both traditional and popular Gambian music
performances. And the jali had to be paid, thus increasing OHAD's bur-
dens but also elevating the prestige of jali knowledge. In the midst of these
practical considerations, OHAD needed to make crucial decisions about
the role of jali. Two central dilemmas were raised about OHAD's vision
of the nation in this process. First, how would national history distinguish
itself from colonial collecting of culture: would Mandinka traditions have
the same status as those of the Wolof, Fula, Jola, and Serer? Second,
would Mandinka jali be central informants and interlocutors in making
national history? The next two sections illustrate how national history
was made in relation to these two questions.

Redefining "Culture"

An initial task of critical significance for making national history possible
was the differentiation of OHAD's work from that of previous scholars
who had studied Gambian folktales and traditions but with a different
set of goals and frameworks. During the colonial administration of The
Gambia, significant work had been achieved in collecting and defining
cultural traditions. In a number of instances, this scholarship was responsible and thoughtful in an attempt to catalogue particular ethnic traditions. Yet to the extent that much of this work accepted the epistemological neutrality of colonial rule as the starting point from which to
understand the specificity of Gambian cultures, it could not serve the purposes of postcolonial nation-making. The collection of culture under colonial authority limited the expansive potential of African cultures by mak-

ing them historically and regionally particular objects of an overseeing colonial attention, which imagined itself as universal.

A national culture must take on some of the epistemological authority that colonialism held for itself. Indeed, it must be able to expand to meet new political and cultural challenges; it must inspire knowledge-making rather than being only an object of scholarship. In this context, "culture" has to take on new purposes and meanings, an atemporal functionalist paradigm has to give way to history, colonial pluralism must cede to national direction, exotic gender specificity must become masculine leadership, and the imagined archaic quality of customary heritage must forge a legacy of working politics. Throughout Africa, anthropologists lost authority to historians after national independence (Hart 1985). Yet culture was not abandoned as an object of scholarship; it was redefined in the context of national histories.

OHAD's job of redefining culture as national history required, in particular, a respectful yet distanced stance apart from the work of an important foreign scholar, David Gamble, whose work spanned both colonial and post colonial eras. Gamble's dedication to charting the cultural history of the Senegambian region has made his work an indispensable resource for all scholars in this area. Thus, for example, Gamble has done extraordinary work compiling and annotating bibliographies of the region, updating them regularly, and maintaining an inclusive reach to both African and foreign scholarship. No scholar of the region can ignore these resources. Upon meeting Professor Gamble in 1990 and discussing his work in The Gambia, I learned to appreciate his commitment to recording and collecting everything available on Senegambia. In many ways, his work is similar to one of OHAD's own goals. Gamble has been committed to gathering oral materials that might not otherwise find themselves represented in the written record of the region. He has assembled folk tales and historical narratives and has described ethnic cultures. He has compiled dictionaries and produced grammars and language guides for a number of regional languages. He has a continuing interest in social and ethnic histories, as these show the spread and retreat of regional cultures. Benedict Anderson (1992a) offers an insightful appreciation of the role of this kind of scholar of Third World social history; colonial scholars immersed themselves in the regions they studied with an intensity that is rare in the postcolonial First World academy.

Yet Gamble's interest in the diversity of regional cultures and their changing interactions marks his difference from the nation-building project. Gamble is evenhanded in his treatment of varied ethnic traditions in The Gambia, and has paid as much attention to the Wolof and the Fula as to the Mandinka. From the perspective of national historians, this pluralistic commitment rests on colonial authority; it succeeds only to the extent that British culture and history orders the region. Instead, OHAD has looked to other possibilities for a nation-making heritage. In The Gambia, Mandinka culture and history has seemed by far the most suitable. Mandinka constitute the largest ethnic group in The Gambia. Under British authority, Mandinka chiefs residing primarily in the Upper-River division of the country formed the backbone of the system of indirect rule. Mandinka culture became the unmarked "native" culture of colonial discourse in The Gambia. At independence, important Mandinka families maintained political prominence. Furthermore, Mandinka had the heritage of kingdoms that could allow the nation to imagine a politically powerful past and future. They were not merely a circumscribed ethnic group; they were the descendants of kings. The heritage of kingdoms allowed national historians the possibilities of imagining once and future political power and independence. It allowed a sense of the kind of political relationships that might productively order an independent and active political space. Culture as custom simply orders everyday life; culture as imperial heritage makes possible a politically powerful present and future.

Thus, David Gamble's pluralism, at least at some level, was rejected by the historians at OHAD. OHAD did not ignore the cultural diversity of The Gambia; however, its significance was reformulated (cf. Bhabha 1990). Minority traditions formed part of the nation's wealth and so were worthy of study and preservation. In contrast, Mandinka traditions formed the core line of national heritage. Gamble himself expressed his disappointment during our conversation in 1990 in the privileging of one ethnic group over the others in national cultural histories. His own vision, however, did not promote the making of national culture in and of itself. In the opening essay of his 1988 bibliography, for example, Gamble traces the history of The Gambia by moving directly from archaeological "prehistory" and ethnic diversity to the explorations of Europeans and then colonial rule. There is no mention of precolonial African "history," only ethnic culture. In contrast, OHAD has "recovered" the history of Mande kingdoms, the heritage of the Mandinka, as deserving of the same respect as the European heritage of exploration and rule. It is history. And in this context, Mandinka culture takes on the authority of civilization, not the limitation of ethnic culture and custom. Its political heritage is expansive and developing, and it can thus inspire national politics, education, and scholarship.

One site in which OHAD was forced to articulate this vision of culture and history was the displays arranged in the museum housed in one wing of OHAD, which I viewed in 1989. Here the curators did not ignore the kinds of customs and artifacts that might have served ideas of "culture" under the colonial administration. The items, however, were assembled from varied ethnic groups, and the display placed contemporary and older pieces in close proximity, creating a display of national ethnic culture. This display inspires respect for cultural ingenuity and diversity as the wealth of the nation. In contrast, another area of the museum displays history. In this chronicle, the story begins with a brief display and discussion of the regional kingdoms and the possible causes of their demise. The story of the Mande kingdom takes the viewer from regional Muslim rulers to colonial administrators, and, finally, to more contemporary political and national leaders.

The Mande kings are shown in the context of the regional progression of precolonial African kingdoms: Ghana, Mali, and Songhay. Sketches remind the viewer of colonial and national photographs, offering an equivalent visual "truth," and narratives of the kingdoms' rise and fall bring them into the same chronological frame. Thus the transition between these kingdoms and colonial rule is not difficult because they can be displayed with the same conventions. Political memorabilia and photographs of British royal visits draw further parallels between African and British moments of rule. Muslim leaders, colonial bureaucrats, and national statesmen form the counterpart to kings in the narration of this continuous history. In the context of the museum, national history is a single story in which Mande kings prefigure later rulers and offer an origin to the independent nation.

Historical narratives as well as visual displays are key to this national transformation of history and culture. Perhaps the most important narrative for this process is the epic tale of Sunjata, as described in the opening of part 2. Sunjata was the founder of the thirteenth-century Malian empire. In colonial archives, Sunjata's story is just another mythic tale, yet he is the ancestral founder of national history projects. OHAD features his story as a grade-school textbook, *Sunjata* (Sidibe 1980). In the introduction to the text, the OHAD staff suggests that the history can be appreciated metaphorically as well as literally. Just as grade-school histories in the United States feature the moral purity of the pilgrims and the honesty of Abraham Lincoln as national historical heritage, the Sunjata text can teach about leadership and social values. Sunjata has the indigenous priority of his buffalo heritage (his mother was a buffalo). He has the almost superhuman strength of the boy who, despite his crippled condition uproots a baobab tree, as well as the imperial conviction to nurture his leadership even in exile and to bring it to a triumphant homecoming. Thus he tells the contemporary nation about the social requirements of successful political leadership: genealogical authority, perseverance, bravery, travel, fighting skill.

Two further elements stand out in my reading of the epic of Sunjata: first, masculinity, and second, the interdependence of social strata. Only Sunjata's masculine authority silences the squabbling of co-wives, who compete for their respective sons' precedence. Sunjata needs the loyalty, knowledge, and skills of his mother and sister; he cannot succeed without their support.But it is his masculine leadership that, with their support, allows him to found the empire. Meanwhile, Sunjata depends very heavily on his jali. His jali are his legacy from his father; they create and recreate his royal nature. They stimulate his generosity, his bravery, and, indeed, all his leadership qualities; it is also they who speak for him, articulating his leadership for the audiences that then allow him to lead. If Sunjata offers his jali flesh from his own leg, it is because their support is a necessary condition for his leadership. Sunjata's story thus shows the necessity of the division between speakers and leaders and the importance of their interdependence in creating political strength.

Sunjata's story is told in many versions. It is known for its performative qualities and the multiple contexts in which it can be made relevant. The OHAD text does not attempt to tame and codify this performative multiplicity, but presents itself humbly as a basic teaching outline. Indeed, the repetition of the Sunjata story and its possibilities for creative embellishment make the tale suitable for a central role in building national heritage. Yet this variability also foregrounds the central dilemma of OHAD's task in making national history: that it must strike a balance between performative and textual aspects of cultural history. For Sunjata's story to count as history, it must have enough textual stability to enter the annals of historical truth, as measured by European standards. But to work as national heritage, it must draw on the liveliness of jali performance and its multiple uses and interpretations.

The centrality of this dilemma is even clearer in considering OHAD's negotiation with foreign professional historians over the meaning of historical accuracy and its appropriate sources and informants.

Predicaments of History

To create a national history, the OHAD staff by necessity entered into a dialogue with professional historians, based mainly in Europe and North America, who were also concerned with the making and remaking of African history. This dialogue offered insights for historians both in The Gambia and abroad. At the same time, it was marked by divergences and disagreements. One of the most important divergences concerned the role of Mandinka jaliya as a privileged repository for regional history. Foreign historians of Africa refused the guidance of jali accounts or circumscribed jali authority by showing it as a particularly biased performance tradition. In contrast, Gambian historians during the same period came to respect jali authority more than ever in making history.

The disagreement about sources for learning history was more than a minor difference of approach. Consider the problem from both directions. From the perspective of OHAD historians, jali were traditional experts on history. For foreign historians to reject them was not only imperious but also reflected a refusal to accept African cultural standards for understanding the past, particular as that position may have been. Yet from the perspective of foreign historians, jali were just not trustworthy as informants; their accounts were shifting, flattering, biased, exaggerated, crafted more for show than for truth, indeed, everything that proper historical accounts should avoid. For OHAD historians to take the accounts of jali as "historical truth" required a reinterpretation of what counted as worthy history. Either position, then, involved an argument about history that went beyond the details of Gambian social life to erect standards for the relationship of performance and text, and memory and truth, for the making of history. The section that follows explores the commitments of foreign historians and the implications of these stakes for national histories in The Gambia.

In the 1960s, when foreign professional historians began to take the study of African history seriously, they faced a formidable challenge: Africa was thought of as the place with no history. Any historical research, by necessity, began by challenging this portrayal. The challenge was met in part because many historians at this time were extending notions of what counted as an historical problem to include social groups other than politically elite families. In this context, these historians of Africa found themselves in alliance with social historians of Europe and North America who were creating histories of working-class people, women, and minorities, previously thought of as marginal figures in history. Provoked by a crisis in representation, these social histories, like the new African history, could create richer versions of the past than those accounts that focused simply on elites: kings, presidents, generals, and colonial administrators.

For the historian of Africa, however, this task required an appreciation of new kinds of cultural artifacts. An overabundance of oral traditions best characterized the resources available in most African contexts from which histories might be generated. Oral genres including folk tales, poems, and songs, could now become legitimate material for social historians; these could be the source for understanding the past beyond official archival, often colonial documents. How would Gambian voices be heard amid the colonial papers on political administration? Still, to use this resource, historians had to overcome the formidable prejudice of most traditional historians resistant to the use of oral testimony as historical source. One historian of West Africa quotes a critic of the use of oral traditions: "For the simple truth is that much oral tradition is mutually contradictory, biased, garbled, nonsensical, and essentially codswallop" (Wright 1991,

399 citing Latham). In contrast, a number of foreign social historians of Africa, including Vancina (1985) and Curtin (1975), began to argue that oral traditions, when used carefully, could provide historians with rich material unavailable through any other source. Certainly the historian needed to be wary. Some informants have better memories than others; some are more inclined than others to be fanciful. Yet by moving cautiously and using an adequate sample, exciting materials become available.

In this context, it is understandable that historians of Africa worked to generate the stable text, one that could stand up to the rigorous scrutiny of those who invoked rigorous procedural methods. As a result, these historians shunned the performative aspects of the oral interview—the features prone to revision, embellishment, and fanciful expression. To create legitimate, real history, historians wanted more than custom; they needed facts about the past, not poetic orations or mythological histories. In collecting oral histories, historians needed to reverse and reform then-current ethnological practice in which life histories and other oral materials were used to understand the functioning of the contemporary social order.

Oral traditions were treated by ethnologists as mythical charters for current social hierarchies. Instead of depending on these traditions, foreign historians worked to winnow oral materials for events and experiences that provided a "truthful" window on the past. The more a particular account of the past seemed to justify hierarchy or recapitulate myth, the more suspect it was to these historians. Jali, professional *performers* of oral traditions, were then the least trustworthy of all informants.

As historian Charlotte Quinn notes, speaking of the sources for her study *Mandingo Kingdoms*,

> An omission from the list of informants which is perhaps obvious to the reader is that of praise-singers, or *griots* [jali] whose profession it is to collect bardic tales, songs, and poems which honor their patrons and vilify their sponsors' enemies. A fascinating study in themselves, the *griots'* tales collected during 1965 proved to be less valuable for the history of Gambian Mandingo society than the traditions and memories of nonprofessional informants whose livelihood was not dependent on the aesthetic or hortatory virtues of their presentation. (Quinn 1972, xvii)

For foreign historians, performance was a problem to be avoided. Ordinary, "nonprofessional" narratives offered accounts that could more easily be imagined as lacking stylistic and performative conventions. Furthermore, translation was described as a "technical" issue; as long as it was competently done, the fact of translation had no bearing on the history it produced. Words were transparent vehicles carrying us toward the truth about the past, for it was this transparency that allowed the possibility that oral histories could contribute to real history similar to that established in places with written archives.[2] Even as oral histories could pull back the curtain hiding our knowledge of the past, the words in which these histories were elicited and told were only passively useful, accomplishing nothing in themselves. This was an effective historical program. But its strength, and its ability to assert that Africans could have "history," produced characteristic limits and insensitivities to its tools of analysis. Africans had "history" only to the extent that they did not perform it.

What is history if not performance-based tales? Foreign historians uncovered an African history that highlighted the movement of various distinct groups of people across a precolonial landscape not yet marked and divided by the authority of the European treaty. The stories of these ethnic migrations were gathered from archival sources as well as through the assistance of local African informants. The power of this kind of account is that it speaks to, yet disrupts, anthropological accounts of ethnic groups occupying the African landscape. Rather than the static order of structural-functionalism, here is dynamism and territorial movement, conquest and assimilation.

Remember, however, that this is not the only possible model of African history. Nationalist histories refuse the rupture of European treaty-making, with its opposition between precolonial fluidity and colonial boundaries; they also reject the precedence of pluralistic ethnic interactions as the key feature of the history European colonialism inherited and remade. Instead, powerful political legacies from the past are shown as relevant to making the terms of ethnicity, colonialism, and independence. Certainly, Europeans imagine their pasts this way. Why shouldn't Africans? The subject of history need not be ethnic migrations; it could equally be political legacies.

Some foreign historians of Africa considered European archives essential to learning the framework of African history. From a nationalist historian's perspective, this reliance on European archival sources biased history toward that colonial perspective that monopolized the definition of history and politics for itself and objectified Africa as only a place of cultures, which may move around and fight each other but never determine the historical frame of moving and fighting. From the foreign historian's perspective, in contrast, one had the obligation to be as thorough as possible, and the archives were the appropriate place to begin one's search into the past.

This latter perspective informed the work of historian Charlotte Quinn (1972), whose study of West African kingdoms has remained essential reading about the region. Quinn spent a year in the European archives, studying travelers' accounts and administrative records in order to trace African social groups. She did not find these archival sources adequate for her research, and after collecting the available records she shifted her research to The Gambia to fill out her account with oral sources. Once there, however, her first discovery was that not all oral accounts were very helpful in augmenting her archival frame. Quinn refuses jali accounts because of their stylized and performative portrayals of history. In contrast, she prefers the accounts of ordinary Africans. These, at least, have the truth of personal experience. "There are still people who can report from first-hand experience events of the Muslim jihad in its later stages," she writes enthusiastically. Second best, firsthand experience may be relayed through family connections. She continues: "In most cases, however, informants have gathered their information second- or third-hand from their fathers or grandfathers who themselves lived during the period" (1972, xvi). Quinn's "history" requires the truthfulness of personal memory, which she imagines as unmediated by performative convention. Jali histories will not suit the purpose.

In contrast to Quinn, another historian of the Senegambian precolonial past, Donald Wright, began his study by avoiding European archives as a starting point.[3] Instead, he traveled to The Gambia to search for material that would allow him to "write African history on African terms" (Wright 1992, 400). Wright's research began in The Gambia in 1974, almost ten years after Charlotte Quinn, and his hope was to write an account of the West African state Niumi, which dates back to 1440. Wright recalled his initial enthusiasm, heading first to The Gambia, by-passing the European archives altogether to conduct nearly one hundred oral history interviews for his history of the Niumi region. But, comparable to Quinn's approach, he was in search of facts, evidence of an historical truth. And, thus, he too came to reject jali as a reliable source of historical information. "One of my biggest disappointments was in Gambia's griots—their 'caste' of professional traditionalists, musicians, and entertainers. There were quite a few of which I could almost never make heads or tails" (1991, 401).

Unlike Quinn, Wright decided not to ignore the accounts of jali, despite his disappointment in them. Instead, he collected their accounts, but he was not certain he could rely on them. He came to The Gambia at a moment when historians had begun to be self-conscious about the construction of their sources. In this context, Wright produced a special volume of jali accounts, not as the true account of history but as a source book that requires readers' attention to their limitations as well as their knowledgeability.

Later, when he returned to this material to write his retrospective reflections on his methods (1991), he was quite severe with himself, suggesting that he chose research problems—such as quite ancient events—

that were impossible to research with the oral history methods he favored. In the process, he was thoughtful about his historical interviews. Wright considered the tensions between his expectations for historical truth and the formulaic oral recitations he elicited. Furthermore, Wright's expectations for oral history required it to retain an authenticity that was innocent of the written record. In fact, his informants often relied on written sources. This was one of his major complaints about jali. "Their information was contaminated," he wrote, referring to his jali informants' reliance on written accounts as well as mnemonic technologies of history (1991, 401). In this context, Wright was self-conscious about the set of assumptions that made him reject jali knowledge even as he gathered it. His idea of good history during his dissertation research required independent, authentic sources of knowledge, and he imagined an oral history practice that would draw these together to challenge and replace historians' reliance on the archive. The jali in particular, because they foreground performance, disturbed this ideal. In retrospect, he insightfully situated the ideal as an ideal, and not the only form that historical research can take.

Wright's self-consciousness about historians' assumptions in confronting the challenge of writing African history is a useful node for returning to the predicaments of writing history the OHAD historians faced. As discussed above, the OHAD staff experienced as many personal frustrations working with jali as did foreign historians, but they could not abandon jali as irrelevant or even circumscribe their knowledge as a limited cultural performance repertoire. Instead, those who ran the institution chose to conceive of history in a manner quite different from that of foreign historians. Self-conscious about the performative aspects of jali history, they chose to make these central to good history, rather than its opposite. Indeed, performance is what makes history relevant to the present.

In recent years, international historians, literary critics, and philosophers have become increasingly self-conscious about the performative nature of even the most textually inscribed historical sources. The reading of an archival source "performs" it for the present by enunciating its legacy, making it a "genealogy," in a Foucaultian sense, rather than a dead document. Gambian national historians have been exceptionally self-conscious about this insight; rather than banishing performance, they have viewed their job as balancing performance and textuality.

The mythic character of jali accounts, then, does not disqualify them. In this instance, myth defines historical agency. Mandinka historical myth takes historical agency away from colonial rule, which always claimed its precedence in ethnic-migration accounts. From the perspective of national history, Sunjata's story is as relevant to forging a genealogy of the present as are precolonial European travel accounts or colonial administrative records. OHAD historians, however, also could not afford to merely transcribe the expertise of jali as history. Jali commitments to the performance of history intersected with the goals of national historians but also diverged from them. Thus, for example, where national historians aimed to trace genealogies of leadership, jali perspectives stressed the genealogy of patronage that overlaps with leadership but is not always the same. Where national historians wished to build a continuous narrative of regional politics in which colonial rule could form one link in the chain, jali were more interested in building a regionally syncretic Islam as a basis of authority. Where national historians planned to use jali performance to build up national politics, jali were more interested in using national politics to increase the power of jali performance. Thus, in this sense, national historians were engaged in a complex and sometimes oppositional dialogue and practice not only with foreign historians but also with their most important informants. To explore this perspective further, I turn to the performance conventions of jali themselves to discuss how jali imagine history.

Performing History

In their interactions with foreign historians, OHAD historians appear committed to regional African traditions. In their interactions with jali, however, OHAD historians find themselves endorsing many of the same historical conventions as foreign historians. Thus, for example, OHAD historians imagined history in relation to stable chronologies tied to dates and a progression of historical events that in every telling occur in the same order. They imagine historical eras in which events cohere through related logics. They imagine a history in which performance styles may vary, but different versions collapse into each other compatibly. None of these conventions hold for the histories offered by jali. Yet many jali present themselves as professional historians.

OHAD historians must nuance their relationships with jali with great care, respecting them as peers or fellow travelers with an interest in ideas about the past while they draw from them as sources and transform their histories to create rather different histories of their own. This complex and tense relationship became particularly clear to me in a conversation I had with a patron of jali with a keen interest in history, who offered me suggestions on how to interview a particularly important woman jali. From his perspective, the history she could offer me would be key—yet limited. "She will only tell you about that which she has experienced. You will want to get her full repertoire, have her perform for you so you can hear how she develops her life story and what important people are there and where she has been." The jali offers a specific kind of source material: the performance-based story of important people as known through the jali's own relationship with them. The jali will rarely go beyond this relationship-based repertoire to offer the impersonal, general history imagined by both national and foreign historians. At the same time, the national historian recognizes that this performance-based story of important people and their followers is a significant piece of the historical chronology of leadership that forms the core line of national history.

In the context of the dialogue between national historians and jali, a number of features of jali perspectives on history stand out. These perspectives, to which jali are committed but about which national historians are wary, include the following:

1. History is performance; indeed, performance creates history.
2. History is genealogy, and historical memory is cued through family names.
3. History is religious authority, which links Islam and jaliya in a common line of descent.
4. Historical agency is created through the generosity and bravery of great men and women, as stimulated through jaliya, and is thus a product of the interrelationship of these great figures and their history-making dependents, the jali.

My own appreciation of these perspectives derives particularly from my interviews and informal discussions with jali. I illustrate my points in the following section with quotations from a published narrative of an acclaimed jali known internationally as a performer, Foday Musa Suso. He has discussed jaliya in a photographic essay, accompanied by a compact disc, that is, a kind of docu-pictorial music box, *Jali Kunda* (Kopka and Brooks 1996). By using a written source, I hope to make the dialogue between jaliya and international standards of history even clearer; the text is a jali's discussion of history as practiced at home and abroad. This source becomes a further extension of the how jaliya circulates and how ideas about the Mande world gets codified for different audiences. Foday Musa Suso's project is particularly compelling and articulate in forming an imagined dialogue with the international audience that frames his memoir. Suso's project raises the issue of the double responsibility of jali to speak both nationally and internationally as performers, particularly musicians, as well as historians. This two-sided commitment forms an important aspect of the next section of my discussion.

History Is Performance

A traditional performance of historical narration might take place in a patron's compound and unfold during the course of several hours. Events that commemorate deceased relatives form particularly important occasions where the life history of the departed, told in relationship to other important figures and significant events, enriches a jali's repertoire of historical narrative. While articulating stories of people and events, jali simultaneously demonstrate their expertise in organizing the details of life-cycle ceremonies. Jali narrations form a part of children's naming ceremonies, circumcision ceremonies, and weddings and bride transfer rituals, as well as funerals. Jali narrations are also offered during political rallies and meetings, and on public holidays. Radio Gambia features performances by jali that may include historical epics and other types of narratives.

These historical narratives are rendered in performance with kora or balaphon accompaniment; women jali often serve as background singers. Men jali are most commonly known as experts in history; however, a few women claim expertise in this area as well. Some jali are known more for their knowledge of history than others. Where some jali stress their musical talents or their ability to stimulate and educate audiences, others, especially older jali "masters," are known for their ability to offer extensive historical detail as part of their performance repertoire.

For jali, performance is not just a medium of transmission for history. History is made in performance, as one can see in the telling of the story of Sunjata; a jali's words move the patron to action. Words themselves have the charisma to make history, and jali performance is the enactment of the mastery of words. Jali are responsible for ceremonies in which the name of a child is announced to the community; the name makes the child part of an ongoing social narrative, stretching from the past to the future. Jali goad their patrons into making history that can be told. Foday Musa Suso explains: "Griots would ride along beside kings, singing their praises. They recited the warriors' names and words of inspiration and encouragement: *Tell me what you will do on the battlefield*, they might sing. *Do something that I can pass on to future generations so you'll never be forgotten*" (1996, 36, original emphasis). Jali performance is an active process of appropriating and linking the past to the present in a way that can chart the direction of future action.

The length and complexity of songs is thus the length and complexity of history itself. "There is so much history. Some of our songs last two days" (Suso in Kopka and Brooks 1996, 32).

History Is Genealogy

History as a set of social relationships that extend over time is exemplified by family relationships, as these link ancestors and descendants as well as the collaterals who jointly remember these links. Jali are experts in family genealogies, and through these genealogies they remember and perform the past. In several of the interviews I conducted among jali men and women, particularly older jali, the mere mention of a particular name would engender a list of interrelationships. When asked, jali construct histories of prominent families and their travels, their dependents, and the spread of their fame and influence. These histories are simultaneously narratives of their own families; they remember their patrons through their interrelationships with their own family line. When jali recite histories of great men who lived before their time, they are often the patrons of their own fathers or grandfathers. Historical narrative is thus inextricably tied to the interconnected genealogies of jali and patrons over time.

Family is understood as a principle of spreading interconnection among people, rather than as a line of difference. Genealogies include dependents and superiors, conquerors and their conquered, travelers and their hosts. "We have a cultural tradition called *sanau* that binds together families with different names," emphasizes Foday Musa Suso. "If a Suso meets a Turay or a Darbo, there is instant familiarity and friendship" (1996, 40). It is this understanding of spreading linkages among family lines that provokes a history of radiating influence, not ethnic conflict and division, as in foreign historians' versions of the West African past. Family genealogies and their interlinked ties of influence become the core line through which history is put together as well as the model jali offer as history. For them, family genealogies, which include the relationships among patrons and their dependents, account for the historical endurance of West African culture. "We have a saying," reminds Foday Musa Suso, " 'The man with the biggest family is the richest man in the world' "(1996, 22).

Family genealogy is also a technology of memory. Jali are experts in family names; they remember the past through connecting family names in a story of spreading influences and interlinked lines. I was forced to acknowledge the remarkable feats of memory of which jali are capable when a colleague from the United States visited one of my jali informants with me. The colleague had met the jali five years before; when she bid her adieu at that time, she told him she was going to visit her father, who was ill. Five years later, he greeted her with the question, "How is your father doing?" Through connecting acquaintances and family ties, jali are able to develop an impressively precise memory. Older jali, in particular, are known for their prodigious historical knowledge, created in part by their ability to make genealogical references tell of the past—and not just the past as experienced but as traced through the experiences of all those brought into the story of interconnections. Far from being a disability, old age heightens jali expertise; the jali who has known many people and places can produce an exponentially greater depth in his or her accounts.

Furthermore, family genealogy is a model of history that brings the past into the present and future. Jali are then repositories of a past that can be used to make the future; in this sense they mimic the archives as used by foreign historians. "The Griots are walking libraries," says Suso, "with knowledge of the past, present and future of our people" (1996, 26).

History Is Religious Authority, Tying Islam and Jaliya

Where national historians wrestle with the question of the relationship between national independence and colonialism, constructing a history in which independence flows from precolonial kingdoms and thus corrects the interruption of colonial rule, jali are more worried about the relationship of jaliya and Islam. As the foreign historians tell it, jaliya in the nineteenth century was closely connected to a network of indigenous patronage originally hostile to Islam, and only converted rather late to Islam. But foreign historians have inherited a long colonial tradition of working to separate Islamic and indigenous cultural influences. In contrast, contemporary jali construct a history in which Islam and jaliya emerged together and have created a linked authority in which each requires the other.

This linking of jaliya and Islam is constructed by joining the origin of jaliya with the origin of Islam. The Prophet Muhammed appears in jali narrations as a figure who would fit easily into a West African system of patronage. His religion would never have spread if he had not had jali announcing his message in the villages to which he traveled. As one of my jali informants explained, Muhammed had a very devoted and charismatic jali. "On arrival at every destination, he would sing praises of [the Prophet] such as: 'Oh people come out, here comes the righteous; anyone who believes in his teachings will not go astray'; and so on. He would be given alms for his praises." Why would the populace convert if they had not heard about the religion from Muhammed's jali?

Muhammed is often portrayed by jali as living in the same era as the West African leader Suraqata, in the sixth century; Suraqata is a leader known by foreign historians for his early opposition to Islam and his subsequent influential conversion. According to one jali who recounted this story to me, two linked jali traditions arose at the time of Suraqata: religious jali (*fina*) and ordinary jali. Both jali were devoted to the prophet Muhammed. Suraqata's jali sang praises to Muhammed, saying "Here is the apostle; he is the highest among all creatures. He is the leader of all created beings." Because of this praise, people came out and offered donations; both Islam and jaliya drew from this public generosity.

Another jali incorporated Suraqata's initial hostility to Islam into her story: "Jaliya started during the time of the Appointed One [the prophet Muhammed]. Suraqata was the disciple and student of the Holy Prophet.

But before he was made his student, he was a soldier. He was among the envious people, enemies of the Holy Prophet. Those who did not like the Holy Prophet came to wage a war; they said they would kill the Prophet." During this war, Suraqata, a brave fighter, confronts Muhammed but is unable to defeat him. This settles his conversion, after which he praises Muhammed and his religion. Thus far, the story is similar to that told by foreign historians, except that Muhammed is brought to life for religious conversions of a much later date. The jali story, however, privileges the Islamic origin of jaliya and not the historical specificity of Islamic conversion. After Suraqata's conversion, the jali continues, "everywhere the Prophet went, Suraqata would sing his praises. He would praise him just as we are praising people now. That is where the jali took the tradition of jaliya." The common, noble origin of Islamic reverence and jali performance offer each a combined authority.

History Is Made by the Generosity and Bravery of the Great—And Its Telling by Their Praisesingers

For national and international historians (with the exception of social historians), history is made by great people and events. And greatness is difficult to question because it rests on a tautology. Everyone should recognize their greatness because it is part of history; but, since history merely reports on the past, their greatness precedes its recording in history. It becomes difficult to ask how the historical agency of greatness is constructed; one can come up with many examples of "great men"— presidents, generals, ambassadors—but defining in general the kind of persons who should be included and excluded is more difficult. In contrast, jali are much more self-conscious about the making of greatness. Their business is to make greatness, and to make sure that the greatness they make becomes history.

Jali stimulate their patrons to acts of bravery and generosity. In the historical epics jali tell, they continually taunt their patrons, reminding them of their cowardice and their stinginess or poverty to make them more courageous and more giving. Without such stimulation, even those of the most noble ancestry might not live up to their great names. Patrons are thus dependent on their jali for their greatness. They are also dependent on jali willingness to tell people about it. A great man without jali will not be appreciated. His greatness will not become history.

The importance of the work of jali in making greatness, first as deed and then as word—that is, as history—was instilled in me over and over by my jali informants. One story was particularly helpful in stimulating my understanding of historical agency. Even an ordinary person, perhaps even an undistinguished young woman, can become a personage in historical narratives if she is stimulated to bravery or generosity by the work of jali. She rises from her ordinariness to become the heroine of song and story. When she dies, she is remembered; her greatness, interwoven with that of others, becomes part of the history that jali tell.

Here is the story as one jali conveyed it to me. A jali informant was listing his best songs for me. He came to one song dedicated to a young woman who had since died, but who continued to be remembered. He had not expected to dedicate a song to this young woman; in fact, she came to his attention despite his initial lack of interest in her. The jali had traveled to a village upcountry, and upon his arrival, all of the young women, as well as the family with whom he was lodging, came out to honor him. Each of the girls presented him with a chicken; he noted that he had received sixty-six chickens in all. He stayed in the village for some time and tried to express his appreciation of these gifts, but after a long period he felt ready to leave. The chickens were an appropriate enough gift, but he had stayed long enough. He asked his hosts for permission to move along, and his host, as well as the donors of the chickens, said their farewells. But just as he was about to leave, another young woman ran up and asked him if he would spend just one more night with them. She had not yet had the opportunity to honor him, she said. He was impatient to leave, and the last thing he wanted at that time was another chicken. He was reluctant to pay any attention to the young woman. The woman, however, insisted, and despite his own wishes, he agreed to stay.

Soon an elderly man knocked on his door. "Here is your chicken," he said. But amazingly enough, he was leading a goat, not a chicken. The jali was surprised. "The flying feathered creature has turned into a horn-bearing creature," he said to his companion, a religious griot with whom he had traveled. The jali requested that the goat be slaughtered for a meal; he gave some to his hosts, and ate some. In the evening, he readied himself to express his gratitude by performing, but the young woman appeared again and insisted that he wait until she spread a mat for him. She took money and placed it on the corners of the mat, thus showing again her earnest appreciation of the jali. On that day, he dedicated a song to her and he has continued to sing that song, memorializing her generosity and placing her in a line of other great figures. Although she died young, she is remembered within the jali's repertoire.

Greatness, and thus historical agency, we might gather from this story, is created by acts of generosity to dependents. After all, a great person is a person with appreciative dependents, whether that person is a king or a generous young woman. Jali remind historians of the importance of the historian—jali or academic—in memorializing greatness, withdrawing it from obscurity, and bringing it into history. Yet this self-consciousness is not particularly appreciated by either foreign or national historians, who hope to uncover histories that are less dependent on the explicit detailing of personalistic relationships of the teller.

Indeed, these conceptions of history are both inspiration and frustration to the national historian. Sometimes it is useful to both cordon them off and empower them as "culture." Furthermore, jali are not adverse to this move, and their enthusiasm about "culture"-making is an important aspect of OHAD's efforts to build an interconnected sense of national culture and national history. This effort draws on and blends standards of international legitimacy and legacies of regional politics to construct a cultural politics that can be recognized as "national" from many directions.

History, Culture, and Development

Building a national history joins the project of building a national culture; both have been requirements for new nation-states. And a national culture, like a national history, has distinctive characteristics, requiring refigurations of notions of "culture" that have been institutionally and intellectually situated in other ways. A national culture, for example, must form the basis of a national politics. It must help create a national community. It must also facilitate the international legitimacy of the nation-state at the same time that it draws local loyalties. In this sense, a national culture—at least in the global South, where international standards are not taken for granted as home-grown—is a self-conscious fusion, combining shreds of regional cultural legacies and international symbols and conventions. Even in its dependence on regional cultural legacies, it must be syncretic and transformative; it must form an assimilative tradition, which draws on the forms and knowledges of particular ethnic groups to enlarge them, creating a broader national embrace. And most importantly, perhaps, it must show itself as a kind of culture that is not caught in tradition. History must be forward-looking. It must embrace international development. No mid- and late twentieth century national cultures could survive outside the endorsement of international development standards.

In The Gambia, building a national culture required bringing the traditions and knowledges of Mandinka jaliya into the goals of nation-building. As I have been discussing, Mandinka cultural legacies have been at the center of the imaginative features of nation-making projects; yet jaliya must be tapped and trained into nation-making. One aspect of the nation-making project in which jali have participated has involved building a national forum. Radio played a major role in this, similar to that of newspapers in Benedict Anderson's account of the creation of imagined communities (1992). Newspapers played a less important role in The Gambia than in the places Anderson discusses in part because The Gambia possessed a very small literate intelligentsia, and most of them were of minority ethnic groups whose cultural legacies were seen as less important than Mandinka in building the nation. Instead of newspapers, Radio Gambia became a site for launching the nation.

Radio Gambia was started during the colonial era with the assistance of British advisors. In its early years, it mainly rebroadcast programs made in other areas of Africa or England. Even after independence, Radio Gambia depended on the BBC for programming; however, it also created its own news, educational shows, and music programs, broadcasting in the multiple languages of Gambian ethnic communities as well as in English. Radio Gambia has also featured programs and performances by famous jali. Jali Nyama Suso had a regular program for many years, which drew a devoted audience. When my research assistant, Ms. Mariama Jammeh, and I prepared for an interview with Jali Nyama Suso, then an elderly man, she became quite excited by the prospect of meeting such a famous jali. She remembered the radio programs that featured him during her childhood. "Jali Nyama Suso!," she sang, recalling the jingle that introduced the radio show.

When we arrived at the interview with Jali Nyama Suso, he joined Mariama's reverie about the show, singing the theme song for us as he recalled the program as a national highlight in his career. Many of the other bright moments he recalled involved travel and performance abroad; on Radio Gambia, however, he had an opportunity to become a widely admired performer without leaving home. His popularity contributed to building a national public sphere, an imagined community of radio listeners. Jali performance draws listeners. In addition to sponsoring regular shows such as that of Nyama Suso, Radio Gambia has collected a large archive of recordings of jali performances, which are used in music programming and are an important part of attracting the listening audience, who might otherwise have less patience for news and educational shows.

Another challenge for the crafting of a national culture has been to create internationally meaningful symbols that are still marked with local flair; such local-global symbols are the signs of legitimate nationhood. Every nation, for example, must have a national anthem, national flag, and national coat of arms. Jali Nyama Suso tells an important story of how he was enrolled in the process of creating these national symbols, with their strict requirements for both international and local intelligibility. The flag and the coat of arms, he said, were easy. But the politicians were stumped on the question of the national anthem. So they came to Jali Nyama Suso for assistance. "They asked me, 'What song will you compose for the national anthem?' I replied, 'The tune I will take it from will be the tune dedicated to Fodee Kaba Dumbunya.'" Fodee Kaba Dumbunya was a Muslim reformer and a famous warrior, remembered for his conquests for Islam. Furthermore, he was a patron of Jali Nyama Suso's grandfather. Thus, his praisesongs come to Jali Nyama through his own genealogical training. They are history because of their combined significance for the jali and his audience. They are national history, however, because of their parallels with other nations' anthems, which offer them international legitimacy.

> They asked me, "Why are you choosing that tune?" I replied, "When the Republic of Mali gained its independence, they took the tune dedicated to their great king called Sunjata Keita and made it their national anthem. The Republic of Guinea Conakry also did the same as Mali. They took the tune dedicated to [King] Alpha Yaya Jallow as their national anthem. So The Gambia should do the same." They asked me, "Who [i.e., what famous figure] is it going to be?" I replied, "It will be the tune dedicated to Fodee Kaba Dumbuya." So I played the music and put in my own words. They recorded it.

By writing the national anthem, Jali Nyama Suso forges a relationship with national political figures, and becomes himself a crafter of the imagined community. He even gains status with international political figures.

> By then the Premiere was here, and they took [the national anthem Jali Nyama composed] to the Premiere's office in the cabinet to listen to it. Premier Jawara said he was satisfied with it. So they took it to the Governor General who also stated that he was satisfied with it. Later it was taken to one British Commissar called Sir Jeremy Howe and he translated it in English.

There are other stories, however, about the national anthem. The national anthem is what science studies scholars have called a "boundary object" that gains its solidity because it takes on different significance from different points of view (Star and Griesemer 1989; Fujimura 1992). From the perspective of Jali Nyama Suso, it is a praisesong from his family repertoire, rewritten in the spirit of nation building. But from the perspective of foreign commentators, it is a British expatriate creation that borrows from local Gambian "popular culture." Here is how one American journalist, whose sources appear to have been British residents in The Gambia, tells the story of the national anthem: "Mr. J. F. Howe, a former British administrative officer, wrote the new Gambia National Anthem, with lyrics by Mrs. Howe. He took the music from a popular Mandinka song, 'Foday Kabba Dumbuya'" (Rice 1967, 22). Jali Nyama Suso's creative efforts in this telling are reduced to the transmission of a "popular Mandinka song." Furthermore, according to this journalist, Fodee Kabba Dumbaya's status is internationally questionable. He writes, "Foday Kabba is revered by Gambians as a powerful nineteenth century Mandinka Ruler, while British historians describe him as a ruthless crusader whose fervor for the new Muslim religion led him to forcibly convert or ravage pagan villages" (Rice 1967, 22). In this context, only British authorship allows the national anthem to take on its international role in symbolizing a civilized nation. And perhaps because different versions are possible, then, the anthem works to draw in both foreign and Gambian audiences: those who need to amend Fodee Kabba Dumbaya's reputation, and those who wish to continue it into the present. In this sense, the hybridity of national culture is created through its ability to suggest different origin stories to differently situated observers.

A national culture must by necessity serve the needs of national politics beyond the moment of independence and its rituals. In The Gambia, the national bureaucracy in the immediate postindependence period appears sometimes schematic, but the nation-state cannot function without it. And jali are enrolled to create its status and thus its effectiveness. Jali accompany ministers in their official duties, announcing their platforms and programs to the people, and help create the appropriate sense of respect for the ministers' official positions. The everyday functioning of the administrative apparatus of the state under the regime of President Jawara thus required the making of a national culture, with the participation of jali.

At the same time, a national culture cannot help but look outward toward international institutions. The Gambia's independence could only be guaranteed by its participation in international networks. Perhaps the most significant of these, in relation to the making of national culture, have been those elements of the apparatus for international development that have seen "culture" as a key part of the development program. Organizations that stand out in particular in this regard for their concerns with building development-oriented national cultures, include the Ford Foundation and UNESCO.[4] Both organizations shared an interest in human progress and global development for the goal of peace and world security.[5]

The period after World War II showed increasing concern for "culture" as an aspect of national development. UNESCO's founding constitution, ratified in 1946, dictated support for social science, theater, and mass-media projects in culture. This agenda spread throughout UNESCO's institutional development. In 1988, the United Nations declared a decade for cultural development, which included the following guidelines: acknowledgment of the cultural dimension of development, affirmation and enrichment of cultural identities, broadening participation in cultural life, and promotion of international cultural cooperation (M'Bow 1988, 6). The organization created a World Commission on Culture and Development with the charter to investigate the relationship between culture and development on a global scale.

The Ford Foundation also funded cultural development in the global South. In 1950, the philanthropic organization developed a national and international focus, paying special attention to the emerging nations of the South as well as to disadvantaged areas in the North. The explicit goals of the Ford Foundation included "to strengthen democratic values, reduce poverty and injustice, promote international cooperation, and advance human achievement" (Ford Foundation annual report 1958). They articulated these goals in their work both in poor areas in the United States and in the ex-colonial emergent nations. At the center of many of the Ford and UNESCO projects was cultural preservation and development. Ford particularly supported local initiatives in documenting, preserving, and creatively figuring cultural histories. In their work in Africa, which began in 1958, they offered funding designed to strengthen self-government and development by broadening their cultural effectiveness. Cultural preservation was seen as particularly important in developing countries where rapid transformations and the formation of national politics were eroding cultural legacies.

From the moment of its founding, OHAD aimed for funding from international agencies to support their work in building national history and culture. Indeed, in the 1970s OHAD was successful in obtaining funding from Ford. During this same period, UNESCO support also made its way to The Gambia. Beyond the actual funding itself, the constant search for support from these organizations helped shape OHAD's programs, providing the stimulus to continually consider the relationship between the national culture they aimed to build and its fit with international development rhetorics and goals. One outgrowth of the continual search for international funding was the importance of thinking about culture from a transnational perspective. OHAD scholars' interest in ancient Mandinka kingdoms already predisposed them to thinking about Mandinka culture in a *regional* perspective—one that crossed national borders—which added to its national significance. In conversation with foreign funding agencies, this attention to the regional, transnational significance of Mandinka only flourished.

Furthermore, the search for foreign funding kept OHAD in touch with foreign scholars, another set of international institutional figures who helped shape notions of culture on a regional level. Foreign academics, leaving behind their role as connoisseurs of particular colonial territories, had begun to focus on the histories and travels of regional African cultures. I have already discussed foreign historians who portrayed Gambian history as a series of ethnic conflicts and migrations. Anthropologists, linguists, art historians, ethnomusicologists, and literary scholars also became interested in ethnic regions as these crossed and refused national boundaries. British scholars began discussion of the "Mande world," the cultural area that crossed Mali, Senegal, The Gambia, Guinea-Conakry, and Guinea-Bissau.

In 1972, the first Mande world conference was held in London. A number of Gambians were invited, including authorities on Mandinka culture. The conference had important implications for Gambian thinking about national culture. First, it gave international legitimacy to the idea that Mandinka cultural traditions were "world building" rather than bounded by territory, custom, and tradition. The regional, indeed transnational power of Mande culture, which includes Mandinka, made it even more appropriate for nation builders, who could imagine its regional political significance as a support for their notions of politics, leadership, and national legacy. Furthermore, the regional significance of Mande culture supported the primacy of Mandinka influences on building national culture in The Gambia.

The London conference also raised the profile of jali, a number of whom were invited to perform in London. The success of their performances helped stimulate international interest in jali; by the late 1970s, invitations to perform in Europe and North America began to increase. This international currency of jali performance at times raised their prestige at home in The Gambia. National culture became more devoted than ever to the promotion of jali because of the mediating efforts of OHAD. The prominence of jali in Gambian notions of what might count internationally as Gambian culture was promoted in London when the Gambian scholar invited to the conference contributed a paper on jali: "Griot: A Self-Portrait" (Darboe 1976). (The author of this paper was himself of high status, a patron to jali, but jali were so symbolically important to Gambian identity that a patron wrote a jali "self-portrait.") In building an international presence for The Gambia, jali became for many what would count as Gambian culture.

International interest in Mande culture only increased after the London conference, and academics kept it alive on a number of continents. Thus, for example, linguist Charles Bird at Indiana University formed a group of scholars whose focus was the Mande world. In The Gambia, communication with foreign academics came together with attempts to seek funding from such agencies as the Ford Foundation and UNESCO in supporting the notion of a region-wide culture, which could also form the basis of national political and cultural development. A growing, transnationally active "Mande culture" thus became an object of observation and nurturance by both foreign and national scholars in their communication with the institutions of international development.

OHAD members sustained attention on the Mande world as an aspect of their work in building national culture and history, as was particularly evident in their promotion of regional sites in which Mande culture could be performed and displayed, crossing the boundaries of contemporary West African nation-states; these sites gave Mande cultural politics a transnational African presence that raised the profile of Gambian national political culture. One such site was the Sedhiou cultural festival (discussed in chapter 2). The OHAD staff played a prominent organizing role; the OHAD conservator chose the Gambian delegation. He was partial to jali from the eastern, rural part of The Gambia because he knew their cultural knowledge could be perceived as regionally more authentic. The Gambia would be a showcase of the best Mande culture, with its historical ties to the Malian empire, whose center lay to the east of the Gambia. Meanwhile, Gambian jali would join those from Senegal, Mali, and Guinea Conakry to celebrate the Mande world.

At the festival, performances were organized according to country of origin. At the same time, the event was self-consciously constructed to increase the transnational prestige of Mande culture. Indeed, there was a sense of the Malian kingdoms come again, with the delegations' spread of Mande cultural and political space across the region both through and across the varied nation-states. In some of the nations represented, Mande culture was more central to national culture than in others. In Senegal, for example, where the festival was held, Mande-speaking people are a minority and of little prominence in national affairs, which are administrated from northern Senegal. The festival was held, however, in an area where Mandinka were in great numbers, thus raising the political prestige of the peoples of that area through their alliance with Mandinka delegations from The Gambia as well as other Mande-world countries. In this context, Gambian national culture and transnational Mande culture worked together to form a regional presence.

There were also other models of politics and culture at the festival. As I discussed in chapter 2, some national delegations offered multiethnic performances or featured village plays with state administrative messages rather than jali performances. OHAD's efforts to build a jali-centered vision of a living and expanding regional Mande world to support the Gambian nation had to compete with other political agendas.

Meanwhile, the goals of Gambian jali also had expanded beyond the terrain of national culture. By the 1980s, the most prominent of the Gambian jali had found places on the international circuit for West African musicians. The presence of international tourists in The Gambia had increased, and their demand for jali performance expanded the repertoire of jali self-presentation. These developments both supported and transformed OHAD's efforts to preserve cultural legacies to build a national culture and history. Jali were more important than ever as spokespersons for The Gambia. They traveled abroad as national representatives; their performances were funded and supported by forms of internationalism that made them appear to be representative of The Gambia, and, sometimes, of Africa in general. These activities made jali one important symbolic reference for the nation, and also allowed jali to demand higher fees and more personal recognition, thus hampering OHAD efforts to collect their knowledge as national treasure. By the 1990s, it was time for a new kind of OHAD.

In 1989, Mr. Bakary Sidibe retired from his position as conservator of OHAD. He was replaced by Mr. Sanyang, who immediately began plans to reorganize the institution; among the most important elements of the reorganization, at the insistence of governmental officials, was the plan to make the institution self-sufficient. No longer was OHAD a mainstay considered crucial to nation building; therefore it must seek funding beyond government support. In the spirit of new economic plans advocating privatization and self-sufficiency, the institution was now encouraged to market national culture. Rather than remaining under the primary directorship of an individual, the new institution would be managed by a cultural committee, which would oversee the programming and broaden the vision of OHAD beyond the immediate postcolonial era. The agenda would aim to become more culturally pluralistic, with less emphasis on building national culture from Mandinka roots. In a context in which the marketing of culture was more important than nation building as imagined in the postindependence era, the whole spectrum of Gambian ethnicities could be gathered and put to use. The new director had several plans for generating income, including museum entrance fees and the development of a gift shop and dining facilities attached to the museum that would draw tourists. This would eventually, it was hoped, allow OHAD to become a self-sustaining institution.

In the late 1990s, then, even national culture became a commodity. In an entrepreneurial age, an era of international structural adjustment, it was no longer nationally respectable to rely solely on grants and government support to sustain research on culture and history. Culture and history must support themselves. As tourism became the most hopeful prospect of economic development, the importance of The Gambia in the world increased hopeful possibilities. Still the revenue generated through tourism rarely amounts to more than getting by. Like many countries, The Gambia does not garner a profit from tourism.

This chapter has traced history-making projects developed during the postindependence era, and how they have challenged and redefined national history and culture. In the early 1990s the range of projects of building national identity, legacy, and direction was transformed. Now the nation, and its suddenly more multiple cultures and histories, must sell itself to the world. At each turn, history-making projects have been intimately bound to multiple social projects: modernization and development theories, and models of nationhood and civilization that travel along with these visions; contests over which visions should be foregrounded in postcolonial states; and philanthropic and commercial interests that help set the agendas of what history can be. Thus charting the contours of the Gambian history project provided a way for understanding the institutional setting of a history-based project that attempts to insert its unique concerns within an internationalist vision of nation-making.

CHAPTER FOUR

Personalistic Economy

SETTING: 7:00 A.M., BANJUL, 1989

Early in the morning on any given weekday in the capital city of Banjul, people made their way to offices and to the markets. The slow opening to the day had taxi vans and buses making their way through the main street bringing people from the surrounding areas to work. Some of the men, civil servants, were dressed in dark Western-style suits and others in gray nationalist "African" suits and plain cotton shirts and trousers. Scattered among the civil servants in their modern attire were jali, many of whom appeared distinctive because they were wearing brightly colored, elaborately embroidered robes. Following their patrons, the jali were also on their way to work. Their occupation was to make their daily rounds to the offices of their patrons who were civil servants. Somewhat like congressional pages and lobbyists in the United States, they were responsible for attending to the needs of their sponsors; they must be ready to offer their services at any point during the day.

An office that I happened to visit one day when I was newly arrived in The Gambia introduced me to the protocol that would become familiar as my visit in The Gambia lengthened. The first thing I noticed was the expectation around interpersonal interaction; the requirement around sociality with coworkers put many U.S. practices to shame. My hosts exchanged a standard greeting: "Salaam aleikum," "Aleikum asallam"; and in Mandinka: "How is the morning?" "It is fine"; "How are those at home?" "They are all there"; "How goes the work?" "The work goes fine." And the ritualized exchange went far beyond this opening gambit. The elaborateness of greetings gave me my first sense of the importance of personalisms and the importance of interpersonal connections. This notion further developed as I met with the person who caused me to be in that office on that particular day.

I was visiting a man who worked for the government to discuss my research. He and I had met during my previous trip in 1983, and he had kindly arranged for me to take lessons with a kora teacher whom he greatly respected. This time, upon my return, I wanted to discuss my interest in deepening my understanding of jali and their social importance and particularly the relationship of women to jaliya. Upon entering his office, after we exchanged the standard greetings, I was immediately alerted to the presence of a man, clad in a dark maroon suit, who sat quietly as if he would go unnoticed. He was a jali, and he remained there for quite a long time sitting in silence. An occasional glance suggested he was listening, but he never joined in the conversation. Eventually, he perhaps thought he had been there long enough and decided to leave. As the jali got up, the civil servant got up too, said a few words, and then gave him some money. And when the man left, my host said, "That was a griot. He is going to tell everything about our meeting. He's the recorder of all things." The double-edged power of the jali's knowledge of the conversation escapes no one; he can use it to promote the interests of a patron, or take his information to please and flatter another patron with different ties and aspirations to power.

Later the civil servant excused himself momentarily and left for another short engagement. Another jali walked in, seated himself at the civil servant's desk, and decided to use the telephone. When the civil servant returned, he was hardly pleased to see his office so fully occupied. The jali made way for the civil servant; the civil servant offered him some dalasis (Gambian currency), perhaps for his appearance and in the hope that the jali would reciprocate with loyalty.

The power relationship between civil servant and jali is ambiguous. On the one hand, the civil servant is the patron, the one of noble or elite background and therefore entitled to rights, privileges, and authority not afforded others in the society. On the other hand, several features differentiate this relationship from easy stereotypes of typical patron-client relationships. First, the civil servant depends on the jali for his reputation, which is made and remade by what the jali says about the patron. Of course, the patron is perfectly capable of conducting private conversations to his own benefit, but his public image depends to a large extent on the activities of jali. The official is made by what the jali says about him. This reputation-building is more than a matter of rude mumblings of little consequence—the jali is a professional character builder. The civil servant cannot speak his own power; only the jali can articulate his position for him. Second, both loyalty and status are always in the making. The civil servant cannot rest on his position. To form networks with other powerful people to maintain his status, he depends on the communicative skills of the jali. But the civil servant cannot trust the jali, who may shift his loyalty or play one patron off against another. From the jali's perspective, the civil servant must be constantly cajoled into acting like a patron. And the jali must continually expand his network through his ability to *make* patrons through performing attendance on them. The civil servant dismisses the jali as a "beggar." But only through his appropriate generosity to those "beggars" can he become a great man.

This chapter explores the processes for making power and status in which Gambian jali participate, in their own country and beyond. My discussion foregrounds the use of performance in forging power-laden relationships, for this is how jali themselves describe their role in activating this important aspect of social life. The idea of performance here is not so much focused on formal concert performances, like those I discussed in chapter 2; rather these everyday performances involve praise, gossip, deference, harassment, secrets, "begging," threats, generosity, renewals of loyalty and kinship, and all the oral skills of everyday performance associated with jaliya. The necessity for interpersonal performance to make and reaffirm status and interconnection also highlights the importance of personalistic ties in the dynamics of authority and influence. I use the term "personalistic economy" to point to the structured ties created among jali and their patrons not only in The Gambia but also internationally, as jali attempt to bring their interpersonal performance skills to bear on making international connections, signing recording contracts, and booking concert engagements. A culturally distinctive arrangement of performance, personalism, and power, this perspective also alerts us to the force of performance-based personalism in all kinds of cosmopolitan social relations—even where local commitments to other status dynamics may hide them.

To show how the everyday performativity of jaliya inflects social life in The Gambia, as well as jali social contacts outside The Gambia, I move back and forth in this chapter between presenting theatrical "scenes" of jali interaction and discussing the dynamics of culture and power. I begin with some general characteristics of performativity and power in West Africa to ask how these affect that status hierarchy most commonly translated into English as "caste." I show that Mandinka caste is not a classificatory principle of hierarchy that underlies all subjectivity, but rather a frame for the active pursuit of performance-based personalistic ties. Then I consider how this way of making relationships is used in the international work of jali—and their work at home.

The Public Sphere

SETTING: AN OUTDOOR EVENT IN A RURAL PROVINCE ON A SATURDAY AFTERNOON, 1989

The minister of water works had arrived to present the news of an exciting development: the installation of the water system in the village. The celebration had been prepared weeks in advance, and this was the day for a display of local pride and the welcoming of an important guest to the village. Praises from the village jali announced the minister's arrival, which was followed by a procession. The minister, formal in his appearance, wore a shirt and trousers not unlike that of the more prosperous village men. In contrast, the jali were in traditional, ceremonial regalia. The minister slowly made his way to the front of the gathering to stand and face those assembled for the event. Some in attendance were already seated; a number of people, including village women, each wrapped in matching patterned cloth, lined the edge of the reception area to enliven the atmosphere while awaiting the minister's message. The minister's way had been fully paved by the eloquent words of the praisesingers, and praises from the jali continued to welcome more honored guests still arriving. When the minister finally reached the center of the stage and was ready to deliver his message, he stood and waited for those guests to take their seats. He was not alone on stage. As the minister readied for his presentation, a jali stood at his side. In familiar fashion, the minister's words were first softly conveyed from the minister's mouth to the jali, and then the message was repeated by the jali directly to the audience in a louder, stronger voice. The audience could see the message being relayed, and certainly some could even hear the rather muted voice of the minister in the background while he was giving the jali his speech. Also nearby was an operative amplification system that easily could have delivered the minister's message for all to hear. But this was a moment of ritualized performance. Important men do not speak directly to each other, but only do so through their jali. The minister could not speak directly to the crowd; that was the responsibility of the jali. The public sphere, where politics is brought into presence through the circulation of words, is made by the joint activities of political officials and their spokesmen.

James Scott (1990) has usefully drawn attention to the relationship between performance and power in constituting public space. Scott argues that public spaces are made by performances of deference on the part of subordinates, who perform from sanitized "public transcripts" in obedience to the agendas of elites. The humiliation of this deference drives "backstage" dissatisfaction that, he argues, functions with important similarities across cultures in producing "hidden transcripts" through which subordinates privately air their grievances. In public, these hidden transcripts tend to appear only in disguised forms, where they offer an ambiguous accompaniment to the performance of flattery for elites.

Scott's formulation seems relevant in a number of ways to the relationships of jali and their patrons. Born to social locations within a caste system and offered different options for work, prestige, and wealth by these birth positions, jali and their patrons seem in some ways exemplars of the kind of unequal status relations from which Scott has formulated his ideas. Furthermore, jali stress the performative aspect of making status; they would agree with Scott that power is always made in performance. And much of that performance consists in the flattery of elites.

Yet the West African dynamics also contrast in striking ways with Scott's thought-provoking generalizations. Certainly, the West African public spaces where important men compete for power, patronage, and authority are theatrical. But they are spaces in which the important men are themselves rendered inarticulate while their subordinates hold center stage. From the perspective of the elites, the "public transcript" is rather out of their control; powerful men cannot, as Scott describes, control their appearance through it. They can try to influence it with their soft words, but they can never expect to banish the ambiguous mixing of their own intentions and their jali's intentions since jali performance holds the floor. In this context, a separation between "public" and "hidden" transcripts becomes difficult to imagine since public discussion is constituted precisely by the predominance of jali speech, with its mixing of flattering deference and dangerous gossip, conjoined with the withholding of secrets.

The call for attention to the culturally specific relationship of language and subjectivity forms a helpful intervention here, as Susan Gal (1985) argues; the linguistic construction of domination and subordination varies across different cultures and contexts. Gal urges researchers to begin by noting how identities are constituted in relation to language in particular cultural-historical moments. Without abandoning how power is made in performance, it is possible to formulate a framework that seems more suitably tailored for the relationship of West African praisesingers and their patrons.

This framework must begin with the separation of the power of being an important man, on the one hand, from the ability to speak in public and to make reputations, on the other. I recall asking one patron, and being misunderstood and also misunderstanding what was at stake: Why do you care what jali say about you? Why couldn't you stand on your own reputation, which you've made? Unaware of my own cultural assumptions, I was told, "Obviously, you don't understand. I am powerless to make my own reputation. Without jali, I am nobody." What he meant by this was that he could not gain the ear of other powerful men; he could not effectively influence the workings of society. Indeed, in the West, too, personal connections are required for influence, although the ideology of individual initiative masks some of the parallels and overlaps. Gambian patrons are afraid of their jali, just as jali are afraid of their patrons. Patrons have the ability to make important decisions and policies, but only as long as they hold on to the loyal performance of their jali.

The question of speech and power has been much discussed in the literature on the Senegambian region. One useful portrayal is Bonnie

Wright's (1989) essay, which helpfully argues that West Africans distinguish between those who have the ability to speak and those who have the ability to act. Writing specifically of Senegalese Wolof, she shows that caste rankings correspond not to a single underlying principle of hierarchy but rather to the attribution of different forms of "innate capacity" to different caste groups. Nobles have the capacity for action; praisesingers have the capacity for speech. Other caste ranks have other capacities, such as the capacity for "*transformation* (the other occupational castes) and *servitude* (slaves)" (Wright 1989, 42, emphasis original). One worries here that attention to power has been banished from the analysis. Can it be possible that some people identify themselves only through their capacity for servitude? Wright, however, usefully shows how people agree to talk about caste. Caste differentiation works together with other principles of difference, including descent lines, ethnic groups, places of origin, gender, and age, in defining capacity and identity. She stresses how praisesingers and patrons feel interdependent rather than situated within a clear relationship of domination and subordination.

Wright's discussion of these cultural principles of identity-making is insightful for the Gambian Mandinka as well. Mandinka jali perceive it as their responsibility to drive their patrons into action rather than to act themselves. They articulate the patron's power and commit it to memory; they forge connections among patrons. Important men are all indebted for their power as well as what they can do in the world to jali performances. The ability to *hold* public power and the ability to *create* public power—to speak about it and negotiate and join its separate sources—are distinct. And, as many reminded me, while "a jali and his patron will never be the same," both have the ability to influence public action. My understanding of power-making performances requires, then, particular attention to these contributing distinctions and interdependencies as they are wrapped in local notions of "caste."

To move toward rearticulating personalisms, social location, and social dependencies, one can imagine the limits and creative possibilities of the jali-endorsed frame of personal networking from the perspective of the paradox of a divided literature on West Africa. On the one hand, a rich literature speaks of the need to build a personal entourage, often called "wealth in people," and of the importance of specialized dependents, including praisesingers, in building this entourage of power. On the other hand, an equally rich literature on peasant economics, urban migration, and development never mentions "wealth in people." This separation is surely in part because of conventions in the U.S. academy that segregate cultural and political economic studies, allowing students of the former to ignore class and livelihood while students of the latter assume such matters are entirely noncultural. Yet even when an analyst tries to avoid this segregation, these differences draw one's attention one way or the other. In The Gambia, two kinds of social distinctions frame the varied importance of jaliya-based personalism: urban-rural distinctions and ethnic difference.

Social Opportunities

SETTING: A PATRON'S COMPOUND, 1989. WE ARE SEATED IN THE LIVING ROOM, DRINKING *FANTA* ORANGE SODA

Lamenting that relations between nobles and jali are no longer what they once were, a patron explained his predicament to me. Jali, he said, are no longer under the control of their patrons since they can no longer expect that all of their needs will be cared for by any one patron, as they once could. Instead, they play patrons off against one another. As a result, the burden of patronage responsibility toward jali feels heavier all the time. Besides, it is harder and harder to keep up with such responsibility financially. A civil servant's salary does not afford one the means to maintain jali with ease. If jali are not supported properly, they are not loyal to their patrons. Jali these days build a network of benefactors, but without clear loyalties to any. "The jali has lost his sense of place here in the city," he complained. "They moved to the cities following their patrons. But they cannot be controlled. They should be sent back to the farm."

The patron's sense of frustration was particularly acute because at the time he was in need of a loyal jali. His position within the civil service was in danger; he had reached the age of retirement, but he believed these things could be negotiated. But he needed the ear of an important man to rescue his job, and the only way to one who might lend an ear to his plight was through his jali. Now the patron was aware of a particular jali who could talk for him, if only the jali would just agree to cooperate. He wondered how he could properly court the jali to get him into his retinue. Our discussion turned to how I might be of service, offering some opportunities to the jali in question to cement his patronage relationship with the patron.

In many ways, the patron's complaints are reminiscent of the comments made by elites in many places in the world who lament the difficulty of finding good servants these days. Yet the patron's comments also appeared to me to address the real force of interdependencies between jali and their patrons. The patron would certainly lose his job if he could not enlist the help of a jali to establish the connection that would allow him to present his case against retirement. His acquaintance with the jali whose help he required was not enough. Although their families had a long history together, the patron felt that he must court the jali and offer him significant advantages to obtain his services. Meanwhile, it was also true that jali were unable to wield any influence, and indeed unable to practice as jali, if patrons such as this did not provide them opportunities.

Scholars of Mande society explain precolonial social structures as divided into three tiers and held together by their interdependence. The first tier was composed of nobles, traders, and peasants, collectively referred to as "freeborn." The second tier was composed of artisans, which included male blacksmiths and female hair-braiders, male leather workers and female potters, male and female jali, and religious singers. The third tier was composed of slaves.

The third tier was officially abolished by the British early in the nineteenth century, leaving the freeborn and the artisans, whose distinctions were acknowledged and sometimes even encouraged under colonial rule. The asymmetry in this classificatory distinction is recognized by the common description of the system, in English language sources, in the odd anomaly of a one-caste system: Only artisans are referred to as "caste members"; freeborn are described as unmarked by caste. Of course, the whole point of caste—based on the South Asian model that fashioned the term's focal English uses—is to designate a system of hierarchy in which all participants know their ranking in relation to others. There can be no one-caste system. Yet the Mande world is not India. Artisans are marked by their birth into an endogamous descent group; they learn their professions from their parents and other close relatives. Artisans know who they are because of their lines of descent and close intermarriage. All others are imagined in relation to a much more open set of opportunities and constraints; they are thought of Mande, not as "caste members." At the same time, they depend on their relationships with artisans, including jali, in imagining and making the Mande world.

Artisans are the marked category; freeborn, the unmarked. Thus many aspects of the customary functional repertoire of artisans are imagined in relation to category-breaking, uncontained power, and danger. A set of stereotypes keeps in circulation ideas about the distinctiveness of jali from other members of society. These include the fact that jali are known for their transgression of "ordinary" gender roles. Jali men are given speech in contrast to their noble patrons, who are spoken for. Jali women go to public places where women of elite status would not be found. Jali were once buried in baobab trees so that their corpses did not pollute the ground. Jali travel in many worlds, crossing borders of status and knowledge as well as physical locations. Like other artisans, they have an inexplicable power in learning and making their crafts. They have occult knowledge that nobles and other freeborn do not possess. They inspire reverence by moving with a particular mystique. They *name* people and bring them into the social world; they can make and break the reputations of those names. They sing praises with an excessive show of affection; if angered, they can turn the other direction and take those praises away. They carry the power of the word.

Some of the jali with whom I spoke had an ambivalent relationship with this charisma. On the one hand, they used it; they reveled in it; they made careers of it. On the other hand, they resented their subordination and their dependence upon elites. They complained about the high-handed behavior of their patrons and their own demeaning obligation to service their patrons' every need, while still flattering them. Nor were their patrons oblivious to this ambivalence, which charged their relationships, making it possible for the jali to make more demands and yet also drawing more resentment from their patrons. The working relationships forged in this atmosphere were far from settled and easy. This expectation of tension created an even greater emphasis on personalism. It was up to an individual patron and an individual jali to forge proper ties of patronage; the whole arrangement could fall apart in an instant if expectations on either side went unmet. But despite this sense of unraveling arrangements, the relationship between jali and patron continued to form the frame for Mande politics—and everyday social life.

The importance of caste was reiterated again and again when my research assistant, a freeborn woman with a Western education and "modern" ways, called caste principles into play in every social interaction through which she led me. Each time she introduced me to someone, she led me through a series of inquiries about the social status and identity of this new acquaintance. We spoke of the place he or she was born, and the family name and its history. She commented on the status implications of the name, and its association with traders or artisans or nobles. She noted its ethnic connotations, particularly when names indicated a non-Mande origin. And when she felt I was still too slow in understanding how to treat acquaintances according to their status, she presented me with an essay she had copied in her own hand, offering a nutshell description of caste and status differentiation. In this way, she led me to appreciate that caste works together with places of origin and ethnicity in creating social identities. And she pushed me to recognize the continuing importance of such identities in the midst of the urban cosmopolitan business of the nation and the world.

The Force of Recitation

SETTING: A TEACHER'S OFFICE, 1989

Jaliba Kouyate had been a primary school teacher. As he explained during an interview, jaliya began to take on greater importance in his work when he was approached by the minister of education to work together with a program that hoped to use traditional music to promote state projects. Most of this particular era's projects were aimed at rural women, and support for these projects was found through international "women and development" programs. The programs promoted the importance and benefits of literacy, and they endorsed state-organized women's gardening cooperatives. This was part of the development agendas of the 1980s (Schroeder 1999). With the use of a variety of venues, including radio programs, political rallies, and community gatherings, the team, which included the jali, would promote an awareness of the new programs.

Although many of these development programs were intended to enlist women's participation, I noted that it was a jali man and not a jali woman who was tapped for the job. Jaliba's appeal and reputation, however, no doubt would be quite effective. He was often described to me as an idol, like a rock star. Still, no member of the targeted community of these programs was asked to make the educational address; the state wanted a professional. A jali was chosen not for his immediate rapport in an intimate way, but rather for his expertise as a performer.

The continuing importance of jali in Gambian political life in the postindependence era, under the presidency of Sir Jawara, was extended by the state bureaucracy's use of jali for purposes of national education and promotional campaigns. Sometimes, as in Jaliba Kouyate's team project or the minister of water work's speech, state messages could be more effectively conveyed by jali. As professional communicators whose performance repertoires expand to convey development slogans and administrative programs, jali transformed their traditional repertoire to incorporate these new plans, even while supporting and reproducing the institution of jaliya. Jali continued to offer praises, historical genealogies, epic tales, and naming ceremonies—the forms commonly associated with their duties—even as they seasoned these with affairs of the contemporary state.

The use and transformation of the Sunjata epic is exemplary of this process of simultaneous reproduction and retooling. The Sunjata epic has all the characteristics of the "premodern" performance repertoire: the epic is performed orally, and while there are certain set features, its versions can differ from one teller to another; the form mixes myth and history; it is long-winded and teleological, without the "simultaneous, empty time" that Benedict Anderson (1992) sees as the distinctive break marking national consciousness from the time of empire. The epic of Sunjata cannot join the novels and newspapers Anderson describes as promoting the "imagined community" of the modern nation. And yet the story has continued to be immensely popular, both with and beyond the support of the nation-state. As I discussed in chapter 3, the story of Sunjata is used in Gambian textbooks (Sidibe 1980) and has been made a part of national history. It is also the subject of several literary reworkings (Niane 1965; Laye 1980), and has been rendered into a film (Kouyate 1995). These literary and filmic versions cross the borders of nation-states in an effort that attempts to build a regional Mande consciousness. Nation-states, including The Gambia, draw on the energy of this regional cultural consciousness to vitalize their national political cultures. Jali are essential agents in making this complex imperial-national-regional, premodern-modern, epic-novelistic-filmic, community-building hybrid.

Dani Kouyate's film, *Keita: The Heritage of the Griot*, illustrates one version of the tensions of community-building hybridity. Kouyate himself comes from a Mande praisesinger family in Burkina Faso, and his film portrays the importance of the praisesinging tradition in educating the modern children who will build the region and the nation. Kouyate's father plays Djeliba, the praisesinger come from the countryside to retell the epic of Sunjata to a new generation of children in the city. The children are portrayed as Westernized and schooled only in "modern" knowledge. They learn to love the Sunjata story despite an unresponsive teacher and ambivalent parents. The Sunjata tale adds depth and purpose to their school education and stimulates a new commitment to an African future. The Sunjata story itself tells them—through young Sunjata's own struggle to overcome his inability to walk, and then to win a kingdom—how to blend a mixed heritage of learning and spiritual power to create personal effectiveness, a great polity, and a lasting culture.

The layering is striking here: the director is a jali making a film in which the lead actor is a jali who plays a jali telling the story of Sunjata to a modern audience, both on film and in the movie theater. In the film and in the theater, the story performs jaliya to guide an audience through the political dilemmas of the contemporary world. Through the jali—in their multiple guises as film director, actor, and bard—Sunjata still speaks to the world, offering a legacy to guide the future.

Intersections

SETTING: A SUBURBAN TOWN KNOWN AS ONE CENTER OF JALI ACTIVITIES, 1989

While in The Gambia, I spoke with another foreign researcher who had come to study the music of jaliya. As we talked about interviewing, we compared our experiences on how best to work with jali. One issue concerned the kind and amount of remuneration most jali expected to receive for their services. He sat aghast to hear how much I said I was expected to pay for my interviews and work sessions with jali. I explained that the conditions had been established by OHAD, the office collecting village narratives told by jali. I had been warned, a warning confirmed by my early attempts to do otherwise, that jali would be uninterested in working with me if I didn't pay for their professional time and on terms they could accept. He told me of how he tried to adjust the fees to work within his limited budget. Moreover, he was determined to work with the jali on what he considered fair and reasonable terms. He offered a fee and paid only that fee. We had very different experiences.

Although jali with whom he worked appeared to accept this arrangement the researcher was met by repeated jali evasions. His informants told him that they "just didn't know" the answer to many things he asked. I received a different answer in some instances from the same jali. Our two experiences set up our projects differently: He learned to specialize in gathering fragments; I was pressed to worry about the dilemmas of personalistic power. Jali negotiated with foreign researchers on terms congruent with their understandings about the making of relationships of patronage and power through performance. They expected to be able to demand more relative to the extent that they used their knowledge to build the researcher's career; they made every attempt to make themselves part of the researcher's retinue in a long-term relationship of personal service and dependence.

Most foreign researchers are not accustomed to this understanding of their relationship with informants, although intellectual property rights and the commodification of culture has greatly heightened awareness and concern about these issues. In many U.S. research settings, the "information" we gather from informants is supposed to be the raw data which we are then able to process in the analyses that establish our authorship; we do not expect to give up our power to speak to obtain articulate versions of this "raw" knowledge. Most foreign researchers, indeed, are tone-deaf to the status performances through which jali attempt to cajole us into becoming patrons. We understand that jali are world-class musicians and that we should pay respectful attention to them as such. We can tell that they are making personalistic connections with us that they hope will outlast any particular period of research. But we rarely know how to be Gambian patrons.

This partial and mismatched comprehension of the frame of interaction is similar for the other foreign interlocutors who deal with jali, such as those who arrange their concerts abroad or for foreign audiences in The Gambia, those who sign them up for recording contracts or to play with foreign musicians, and those who look to them for a renewal of African roots. These contacts produce an appreciation of jali musicianship that travels beyond the region; they also produce a network of personalistic ties through which concert and recording engagements are extended to new areas and for new tours. In these foreign engagements, then, jali performance of power relations leads mainly to a mutual agreement to embed musicianship in personalistic entrepreneurship, as a condition of the relationship. The question of status differences is left amorphous and ambiguous. Instead, personalism becomes the main message communicated about interconnection.

Personalism, however, works on multiple levels. Many of the jali who had established reputations abroad through international travel began this travel through a tour arranged by the Gambian minister of tourism. In the 1980s and 1990s, the ministry of tourism drew heavily on the popularity of jali music to market The Gambia. This involved the packaging of jali performance not only for foreign tourists who had already found their way to The Gambia but also for foreign audiences abroad.

Not all jali who traveled with a ministry of tourism tour, however, were able to use the tour to build international careers. My jali informants complained about the barriers that kept them from forging personalistic connections that might have allowed them to continue to travel and perform abroad. Language was a problem. Some tours carried jali across many linguistic environments—for example, traveling across Europe from Germany to Amsterdam to England to the Soviet Union. Even a jali with some (albeit uncertain) skills in English found them of only limited use; he was forced to communicate in a creative, on-the-spot sign language. For professionals in the performance of the spoken word, the enforced silences of language incomprehension appeared a formidable block against all meaningful social relationships.

Jali who were successful in repeating their foreign tours pinned their success on their ability to find foreign managers who would serve as personal conduits to concert and recording arrangements. Through the connection with a particular foreigner, a jali could extend his circuit of travel to another corner of the world. This image of responsible personalism was always explained to me in contrast to the alternative nightmare of being used as a foreign guest worker: informed at the last minute of a concert tour and told to obtain a visa; whisked from the airport to a concert hall to a hotel and back to the airport; and returned to The Gambia with no sense of where he had been or how to get there again. Jali obtain agency in their international travels only through personal connections; institutionally impersonal arrangements leave them as puppets of a social system in which they find little room for their hopes and desires. Steven Feld (1989) describes the circuit of a music group from the South in which the musicians become the workers for Northern music managers. Jali reports of their alienation on international tours without personal ties recalled Feld's account of the political economy of Southern music. Only personal connections could bring the tour to life as part of building a set of social relationships.

Of course, personal connections do not always work out as well as jali would like. One jali complained bitterly about his relationship with a foreign concert producer. The relationship had begun full of promise; the producer had arranged several tours to Europe. But they could not understand each other's expectations. Ultimately, he felt that the producer was irresponsible, unwilling to listen to his needs and requests. The relationship broke off, and with it the possibility of travel for the jali. The management of personalism, then, is never simple.

The Personalistic Economy

SETTING: A JALI'S COMPOUND, 1989

Jali Suso greeted me enthusiastically and brought me into his home. We had met on a previous occasion at a patron's house in Banjul. He urged his wife to offer me a more generous hospitality upon his departure. What a contrast, I thought, from so many of my jali informants, who brought me through opening negotiations over payment before we could even begin to speak to each other. Instead, Jali Suso was freely giving of his time. "Ask me anything you want to know," he encouraged.

Jali Suso was well traveled. We spoke of the cities in the United States he had already visited and of those he hoped to visit. And upon my return to the United States, I received phone calls that were meant as greetings, "just to say hello. " But an underlying assumption was there; perhaps I had found some new opportunities for him to perform. Had I had a chance to talk to my university about sponsoring the concert he had suggested? I was not to forget about him. In hindsight, I could see that his freely given services in The Gambia were an investment plan. We forged the sort of patron-client relationship that implicated our mutual obligation to one another.

Jali Suso once worked in The Gambia for the government. In his capacity as a civil servant he accompanied the minister of tourism on a trip to Jamaica so that The Gambia could learn more about the tourist industry. Upon the return trip, the jali and the minister of tourism stopped in New York City, where Jali Suso was able to establish an important personal connection that convinced him to change his career from civil servant to jali. Although he was born into a jali family and had learned the practices of jaliya, he had not planned to pursue this profession. When he considered the possibilities for using jaliya successfully and that he could find opportunities for travel and performance, he decided to make the shift away from his government position to the international performance circuit. The jali did not view his talent primarily as resting in music; he felt that the jali skill of speech would offer him the opportunity to communicate about culture, across cultures. On his trip back through New York City, he connected with a sponsor who was able to link him with a world music organization that sponsors musicians from around the world. He returned to New York to pursue jaliya in the United States.

The organization offered him a regular salary; however, he refused their offer, insisting instead on the method of compensation he viewed as more closely linked to a jali's talents. Instead of letting the organization arrange his concerts and pay him for them, as if he were in their service, Jali Suso negotiated with the organization to arrange his own schedule. He offered to pay the organization a percentage of the income he earned from what he received. This way, he would be able to use the concerts to make more than payment for the concert; he would be able to make far more extensive and better personal connections. The jali explained how he incorporated and accommodated his skills as a jali in some of his concerts in the United States. After a concert, he met with enthusiastic audience members. Perhaps one or more of them would arrange another concert for him. He agreed to pay a percentage of his take to anyone who found him a future performance. Jali Suso has quantified his valuation of personal connections, both with the organization and with his scouts for future concerts, because he understands that New Yorkers need to know just how much they will be paid. He is not satisfied with a salary, however, because he sees his trade as depending on an expanding network of personal ties arranged in relation to money, on the one hand, and performance services, on the other. He has forged a creative version of jali networking suitable for international entrepreurship. The personalism of this practice allows the jali to keep his professional career going through his ability to cultivate more and more patrons. Like those described in the United States as charismatic capitalists (Biggart 1989), his strategy is to use face-to-face interactions that draw in the sale.

Jali Suso's performance-based, personalistic entrepreneurship is not an isolated arrangement. It is a central feature of the Gambian economy, at home and abroad. Recall that—after smallholder peanut production— tourism is the most prominent economic sector of the country, and that a good deal of the work of tourism is organized informally according to personal arrangements between tour guides and cultural producers. Craft producers as well as jali look for personal ties of patronage to market their goods to tourists, as well as to internal markets. Other prominent economic activities include import marketing, with franchises arranged through personal political connections, and the related regional smuggling, also organized through personal connections and networks.

In this context, jali present an articulate model of economic ties. For them, there is never a market for level exchanges; offering goods and services always establishes personal power relationships that endure beyond the transaction to sponsor further transactions and opportunities in a continuing relationship. Within this set of understanding, words, memories, genealogies, and stories are as much material offerings as crafts or foodstuffs. As anthropologist Judith Irvine suggests (1989) in her analysis of a similar situation among Senegalese Wolof, a praisesinger's words are a commodity, not a sign-system about commodities. They not only enter the system of economic ties, they are central to forming its levels and niches. Moreover, they exemplify the materials transacted to forge power-laden personal relationships. They are never neutral in their assessment of the relationship: They praise; they take away praise. They can never be disconnected from the relationship itself.

Gambian elites sometimes call jali "beggars," expressing their frustration with what many say are the constant demands of jali. These pressures no doubt feel particularly acute given civil servants' salaries. Yet they cannot separate themselves from the system of begging that creates economic and political webs of dependence and difference. These "beggars" are not those who are separated from the system, the disenfranchised who do not meet the normative assumption of wage labor; instead, they set the standards for economic relationships based on personal entrepreneurship. Like futures traders on the stock exchange in the United States, jali as "beggars" demonstrate the possibilities and risks of economic life. This is not an economic system in which industrial institutionalization makes possible a bureaucratic reading of "class" in which working class and ruling class are easy to separate. Performance-based personalism instead sets a frame of opportunity in which at least a few jali are better connected and richer than many nobles, and in which everyone must try to advance themselves by building ties that might lead them to such success.

In the incantation of U.S. discussion of globalization and venture capitalism, everyone must be a personal entrepreneur. And in this guise, too, jali who travel in international circles are able to link up with managers and fans to create concert venues. Working with foreigners in the idiom they best control, they bring out the personalism that is so often disguised and hidden in European and North American commitments to fairness and impartiality. They force their interlocutors to admit and acknowledge the power of personal ties. Sometimes in the process they push too far, aggravating their managers just as they do Gambian patrons. Without such aggravation, however, how can they stimulate patronage?

Jali and their Clients

SETTING: AN EARLIER VISIT, BANJUL, 1983

My kora teacher has come to continue my lessons. He arrives daily with his personal entourage of dependents and peers, and they stay for six to eight hours. I certainly had no idea what I was getting into when I asked to study music here. I sit in the corner willing my awkward fingers to play the complex melodies across the many strings. Meanwhile, the jali is otherwise engaged. His entourage is now up to six, and at times eight young men, and they talk and talk the time away while I embarrassingly play the same thing over and over again. Some of his friends leave and return, running errands. Every so often, the teacher remarks on a mistake and puts me back on the right track, or so he hopes. Despite the unfamiliar practice style, I find that I am making progress.

Sometimes I must take a break. I talk to one of the most familiar visitors, asking why he is there everyday. He reports that he owes the jali a debt and in order to repay him he has become his companion. His original profession was as a dyer, another niche within the artisan rank. But the man borrowed a large sum of money from the jali to buy supplies and he has not yet been able to repay his loan. In the meanwhile, he will be a personal dependent, offering service.

Jali are professional dependents. But, as I learned from the friends of the jali teacher, they too have dependents. Dependency in this instance links relative peers, yet it is imagined on a familiar model of service and loyalty in exchange for support. No singular model of caste hierarchy can explain the nodes and networks of dependency each jali makes for himself; he must craft it from the opportunities presented within his social milieu both in The Gambia and beyond.

Because of my interest in the shaping of ideas of Africa in powerful national and international projects, I spent much of my research effort learning about those influential jali who have been given the most opportunities to represent Mande culture at home and abroad. Some of these jali have a Western education; some have been able to build from jaliya to gain control over other entrepreneurial projects, ranging from a taxi service to owning a shop. These entrepreneurs see themselves as people with many opportunities and a good deal of influence. From this position, they agitate for the preservation and extension of the kinds of performance-based personal networking they know best. They are successful at it. Yet the frame within which they know how to work has no cultural guarantee; they must forge it continually and creatively.

The Gambia is a small country, and the conditions of national independence and participation in the world economy have encouraged many elites to settle in the cities, where civil service jobs, import franchises, and internationally sponsored economic activities are located. Many of the most successful and powerful jali followed their patrons into the cities; those who remain in the countryside spend much of their time as commuters in urban settings. Thus, in contrast to the situation in neighboring Senegal where praisesinging is thought of as rural (see Irvine 1973), the most intense centers of jali networking and performance are now urban rather than upcountry rural, despite the fact that the authenticity of Mandinka jaliya is often measured by its closeness to the rural eastern end of the country.

Urban areas are entrepots for people of many ethnic origins. In The Gambia, perhaps Mandinka are more closely tied in to the political culture of praisesinging. Wolof form a significant Gambian presence, and in Senegal, particularly northern Senegal, Wolof are known for their praisesingers. Praisesinging is practiced in relation to an imagined polity for which it provides a structure of personalistic power relations. This complex social geography does not make jali personalism irrelevant; instead, it sets the frame for jali challenges. Jali forge ties of patronage and dependence wherever they go. When their interlocutors misunderstand their efforts, they forge ties through the partial, fragmented understandings that come through. Debts are repaid through personal service. Service is offered only if a long-term commitment to providing future opportunities can be made. The jali challenge is to move in the world using these kinds of frames for social connection, even in distorted form.

Gender is another aspect of the social landscape that makes a difference in relation to jali opportunities and constraints. Like men, women jali are expected to be entrepreneurial and opportunistic in making performance-based personal ties. Like men, women praise, name, gossip, cajole, and inform elites. But women are hampered by constraints on their ability to travel and to enter key scenes for training, making connections, and influencing the influential. One woman jali I knew had been quite successful in forming personal networks and gaining patrons entirely separate from those of her husband. Yet she complained that he did not allow her to stay in urban areas for long. Since her most important patrons all lived in urban areas, living in a village upcountry, with occasional visits to the urban areas, hampered her effectiveness. Yes, she said, she traveled to see her patrons, but she always had to ask the permission of her husband.

Women jali are also blocked by the expectation that they will learn from their parents and their husbands, but not through the wide network of personalistic ties that jali men seek to enrich their knowledge and performance repertoires. Women must find creative ways to expand the networks through which they can aspire to become a person of influence. In my last dramatic sketch, I tell of a woman who used recorded music to expand her own repertoire. I left her thinking about the constraints of women's training and the networks of dependence that are created through training as well as performance.

SETTING: JALI MUSALOO KOUYATE'S
FRONT PORCH, 1989

My research assistant and I arrived just after lunch. Mariama encouraged the taxi driver to wait: "We won't be long," she said. He didn't seem to think several hours was an inordinate amount of time, although he sat outside the compound with little company to pass the time. When we stepped inside, women and children were in the compound. We readied ourselves to interview a jali woman I had known for some time. Sitting alone on the porch with a portable tape recorder, Jali musaloo Kouyate was playing a song of one of her favorite jali, musaloo Aimee Koita. Actually, she was rehearsing. Stop; rewind; play and sing along. Stop; rewind; play and sing along. We interrupted her and began the conventional greetings: "Tilibalo ba di?" How is the afternoon? How are those there? How goes the work? As expected, everything was reported to be fine. We moved to a room inside the house and began the formal interview through its standard opening, the negotiation of fees.

The interview was rich in details about her family's history and the importance of the Kouyate family to jaliya. I also appreciated the skill in which Mariama thought of questions that were more attuned to the situation than the more general ones we generated before the interview. But the most striking image for me of the structural differences between men and women jali was the sight of the jali musaloo's practice on the porch. Jali Kouyate said she had learned jaliya from her mother and aunt, and now her husband. In contrast, most of the jali men I spoke with had much more elaborate stories of training, learning with many teachers. Still, Jali musaloo Kouyate had spirited dreams and aspirations. She wanted to become an internationally known singer. Her singing had been much praised in The Gambia, but she had not yet made the kinds of connections that would allow her to expand her reputation. She imagined herself travelling abroad, and she did not want to depend on her husband's success for her own career. She was compelled by the music of Aimee Koita, she said, because she was from the east, where jali really know the traditions. The jali musaloo's quiet, solitary rehearsal on the porch, so different from the showy performances of jali men with their patrons and dependents, moved me to consider the difficult avenues for women's aspirations.

After the interview, Jali musaloo Kouyate asked for a ride to a neighborhood naming ceremony. She hoped her performance there would help in her determination to make her own name. Women jali, despite constraints on their networking, training, and performance activities, could sometimes find a way to move in the world. Indeed, in the last ten years a few jali women have begun to distinguish themselves in careers in the international circuit.

This chapter provides the scaffolding of a dynamic social structure in which jali and their patrons form crucial interlocking relationships. The explication of this system provides a sense of the principle ideals of the social structure that will be brought into closer view in chapter 5, when I consider the stories told by individual jali about their professional careers. The performance of status and rank are important aspects in the reproduction of sociality in The Gambia. Networks of contingent relationships are absolutely critical to the system. Yet, what is remarkably telling about this example is what it illuminates about the ways social worlds are configured even beyond the specificities of this social system. It gives pause to consider how personalisms inspire economic relationships—despite the adamant denial on the part of those in various places in the West (the United States among them) that economic relationships are often created and sustained through performed dependencies. Scholarly readers, consider your own plight.

CHAPTER FIVE

Interview Encounters:
The Performance of Profession

Jali musaloo Sakiliba must have spotted us at a distance for we could hear someone singing praises, seemingly in our direction.[1] Preoccupied with thoughts about how this interview might go, and the fatigue of our long trip, I did not see her. We had started early in the morning from Serrekunda, and now in the heat of the day, shaking loose the tight feeling after a three-hour busride upcountry, a transfer by ferry, and finally a truck ride, we were tired; and yet the day had really only just begun. We had met Jali Sakiliba several months before at the Mande Cultural Festival held in Sedhiou, Senegal. Now, long overdue for the visit we had tentatively arranged then, Mariama and I confided to each other in muttered tones our embarrassment over the amount of time that had passed since we had last seen her.

As we approached her house, the figure, barely visible at first, came into view. Jali Salikiba hugged us and danced around us. Her singing of praises somewhat quelled our anxieties. Indeed, this warm reception made us feel welcome. It also made me more aware of how the mere idea of conducting an interview always required a certain amount of courage more difficult to muster in the abstract than what was actually called upon.

Jali Sakiliba had announced our arrival in the way that jali do for patrons. I had observed this type of performance on numerous occasions, when the arrival of a particular patron would inspire a group of jali to rush over and announce the newcomer's identity through an elaborate greeting. These moments of boisterous recitations, often lasting for several minutes, announced to the audience the patron's history and good deeds.

We followed Jali Sakiliba and were soon greeted by family and friends who had gathered around the house. Jali Sakiliba continued to sing until we reached where the guests had congregated and they, too, could hear the words she bestowed upon us. These welcomers would for the most part stay throughout our visit. After extending our own greetings, certainly modest by comparison, we were offered mats and served lunch. Afterward we prepared the tape recorder for the interview that we soon

learned would be conducted on our host's porch. The raised cement plat-
form suddenly appeared more like a stage; those who had gathered to
look on—as if this spectacle could offer sustained entertainment—planted
themselves as an impromptu audience, fixed for the duration. We started
the questions amid the competing sounds of children and roosters. Their
noise provided a fitting ambiance that helped authenticate the conditions
of the "field tape." In contrast to the unrestrained welcoming ceremony,
the interview itself conjured up a more formal atmosphere as Jali Sakiliba
conveyed in earnest tones the practices and the traditions of jaliya through
her own life story.

This moment introduces the theme of this chapter: jali performance
of self and status, particularly in the context of interviews. Jali, of course,
are expert performers. It should be no surprise that they perform interviews just as they do other interpersonal encounters. Yet to discuss the
performance of interviews works against those unspoken assumptions in
anthropology that allow us to "mine" interviews for their content without
examining issues of form. Jali refused to allow me that luxury. Most of
the people I interviewed made it their business to draw attention to the
style of the interview and to the performance of skill, caste status, and role
expectations that form a part of their arts. Just as Jali Sakiliba's welcome
enacted jaliya through a familiar performance repertoire, so, too, the en-
suing interview drew from her performative knowledge and skills. Those
understandings that I drew from interviews and other interpersonal encounters were always performative understandings—that is, ways of
knowing about jaliya through the practice of jaliya.

Challenges in every phase of my research and subsequent review of
the material after the fact drew my attention to the performative dynamics
of my interviews with jali. I was at first surprised and disturbed by my
inability to keep the interviews on the course I had originally intended,
for most of my jali interlocutors inevitably took the interview in the direction of their own choosing. Often I felt that the jali I interviewed were
not interested in the questions I had prepared or what I might already
know about jaliya; they set their own agenda for telling me a story they
wanted told. As I began to analyze the initial interviews, I felt concerned
that the material was repetitive and sometimes included what appeared
to be an utterly rote recitation. This, I might add, is also what previous
researches had found frustrating.

Yet when I reimagined the interviews as performances, these once-
disturbing aspects that seemed to tell the same set of "facts" became vir-
tues. Jali initiatives and repetitions, it suddenly seemed, could be understood as aspects of genre and style as well as sources of information.
Moreover, much of the performance part of the interview was immediate
and sensuously conveyed. I found that my transcripts often contained

little of the vividness of jali presentation in the interview encounter itself. The dramatic gestures swept us—informant, research assistant, and anthropologist—together into an appreciation of jali lives and the practices of their profession.

Since completing my collection of interviews for the project, I have given more thought to the methods and interpretive skills involved in ethnographic interviews, and I have become acutely aware of the importance of appreciating performance in the interview process. Social scientists often assume that interviews will be an open channel to the autonomously generated personal thoughts of other people. By contrast, I find myself trying to explore the interviews as dramatic expositions rather than just repositories of information.

In this context, issues of form and content take on as much importance as the substantive topics I discussed with jali. The mundane and routine negotiation of interview fees, I realized, was intimately tied to jali assessments of the value of their words, which in turn are a central facet of their performance art. I began to hear jali recitations of lists, including places they had been and genealogies of relatives and sponsors, as a genre through which interviews and more public jali art forms could be brought into synchrony. I also started to appreciate the range of idiosyncratic styles at play, and I saw how my assistant and I were being trained in our own performative roles by our interlocutors. I could appreciate jali attempts to tell me in their own words about the importance of performance in even the most intimate of encounters and most personal of narratives.

Issues of commodification and folklorization in jali's practiced presentations of life story and "tradition" also framed my interview experiences. Jali are highly desirable subjects for foreign appreciation, and I was recording their testimony at a moment in history when the international figure of the jali, even if few individuals distinguished themselves, made them increasingly sought after by social scientists, ethnomusicologists, music promoters, and even casual tourists. The expansion of a patronage network to include people beyond the historical configuration of regional connections potentially offered a greater number of jali the opportunity to keep their practices alive and also to solidify and codify certain ideas about jaliya. These developments helped make jali stories about jaliya into a commodified form for international consumption. In this context, many jali had already practiced and packaged presentations to offer about their lives and arts. Indeed, the repetition of facts I heard suggested that jali were often telling me what they thought foreigners expected to hear. Much of this general information could readily be found even on mass-produced compact disc inserts. Still, simply because this information was routinized did not mean that it was not also carefully planned and performed in relation to individual talents and experiences for locally as well as internationally meaningful purposes. The familiarity of jali with the interview, however, did increase their attention, as well as mine, to issues of its uses and conventions as well as content.

The Value of a Few Words

Each of my interviews, with one exception, began with negotiations over the compensation each jali wished to receive. On the one hand, this was a straightforward enough convention; on the other, the whole shape of the interview depended on the fine nuances with which the negotiations were conducted. Here jali proved the worth of their oral presentations. The arrangement of compensation was not just about the short conversation provided in the interview; it was a moment for the affirmation of the value of jaliya. Value was individually negotiated, although for many, this value was measured in the context of other professional encounters they had had.

OHAD had established a precedent by paying jali and other storytellers for their oral histories. Upon learning of this history of payment, I asked what might be a reasonable amount to offer. My persistent inquiries to the people affiliated with OHAD, however, never produced a clear suggestion. These were individually negotiated arrangements not subject to a set amount of money. Many foreign researchers found this expectation frustrating, for they wanted to maintain a distinction between commercial and scholarly purposes, yet I found these boundaries impossible to draw since words and forms of knowledge had monetary value. Not surprisingly, misunderstandings abounded. The intense negotiation of reimbursement to jali for their efforts so bothered one long-time foreign musicologist that she moved her research to another country. She explained to me that she had watched the escalation of payment expectations over twenty years to the level of considerable expense, and she found it disconcerting to her ideas of research. Once, she had been willing to arrange concerts and record contacts for Gambian jali, but in her frustration, she later chose to conduct her business with Gambian artisans only from a distance.

Furthermore, even when payment was agreed upon, some jali would be insulted if they felt they were being offered a fixed sum. After all, jaliya is intimately tied to a range of practices that trace their legitimacy from the age of empire through the present. The issue of how much participants should be compensated for their efforts as research interlocutors was understood by jali in relation to a set of social status-oriented relationships and personalistic ties. The significance of money is both material and symbolic. How I handled these negotiations, with the serious intervention of my assistant, made a statement about how much I respected jali as professionals and persons for whom compensation served to establish a patron/client relationship; a simple individual transaction based on a standard rate would not fit the situation. There was no easy way to stand outside a system that pulled one into the role of patron. Once one jali greeted Mariama and me with the following claims: "Yesterday, I was given a car by one of my special patrons. A few days before I needed a new roof for my house and my good patron gave it to me." He hinted that my contribution could be a record contract, and then there was *Roots*, opening the possibility of international fame. Needless to say, in no way could I approach these expectations. But the point here is that the practice of jaliya *always* involves a demand that patrons—including interviewers—fulfill the needs of jali.

Jali must be compensated for interviews in part because they classify interviews—sessions involving the oral presentation of expert knowledge—as part of their professional services. Oral presentations are their livelihood. Jali create wealth with words. As Judith Irvine (1989) reminds us in the title of her article, "When Talk Isn't Cheap," professional wordsmiths rely for their living on personal networks with those who are willing to listen to them. In this context, too, jali stress the value of jaliya as an institution. They are aware that in the interview they are offering their words as art to those who may not fully understand the value of what they are getting. Many explained to me over and over again that jaliya must be saved because without it society would cease to function properly. Could modern society do without jaliya? One jali responded:

> In my opinion, that should not be done because if jaliya is abolished, you will see lots of things will be lost. Because the jali were the first journalists; they were the authors of history books. If jaliya is abolished, the sort of knowledge sought through it will cease because it will be of no use. I don't mean those things that are happening now but those things that have happened in the past. Apart from that, if people were equal in status jaliya would be abolished. If jaliya were abolished, no one would bring himself low under his fellow man. You will see that the world itself will not be steady. It would be a difficult situation. (Jali MS, in his forties)

In this fragment, a jali defends his profession in relation to a particular historical event: the debate in The Gambia in the early 1970s over a proposal to abolish jaliya. (Some urban people felt that jali "begging" was interfering with business in Banjul.) Jali MS responds that elites could not function without the services of those willing to "bring [themselves] low under [their] fellow man." But this passage does not have the specificity of a single defense; jali must always defend their art in the course of the interview. Thus, too, jali cannot leave the interview to the interviewer, or assume that the interviewer already knows much about the art of word-making. In the course of the interview, jali make it their business to remind the interviewer of the necessity of jali to move patrons to action, to make social activity possible, and, of course, to make research valuable and effective.

> The role played by a jali towards his patron, a patron cannot do that towards his fellow patron. It is the jaloo who narrated the deeds of people whether good and bad. In the first place, if I came and found you all sitting down and, for example, we all happen to be patrons, Hun! you will not get off your chair for my sake. That's where I stand in front of you, but you will never get off from the chair. And if people are assembled as well, you cannot tell me, "Get up and share that bowl of food; get up and distribute those kola nuts among the group." You cannot tell me that since I am of the same status as you. You will see that the traditional roles we use to establish differences between us (jali and patrons) will come to an end. Because each and everyone will feel superior to that. (Jali MS, 41 years old)

Life into Narrative: Oral Histories and Biomythography

It has always been known and often repeated that life has something to do with narrative; we speak of a life story to characterize the interval between birth and death. And yet assimilating life to a story in this way is not really obvious; it is a commonplace that first must be submitted to critical doubt.
—Paul Ricoeur, *On Paul Ricoeur*

As professional biographers and people who must create meaningful narratives of other people's lives, as well as their own, jali are institutionally among the more skilled people in the art of constructing and practicing narrative performance. In reviewing my interview transcripts and related materials, including research notes and journal entries, I have found useful Audre Lorde's (1982) use of the term "biomythography," for it signals the act of merging history, biography, and myth in creating an identity.[2] The creation of a self always involves some act of fabrication, a weaving together of multiple strands to create an outwardly seamless story. The notion of biomythography brings us closer to what I believe jali were trying to accomplish in the performances of selfhood that they offered me in interviews. Indeed, the practices of crafting life stories are parallel to the "fictions" of ethnography, for ethnography, as James Clifford (1986, 7) suggests, is also a partial truth. The partialness is not about hiding or lying, but some things are selected and others are not; selection as well as craft is essential to life story narration.

Oral histories have become standard in scholarly practice in recent years as social scientists have tried to "give voice" to people who were often not a part of "official" histories. This approach blossomed with the revisionist history of the 1960s. Scholars believed that oral histories offer a sense of agency to working-class and disadvantaged people found miss-ing from standard historical accounts. Oral histories allowed scholars to engage the historical significance of the lives of nonliterate people. For feminist scholars, oral histories allowed an attention to women's activities and perspectives. For Africanists, oral histories gave new life to earler histories of Africa as they added to archival sources that privilege Euro-pean colonial powers in their accounts of the African past.

Anthropologists have had their own attraction to life stories. Classi-cally, anthropologists have extended their understanding of societies to encompass the making of individuals and selves by asking informants to organize their memories and observations into the form of a "life." Re-cently, anthropologists have also paid special attention to the genres of telling through which life stories are made. Jali self-consciousness about genre and performance style thus overlap with anthropological self-con-sciousness about the making of lives. Yet jali also refuse to consider them-selves the unrecorded "little people" who have been the mainstay of both historians' oral histories and anthropologists' life stories. Many jali view what they do as providing services like those of a consultant and expert on the histories of their people. Like scholars, they are willing to use multiple sources to ensure their accuracy. (As discussed in chapter 3, one historian had his assumptions about "informants" telling events they knew about through personal experience overturned by a jali who drew his attention to the written sources for the period they were discussing, rather than merely offering his traditional epics [Wright 1991].) In this context, then, my interviews with jali are both examples of jaliya as art and commentar-ies on the art of jaliya. Jali tell their own lives with the flair and expertise with which they would like to be known.

Genre conventions were at play even in establishing the interview format, and multiple genres were at work as models. Mariama had a clear idea of what a proper interview should include. As an employee at OHAD she had internalized the institution's view that interviews must contain valuable information if they are to contribute to future archives. Her goal was to elicit that information, at times repeating the questions until she received an answer that satisfied. Interviews needed to be based on a standardized set of questions, she thought, to elicit comparable information, information that could be interpreted beyond the immediate context of its telling. Thus the aim of the interviews seemed to be to generate an archive of factual information that would provide the basis of ongoing historical reconstruction by OHAD. This is where an interesting break in our projects became clear. I immediately became aware that for many of the jali we interviewed, the context of telling seemed as important to them, and perhaps moreso, than the factual information. A key concern was to convey their abilities as verbal artists. Often they evaded and at times failed to even acknowledge the questions being asked. The interviews, then, represented the interplay between Mariama's attempts to make jali art into codified knowledge and jali attempts to take standardized interview questions and turn them into oral art.

Mariama also had her own concerns about jaliya that derived in part from the high status of her own family. She asked her questions from the point of view of a patron, focusing, for example, on patrons' dilemmas in supporting jali when their own resources were limited. She asked, in various ways, about the obligations of the patron to the client and what would result if a patron did not have anything to give. Everyone answered with sympathy and suggested that they would pray for the patron that his luck would return. But they wanted to make clear that a patron should not cheat a jali.

Mariama believed that the interviews might get jali to open up and tell the "truth" that lay behind the strategic maneuvers of jaliya. She was irritated at the hedging and evasion—the very techniques that allowed jali to gain control of the interview. Her intense interest in establishing stable, standardized moments in the interviews and moving the conversation beyond repetition and performance conflicted with some jali agendas. When Mariama and the jali interviewees found common ground—for example, in lists of patrons and their retinues—their interests amplified each other. At other times, however, questions and answers maneuvered around each other in mutually self-conscious strategies of negotiation. Meanwhile the negotiation process pressed me to be a proper patron, and I often found myself—like a person of power—listening attentively but in the background.

Mariama insisted that we begin each interview with standard questions that she believed would allow us to place each jali in relation to region, cohort, and genealogy. I found it easy to appreciate how these categories defined who a person was by place, age, and family background—all categories that spoke of who one was in a broader social context. Her questions were bureaucratic enough in that they attempted to develop a standard list.

First of all, I would like to ask you your name.
Where were you born?
How old are you?
Where did you spend your childhood?
Who is you father?
Where is he from?
What is your mother's name?
Who taught you the practice of jaliya?

These questions were meant to be a way of opening up our discussions with jali. This survey approach, its own stylized convention designed to ensure a certain uniformity of method, could have easily dulled the replies of the respondents. And this type of inquiry left more than a few jali answering the questions as if they were part of an inquisition. Others, however, and particularly older jali, seized upon the opportunity to redirect the course of the conversation by very quickly abandoning these questions to suit their own particular ways of telling. Some jali responded to the question of where they were born by offering a generous amount of information in the form of a genealogical narrative. Sometimes a jali spoke about his grandparents and parents and located them in relation to where they had settled and traveled.

> MARIAMA: Where were you born?
>
> JALI NS (answering in English): I was born at Kerr Sanyang in Niumi District North Bank Division. I have sisters who were born here. My grandparents were staying at Kerr Sanyang. So my father took my mother there when she was expecting me. And she remained there while my father was in Senegal. During the time of my grandparents, there were no specific kora players in the urban areas. They were from Wuli District in the Upper River Division. By then there were no specific kora players in the Niumi District as well. My mother's father was the eldest in their family. His brother came down from Wuli to meet him in Niumi and then the kombos. So they settled in different villages. Some settled in Bakau, Brikama, and Busumbala because it was indeed a good thing in those days for the country. The people of Busumbala wanted to transfer my mother from here to their village in Niumi and also take her to Essau. Later she went to Kerr Sanyang, locally known as Duniyaa Joyee ["World Island"], then her younger brother went to settle at Juffure, the village where Alex Haley's *Roots* came from. . . .

A single bureaucratic question could thus invoke a rich, nuanced answer. In this way, some jali turned around the conventions of the oral history interview and made them their own. In this process, too, they turned questions about identity—intended to help classify them—into questions of travel and mobility, the practices that made their reputations across the land.

The jali quoted above was not yet finished with his answer to the question of where he was born. The story of his birth offered more details of the travels of his parents and grandparents; then he moved into a recitation of status considerations.

> In those days [the time of his parents], the griots used to settle under kings, marabouts, and wealthy people who could afford to meet their demands. If you were a king and you wanted to have your own kora player, if the kora player didn't have a wife, the king will marry one for him, build a compound, and take care of all his needs. It is the king who is responsible for all those.

No recitation of status differences was complete without mention of the generosity of superiors. Perhaps these interviewers (Mariama and me) would follow the illustrious examples of the patrons of former days.

> Griots don't just entertain the rulers with only their music. Sometimes they sit beside them and narrate history to them concerning the deeds of their ancestors that the rulers don't know about. It is also the griot who can keep personal or confidential business of the king. The kings and great marabouts worked hand in hand. Before the king goes to war, he will send his griot to the marabout. If the griot goes he can sing praises of the marabout about the deeds of his ancestors so as to boost him to prepare some great talisman for him in order to be victorious in the war.

The importance of jaliya in stimulating appropriate action was also something of a refrain in the interviews. All this and more was offered as an answer to the question, "Where were you born?"! In his answer, moving beyond the call for the material of bureaucratic archives, the jali approaches the question of origin by locating his family in a variety of spatial and social locations: their associations, caste responsibilities, and expectations of influential patrons (i.e., kings and marabouts). In further testimony, the jali draws attention to his grandfather and comments on the importance of his grandfather to an influential king, a man sympathetic to Islam at a time when many nobles were less favorably inclined. He notes the role of the jali in a patron's life, as well as the responsibility of patrons toward their jali. Historical events and reiterated status considerations are intimately woven into an account of his own family history. The construction of jali identity is thus created by linking with important patrons, and patrons' identities are linked to regimes of power, such as village kings or marabouts.

It was important to Jali NS that he remain in control of the interview and be allowed to tell the story he wanted to tell. He improvised, evading Mariama's script, and took command of the interview; his answers could not be contained by the boundaries of our questions. Jali NS presented many frustrating moments for Mariama in his absolute refusal to even acknowledge, at times, what she had asked; even if she pursued certain questions repeatedly, it was of little use. A bit of a tug-of-war was going on, with him undoubtedly the victor. The fragments I have quoted are taken from a response that continued at great length before we could ask the next question. The responses generated a number of "factual" issues worth pursuing, but Jali NS rebuffed Mariama's efforts to regain the trajectory of narration. Indeed, the jali's ability to disrupt the "official" plan helped show off his rhetorical agility. "A jali must be bold," I was told repeatedly. He must be in control of the situation.

This skill played itself out in a different yet no less powerful form in another interview. Another jali, a man over eighty years old, decided to explain the elements of jaliya by performing his narrative in a formal epic song style while he accompanied himself at times on the kora. He weaves the people he was performing for into his story, and also a historical figure, Kelepha Sanneh. Here is a short excerpt.

> The jali had come with songs.
> They gave me a hundred.
> The successful of the companions who gave something, Yamariwi, the warlike rulers are finished.
> Oh! It's quite a long time, I haven't played the kora.
> Oh, the bull, Jankek, the bull [a praise term].
> Europeans [the author], Mariama [Ms. Jammeh], the Europeans of Bariyanka.
> Oh, the princes, Kelepha Sanneh Balamang kunbalin fing is dead.
> Oh, Mariama, the Europeans of Bariyanka.
> Oh, the princes, Kelepha Sanneh Balamang kunbling is dead. (Jali BS)

Here, temporal distinctions are collapsed to conflate the present and past—an important convention of jaliya. The past is recalled in an active way to underscore its significance as a political framework for the present.

In another case, an older jali, a lady approximately ninety years old, worked particularly hard to control the terms of the interview. Her challenge was enormous because she had to contest not only Mariama's interventions but also those of her son, who had decided to assist her during the interview. We had interviewed him before speaking with her, but he insisted on joining us and continually interrupted her narration. Mariama began this interview in her standard fashion.

> MARIAMA: Elderly lady, I would like to ask you your name. Where were you born? Where did you spend your childhood?

Yet before she could finish her opening questions, the jali musaloo's son broke in.

> JALI NK: Before going further even, our grandfather called Jali W begot our father called Jali AK, but he had settled at Basse D— Kunda. He was the jali of the D— surnames. When our grandfather passed away, the D— surnames of Briffu came for my father and took him to Briffu to make him their jali. My aunt came to get me when my father had passed away. I went with her to Dankuku and spent half of my childhood there, but I spent the rest in Bakau where I became a full grown-up because I was later brought up by my father's younger brother.

At this point, frustrated by the flow of the son's narration, Mariama broke in:

> MARIAMA: How old do you think you would be?
>
> JALI MUSALOO: Hold on, let me tell you! My father died in the year when Musa Molleh (the king of Fulladu) was exiled in Sierra Leone by the colonizers. I cannot remember exactly when I was born but I was very young at the time my father died. I even met up with the wives of Musa on the way to Dankuku with my aunt. Some of them stayed while the others were taken to Sierra Leone.

In these interviews and many others, jali took over and presented their own performative agendas. Some jali felt more comfortable doing this than others. Age, professional standing, and experience played critical roles, with the most elderly and well-known jali most able to make the interview their own. The gender of the interviewee, interestingly, rarely made a difference in our ability to assert our influence over the direction of the interview. Like the elderly female jali referred to above, jali women were perfectly capable of taking charge of their interviews. These examples highlight performative categories and demonstrate that the skill to lure an audience by their performance was an apparent part of what jali do even in these more intimate settings.

Style

Making her entrance through the front door of the compound as if stepping onto the grand stage, Jali musaloo Suso swept in with an effusive air, greeting and thanking those who in her absence had entertained her visitors. As I stood acutely aware of my social awkwardness, I remember thinking, "If only I could be half so dramatic." With an aura of assurance that allowed her to maintain the spell cast in the moments of her arrival, she whisked Mariama and me into her private room where we could "talk seriously." Now midway through the research project, Mariama assumed her usual role in what had already become a well-rehearsed practice; she offered an overview of the project and explained the terms of our interest in understanding jaliya from the point of view of its practitioners. She expressed our hope that Jali musaloo Suso would agree to participate. Mariama also explained the circumstances that had led us to Jali musaloo Suso, mentioning who had spoken well of her and who had urged us to include her in the study. Reputation was critical here, and it was important that our social connections be established.

During the negotiations over the compensation that Jali musaloo Suso expected to receive for her participation, I surveyed the setting of this event, letting my eyes wander by tracing the ordering of domestic space. I noted how material objects can extend a sense of place and person. The room had a number of signs marking its distinction: The walls were adorned with pictures—framed painted glass found in homes in this region of West Africa, and a picture of then-President Jawara and the Gambian state house; her furniture—a wardrobe, chair, and bed—was plenty for a small yet well-ordered room that did not require much more. As for Jali musaloo Suso's attire, the extra piece of gold fabric that appeared so casually placed on top of her head wrap offered a public sign that she had made the hajj. These details of place and dress helped convey a sense that we were in the presence of a very important jali musaloo. Indeed, the jali herself would frequently remind us of this fact throughout the interview, for boasting and self-promotion form an integral part of the practice of jaliya.

Jali musaloo Suso sat poised, eagerly waiting, as she explained, "to answer all [our] questions." She was anxious to convince us that she would speak only the truth and that her source of knowledge was quite reliable. In an early moment of assuring us of the legitimacy of the claims she was about to make about jaliya, Jali musaloo Suso told us that she had learned jaliya from her father, with whom she had traveled extensively as a young girl. Thus we could be certain that she took the practices quite seriously. Her father had been one of the most prominent jali, known throughout The Gambia and Senegal, and "even the outside world," although he had never traveled beyond the region. But because of his fame, many had traveled to The Gambia to find him.

The reassurance she offered about her credibility provided another clue through which to understand what it would mean to construct a sense of self. Among jali, one's identity could only become significant through relationships. Familial and patronage affiliations helped create personal history. Jali musaloo Suso spoke of a self that was indebted to her parents, mentors, and sponsors. Even just sitting with her parents allowed her to absorb the elements of jaliya.

> When I was a small child, I used to go with [my mother] wherever she was going. On arrival, if [my parents] were entertaining, we used to sit together; whatever they were saying, I must say. If I wanted to go to sleep, even then she would tell me, "Open your eyes and listen to what is being said; join the chorus." They were praising high; I would do the chorus until I became firm on it and used to it, until I could do it on my own.

Although Jali musaloo Suso described a debt to both her parents, it was her father's knowledge and fame that brought her talent into the world, she explained. As the interview progressed, she discussed with an edge of resentment in her tone the inability of women jali to be seen as people with narrative authority. Who had the right to speak in an official capacity about certain kinds of knowledge was too often determined by gender, she asserted. In narrating histories, men's abilities were valued over women's. Jali musaloo Suso told us that jali women were confined to certain tasks, their activities curtailed by conventional and restrictive notions of gender-appropriate duties. If she was able to transcend these boundaries in her own knowledge and performance, she implied, it was not only because of her social debts to great teachers but also because of her own bold style.

Jali musaloo Suso's interview performance, like that of other jali with whom we spoke, reminded me of how individuals are shaped by a social context and yet at the same time attempt to make the interview their own, drawing on personalities that reveal aspects that are idiosyncratic, angry, opportunistic, playful, disordered, or exceptionally skilled at storytelling. My interviews of individual jali highlighted dual processes. The details in narratives about professional careers offered a sense of varied trajectories of jali; they also drew attention to style and genre. Tacking back and forth between these two elements, I gained a sense of jali "voice." Yet, too, I was reminded that "voice" could not be captured in a simple story, but always required an array of stylized gestures conveying personal charisma and heroic force. Recalled in a transcript, much of this performance is lost. To get at the full effect of an encounter with a professional jali required more than a written transcript; jaliya requires presence, the public persona that ensures the status of their patrons and the jali himself or herself.

To be a heroic jali is not only a matter of songs; it is part of your speech. If you hear that such a person is a hero, then he is the one having good wordings, a song to praise people. But who is termed as the hero? Somebody who can establish peace between people. (Jali musaloo Suso, in her sixties)

Travel, Genealogy, Status

Heroic jali "establish peace" and make war; they negotiate society. To carve out this performance niche for themselves, they must establish their reputations across space and time, and within the reproduction of the status hierarchy. In asking jali to tell about themselves, my interviews provoked performances of jali identity that particularly highlighted the making of their charisma through space, time, and status reproduction. Travel brought their names over the landscape. Genealogical connections—for both jali themselves and their patrons—established the seniority of their knowledge. Brought together with a history of regional and international patronage politics, travel and genealogy reproduced the story of caste hierarchy and the position of jali performers within it. This section illustrates these themes, showing their texture within the performances of professional self-making that made up my interviews.

> I used to go with my mother to Sutu-Kooba, Makka-Masireng, Jaa-Kunda, Muroo Kunda, Bantang-tinti, Netebula, Koina-Baako, Fa-toto-, Fata-tenda, Kular, in fact all the neighboring villages besides us, especially the Serahuli dwellings. (Jali musaloo SJ)

Even a listing of places is significant within this genre. Travel is an important part of the jali repertoire. Most jali travel within The Gambia between urban spaces where their sponsors help them make a living and the upcountry rural spaces that replenish their reputations for connection with tradition and authentic lore. Furthermore, in contrast to ordinary citizens, who might also move about, the occupation of jali requires regular visits with patrons. As people once attached to a court and to particular families, the importance of travel has perhaps increased in recent years as now jali must cultivate and serve multiple patrons. Contemporary travel is also transnational in its scope, ideally involving Europe, North America, and Asia, as well as West African regions.

Place names, indicating the scope of travel, are intermixed with the personal names that show extensive relations of patronage.

> We used to travel to a lot of places in the provinces, for the patrons of my father were there. We used to beg something from them. I can name some of [the patrons] because there were plenty of them.

> One of my father's friends was at Niani; he is called BM. He used to go there every year. AS, of Kolonba, is also a patron. ABK of Wuli is also a patron. A caliph was also his patron. He is called Al-haji JB. [My father] used to take those routes every year on his journey. (Jali musaloo JS, in her fifties)

Time is measured together with travel.

> We never settled down in one place in those days. We sometimes traveled for a whole six-month period. We would spend one month in one village, two months, weeks in some place and so on. (Jali NS, 60 years old)

Traveling with parents and teachers turns mobility into knowledge and professionalization:

> Yes! I used to travel with my parents; my father happened to be Al-haji BK. But before I started going with him, his younger brother, called JK, was the one I used to traveled with. Starting from here in The Gambia, Cassamance going up to Portuguese Guinea. I used to go with him to all these places to and fro. (Jali DK, 45 years old)

The practices of everyday livelihood are thus interwoven with patronage relations and movements across the landscape. Many jali, in their professional duties, also have to accommodate agricultural responsibilities. As a result, travel beyond the daily activities is generally undertaken on a seasonal basis.

> If we gathered groundnuts together until we stored them, it was after the trade season of groundnuts that we would go to his patrons. We used to come home a month after the rainy season was over. Then it would be time to go to the farms. . . . It's just a dry-season journey. We don't travel during the rainy season except when the harvest commences; then we proceed for another journey. (Jali MS, early forties)

Within this life of mobility, patrons of course have responsibilities to their jali. In some cases, patrons are so generous that they provide jali with all their needs. Or, from another perspective, they require their services so desperately that jali are unable to farm. Travel, which makes farming difficult, becomes inextricably entwined with the goods available from patrons.

> We used to go to our lodgers and our good patrons. To call upon them and beg something from them. Like what we found our ancestors and their patrons doing. Here in The Gambia, others would be giving us a flock of sheep, goats, and money. Including AS, we set-

tled under him as he was going to Portuguese Guinea because that
was his birthplace and that was where he originated from. We once
went with him to Portuguese Guinea. Then that is how I came to
know about Portuguese Guinea. Then, after that, I used to go to
Portuguese Guinea every year with JK. I used to pay visits to my patrons at Cassamance as well. Others will be giving us cows, goats,
flocks of sheep and money. Others will be giving us costumes for
going up to Portuguese Guinea. Then coming back home again,
with this all taking place during the dry season. We used to set off
from here on the commencement of the harvest season. Our going
and coming period exceeds three months after the commencement
of the harvest season. All these periods, normally found us in distant places. (Jali DK, in his forties)

Whether local day-to-day travel during which jali visit their nearby patrons for such ceremonies as naming rites and weddings, or more extensive travels that may happen during a particular part of the year, travel is
significant in the making of jali identity.

Travel also differentiates men and women. Men's travel enhances
their reputation; women's reputations are made suspect by travel beyond
the local region. Women's travel is thus more circumscribed. Moreover,
the opportunities for men to travel internationally far exceed those for
women. A few women have traveled as members of the Gambian National Troupe; however, women are afforded this opportunity only in the
company of male family members. International standards as well as local
gender expectations privilege men. A man traveling to Europe or North
America will generally be looked upon favorably. While he will be seen
as advancing his career, the same value is not attributed to women. Without the accompaniment of a male protector, a woman's reputation would
definitely be questioned. Gender distinctions were clear in conversations
I had with jali and nonjali Gambians.

Even for men, international travel does not always translate into a
heightened reputation at home. While international connections are an
important aspect of a jali's career, these connections cannot substitute
for travels around The Gambia and West Africa because these create his
following at home. Travel in the region reinforces localized family connections and patronage; travel beyond the region enhances a more abstract
sense of reputation. While all the jali men and women with whom I spoke
had a desire to perform in Europe and North America, as well as in other
parts of Africa, and some of the men interviewed had traveled to these
places, international connections are known to be tenuous, and the status
they bring may be short-lived. Internationally, jali are musicians and traditional entertainers; at home, they are much more. International travel

must then be carefully inserted into a regional repertoire of mobility and networking to produce local professional status.

As one might expect, international networks and travel trajectories tend not to follow the same patterns of seasonal visits to patrons. The elements of self-making differ in transnational spaces, as do the logistics of transcontinental travel. The jali must be invited by a sponsor who will also make the necessary travel arrangements to Europe and the United States. It is much more difficult to turn experiences of international travel into stories of jali professional agency in seeking out patrons. Instead, the bureaucratic requirements of intergovernmental exchanges and immigration rules, the timing of international festivals, and the finances of foreign sponsors become relevant. The jali to whom I spoke had little sense that they could organize this mobility themselves.

> The first trip where I boarded a plane was in 1977; that was in Nigeria. The government sent me there. I went for the Festac festival. From there I came back. Apart from that, my father and I commenced a tour for the United States. When we went there for the second time, my father said he was now weary. And he was not going again. My elder brother and I went back to the United States again. We spent two months and fifteen days; then back again. Since that trip I haven't gone there again. (Jali DK, in his forties)

As in the telling of West African travels, however, prowess is created in listing places visited—even if these places are undifferentiated countries rather than intimately known villages. The same jali continued his story thus:

> A white man came from the United States, but he was settling in Denmark. He came to take me along for us to start a tour of Europe. We first went to Paris, then Brussels, Belgium, Holland, Germany, Denmark, Stockholm, and Sweden. (Jali DK)

Another jali with whom I spoke had developed more knowledge of and influence in international circles. He had honed his skills to cater to non-Gambian audiences, and in the process he had developed a sense of personal agency and professional control in his international travels. He traveled to the United States in the late 1960s and established connections that would eventually allow him to use his skills as a jali very effectively. Blending his sense of the importance of patronage to establish reputation and his knowledge of Western audiences, he created a new version of patronage to spread his name, transforming enthusiastic audience members into patrons. Audience members, attending his concerts, would arrange future concerts for him, spreading his performance territory. In this ingenious syncretism, Western audiences become Mandinka patrons. Indeed, this jali was self-conscious about his translation from Mandinka traditions to North American musicianship. This translation, however, did not always serve him well in The Gambia. One Mandinka patron we both knew acted as if he had no awareness of the jali's existence, for the jali, said the patron, was no longer of any use to The Gambia. Besides, he was out of the region most of the time. He could no longer negotiate society.

Performing Identities

Mariama and I had walked just a short distance from the compound where I lived in Bakau to meet with a jali who lived in the neighborhood. This jali was one of the most brilliant kora players I had heard, with the gift of making the most difficult musical passages seem easy and elegant. Excited as I was to meet such a renowned musician, I was not prepared for his bitterness.

As it was still early in the morning when we arrived, the jali was not ready to receive us. We waited in a small room alone for twenty minutes, heightening our nervousness. Finally, Jali Suso returned and led us to another room, as dimly lit as his mood. Even the bright daylight had no effect in lightening the feel of our stay, which was clearly an intrusion. While he spoke at length of his importance, he was so intensely disillusioned about his position in The Gambia that he could offer little but embittered replies.

Mariama proceeded as usual to explain more about the project, but unlike many of the other interviews, which were conducted in Mandinka, the jali spoke in English and preferred to direct his answers directly to me. Fairly early in the conversation, he began listing his European and American friends, many of whom he had taught to play the kora. Others had arranged for him to teach in Washington and Connecticut. Jali Suso also spoke of his role in assisting Alex Haley in finding his Gambian relatives. For this jali the international arena was the stage, the landscape of his fame. The regional landscape had proved to be a disappointment. He could not make the kind of connections that he desired by forcing his international reputation onto local ground, and he turned to me, indirectly, to draw him out of the local shadow.

Through his account it is possible to see the kinds of transregional patronage networks that become instrumental in international connections. Often these connections are made through former students who have come to The Gambia to learn about the kora and balaphon.

> T, an American patron, had a job at the University of Washington, and he said that the staff was interested in the kora and they asked him a lot of questions concerning who taught him the kora. Not so

long after that, he recommended me and they sent for me. I signed and bought my air ticket. The letter came just in time; he told me, "Please, Mr. Suso, I learned of your condition [he was ill at the time], but please try and come because this is a good chance for you concerning your trip to America." That happened in 1971.

Another man in New York City also urged me to make a kora for him. He heard of me in Freetown, Sierra Leone, then he wrote me a letter saying that he will come. He sent me the money from which I made a kora and he came and spent three months with me. He told me that he had visited many countries in Africa but he had never seen anyone like Jali Suso. I ended up going with him to America. We went via Dakar to New York. Members of his family collected us at the airport, and we went to his house. We stayed together for one week and their school resumed.

Jali Suso wanted to know my questions, but he did not in the least bit feel compelled to answer any of them. Mariama was impatient. In preparing a transcript of the interview a few days later, she could not restrain herself from writing in the margin: "In a haste to answer, and the question is not completed." Yet Jali Suso spoke extensively about things that were on his mind, particularly his anger about being forgotten by his patrons, local patrons that included the Gambian state, even his international patrons.

As Jali Suso recounted his travels, emphasizing in contrast to other jali the important role played by international patrons who facilitated his journeys, he was also quite bitter about his stature in the national context. He felt that his country did not honor him in the ways that it should have. This had not always been so. Indeed, in contrast to jali who had fully turned their attention to international audiences, this jali was recognized in The Gambia, and yet he felt that an appreciation of his importance was lacking. In his account of an earlier period, he described himself as an important performer beyond the arena of ceremonial events. At first, he seemed on his way to really becoming someone.

> I used to travel all by myself from here to Basse until we got a small radio station here in Bakau. In those days there was no popular kora player here except me. That is why the whole of Gambia knew me. Perhaps they will tell you they've never seen me with their naked eyes, but they used to hear my name all the time. So I became the kora player on Radio Gambia.

His success, of course, was not just his own. He talked at length about his responsibilities and obligation to support family members. And he celebrated the patrons who brought him his early success. The interview became a moment not only to convey a sense of jaliya but also to call attention to patron obligations to jali. Jaliya, he reminded us, is a profession, not just an art.

> If they come to know something from me, definitely, they have to pay me for it because that is my job and that is what I feed my family on. In fact there are lots of families in the compound and in the culture, if the father is not alive, it is the eldest son who occupies his father's position to look after the well-being of the whole family, because we don't have family separations here. We all live together and make it an extended family system. If I died my younger brother will take care and if that one is not there, it will be the eldest sisters to provide if there are no males. Even if a young boy is there, he will be the compound head in the presence of the eldest sister.

Here he appears to be conveying custom to me, but he has another agenda. In the midst of this celebration of tradition, Jali Suso's account, inevitably, turned into a complaint—and a plea for better treatment.

> So look, all these families depend on me and it is my duty to meet their demands. That is my job and if you want to use me, please look after me because everybody works for his family and are paid with good salaries. Now why is it that they don't want them to pay us and the money is not granted to anyone, it is granted by the government to do the job but yet and still, you don't want to pay me for my labor. Then why do you have to economize that money just because our status is not the same? I will never accept that because I have faith in God. All these nine countries that I toured in Europe, no one had paid my fare. Gambians just heard that I am gone, but they never knew how I managed to go, and I worked there for the benefit or sake of the Gambians. If you go to the museum in Berlin, you will see my picture there with my kora. I am promoting The Gambia with all that and yet and still they want to use me and don't have recognition for me which I will never accept.

One striking aspect of this testimony was Jali Suso's insistence on comparing jaliya to a job for which he should receive a salary. At the same time, he relied on the conventions of patronage. He recounted, for example, that once, when a patron asked him how things were, he replied that he needed a bag of rice; the man immediately purchased the rice for him. Indeed, his patrons seemed to provide significant things, much more than rice, such as a car and a roof for his house. He also had considerable respect and fame. But he remained discontented with his situation, comparing himself to successful national figures with civil servant salaries and feeling his own talents were underappreciated.

In speaking to us, Jali Suso leapt back and forth between nostalgic reminiscence, excited explanation, angry criticism, and downright bullying. His interview performance reminded me that enthusiasm and élan are not the only forms through which jali accomplish their self-making recitations. The contrast between his self-presentation and that of Jali musaloo Suso (described above), for example, could not have been greater. Jali musaloo Suso drew us in with a magnetic style that kept us charmed and excited. She focused her full attention on the interview, letting us know how seriously she took our questions. Her answers were quite extended and were animated by elaborate hand gestures to emphasize to her points. Everything was heightened by the energy she brought to her explanations. Her charismatic style worked magic.

In contrast, the man I am calling Jali Suso exuded authority, experience, and disdain. He wasted little time on our questions, but instead used the occasion to impress us with the importance of his career and his connections. Jali musaloo Suso felt it necessary to prove to us that she was a highly qualified jali despite her status as a woman; perhaps this made her try exceptionally hard to demonstrate her artful talents, extensive knowledge of history, and deep concentration. The man Jali Suso, instead, allowed us to assume his abilities while attempting to impress us with his illustrious history. Meanwhile, he took the opportunity to remind us that we, too, could help to redress the wrongs to his reputation that had become far too frequent in The Gambia, despite his international recognition.

Not surprisingly, Jali Suso was willing to include us in his litany of patrons lost and found. At one point Mariama offered a story she had heard from her father: "One day a jali was praising a chief near the seashore and the patron didn't have any money with him. So finally, [the patron] threw himself in the river and people went to rescue him." Jali Suso was intrigued. "Who is your father?" he inquired with curiosity. When she told him her father was Alhaji Karamo Jammeh, the jali broke into praise. "Is he from Illiasa? Ranging from Tamba Jammeh, Biran Jammeh, Jatta Selang, Buka Jammeh, Chukulu Salimang, and Bambi Salimang, Wulufa Wulunbango, Soling Joyoo, Sara Biram Jammeh." He paused and then said to me, "She comes from a great family in The Gambia. She is a woman, but she can become a ruler here because she is from the royal family." At this Mariama, appropriately moved, searched her purse for a token of appreciation.

Similarly, Jali musaloo Suso included us in her audience of patrons. But the exuberance of her praises formed a striking contrast with the shrugged-off erudition of Jali Suso. As I stated previously, her aim in the interview was to prove to us that she was as skilled as a man in narrating history, so her answers were quite extensive and she punctuated them periodically with moments of authority such as when she let us know how many generations she could narrate back through time. "I can recite your family genealogy back seven generations, and if I were to do so you might offer me five *dalasis* [unit of money] or ten." Mariama, unable to remain outside of the performance, would open her purse and search until she found the dalasis.

> Mariama, cheer for the day, celebrate it well Mariama, give me something. No one will stand up to praise you with something that will pierce through you. But god bless your generation to be fruitful.

Both Jali musaloo Suso and Jali Suso praised Mariama as illustrations of their art. In the process, they retrained Mariama and me, reminding us of our status as potential patrons. The conventions of a formal performance call for audience members to approach the stage and express their appreciation with contributions of money in gratitude for praises. As researchers, Mariama and I were slow to catch on to the intentions of the jali when they offered praises. At first we both sat there listening and trying to keep to our note taking. But the recurring pleas throughout the interviews made clear the reason that Mariama was being called out to participate.

> If somebody says to you "Give me something," and you happen to know him, you will remove ten dalasi and give it to him or her. I will come with my great praises and you will give me a dalasi. That is why the present generation does jaliya, depending on how you know the person. They lost their tradition, praises, and their birthrights. They say it depends on who you know; that is not part of the traditions. I myself even observed that. (Jali musaloo Suso)

Jali musaloo Suso was explaining how jali obtain a living. But she intended these moments of calling out, as it were, as a participatory activity that established the relationship between jali and patron. We responded. We took on our own performative statuses, as women of substance.

> I know you, I can set off and come to you. I will tell you, "Palm Tree [a nickname for Mariama], today your mother has come to visit." You can give me what you can afford and I can come back to my house. For example, Jali S is your age group and if she comes and says to you, "Mariama, I have come to pay you a visit today," you can give her what you can afford.

To those who chose to use the interview encounter to praise the family name "Jammeh," this became a moment for reaffirming—and teaching—status. At the beginning of many interviews, Mariama acted with deference, based on her young age, toward the older jali. The jali, too, unac-

quainted with her personally, treated her as a young woman. Once they
learned her family name, however, they shifted their performative style
and they began to praise her family name. Nevertheless, her age was still
relevant. Their job was to remind her of the responsibilities of the younger
generation of elites. In turn, she was forced to act with the generosity and
stature of a patron.

I, too, was called into the recitations.

> [If] I beg from you and you don't give me something and you are sit-
> ting in a congregation, I say to you, "Give me something," and you
> refuse to do so, the person sitting near you gives me something. I
> will tell her, "Paulla, you are second to none. You are kind and you
> are not ambitious over your wealth." Know that I am referring to
> you. I will make you feel sad in your seat. Your friend and rivals
> will be sitting at that place. You will be ashamed, whereas God will
> not see you giving me my luck. If God does not see you giving luck
> to somebody, He cannot give you some. (Jali musaloo Suso)

Both Jali Suso and Jali musaloo Suso offered interview performances
that became moments for negotiating and constructing a self in relation
to the other people in the room who could be pulled in as subjects of
narration. Jali musaloo Suso pressed me to be a local patron. Jali Suso,
in contrast, configured my place in relationship to non-Gambians and
urged me not to forget the jali who depend on international sponsors.
Both drew Mariama into the status hierarchy by reciting the genealogical
history of her father's family. In the process, they tutored us in performing
appropriate identities as responsible patrons, women, and young people.

The interview context became an arena for other lessons about social
status. Having already begun the job of teaching us to perform our as-
signed roles, our jali informants also spoke of other roles. We were told
not just of the responsibilities between patrons and jali, but of other caste
distinctions, the roles of men and women, and the respect due the elderly.

> The elderly have a greater role to play than the younger jali due to
> respect. We should honor them since they are the same group as our
> parents. They are the ones who share out the money at ceremonies
> and distribute it according to age as is done in the past. The young
> jali will gain blessings by honoring the elderly jali since they were
> the first to experience the traditions before us. If any young jali fail
> to observe those principles, it will not yield good results. (Jali MK,
> 30 years old)

The jali stressed their own willingness to abide by even the smallest
status distinctions—for example, distinctions among jali as well as those
between jali and other castes:

If all the jali assemble as well, it will be the Kuyateh surnamed who will be the first to sing. Even if it happens to be a child but is surnamed Kuyateh, he is obliged to sing first. The Kuyateh surnames were the purest jali. We join them in the traditional practices of jaliya because we see to it that it is a profession. A system of tribute is offered to Kuyateh surnames; in performances they go first. The Kuyateh surname was the first jali of Sunjata. (Jali MS, age 41)

And, of course, they stressed their own moral care in their relationships with patrons.

I've never established a joking relationship between myself and a patron. I've never loved a patroness. I've never allowed my patron to treat me as a downcast and I am not arrogant towards any of my patrons. Whatever thing I found with my patron and he happens to give it to me, it will be all right by me because a jali must be content. (Jali MS)

Certainly, Mariama and I were implicated here.

The interviews themselves, then, became occasions not only for making claims about status distinctions, but also for teaching and practicing them. From the perspective of jali, reputations, identities, and status distinctions are at base performative. They must be renegotiated in each face-to-face context. Without jali performance, patrons have no status, but the patrons must perform too—and so, too, men and women, elders and their juniors, blacksmiths and farmers, Kuyateh and Suso. The special talent of jali is not only to be experts in performance themselves but also to get others to perform their own status properly. There can be no passive audiences, and no neutral scholarly observers. For jali, social interaction requires the performance of identity.

"Small Lies"

I myself taught [my children] about the traditions of jaliya.
When they were young they sat beside me, and with the
small lies I put together to sing, they too imitated that system.
—Jali Sakiliba

As do artists and performers in many places, the jali I knew framed their life stories with performances, but they contrasted their professional identity with other types of performers. Unlike U.S. rock musicians and movie stars, for example, jali did not create themselves as eccentric "characters" in order to sell their public performances, but instead used their public performances to reaffirm their status as skilled, creative, dependent, even overbearing, and bold caste members—that is, jali—in everyday life. The blurring of lines between everyday activities and staged performances is the trademark of their social position. It makes them always ready and ever-able go-betweens, negotiators, and on-the-spot singers of praise.

When Jali Sakiliba explained to me that she socialized her children into the jaliya art through "small lies," she was referring to this performative aspect of jali self-presentation. In this context, the "lies" she invokes are not arguments against truth or science but rather point us toward the making of truths of status and sociality in well-honed rhetoric and performance. They are learned through "imitation"; put together, they recreate and extend "traditions."

Jali musaloo Suso worried through the concept of "lies" in a rather different way: in giving her interview she was concerned that "with something to be written I do not want to tell lies." Jali musaloo Suso embedded her interview performance in a sense of the permanence of the written word. Where Jali Sakiliba's "small lies" are negotiations of performative roles necessary for face-to-face interactions, Jali musaloo Suso's "lies" are public pronouncements removed from their performative context and presented to the world as if inflexible truths. This distinction between the necessities of performative flexibility and the importance of "getting it right" for the public record was a key feature of much of what jali wanted to tell me. A jali is unafraid to make any moment a negotiation of status and a performative teaching experience. A jali also has a responsibility, however, to the record of genealogy and history. To confuse the record of history and status is to be publicly "shameless"; in contrast, to engage in the performative manipulations of everyday life is a necessary shamelessness required for jali to be useful. A jali must be bold.

> If a jali is not bold enough, he will not possess any means of wealth from his patrons. The silent word for *bold* is *shameless* but that is also of two types. First of all, to be shameless in the presence of an audience, that is the quality a jali should possess. Secondly, there are some people who are even shameless in the presence of the whole world. The jali cannot be grouped in the second group. (Jali musaloo SJ, approximately fifty years old)

This self-consciousness about the limits, forms, and proprieties of performance makes a significant contribution to the ways that social theorists have discussed everyday enactments of gender and status. The creation of identity is always made within the structures that scripted in and yet tampered with those who refuse, misunderstand, adjuticate its possibilities. Performative elements create a space of play in social locations; indeed, social distinctions are not fixed but rather are given new meanings and latitudes through performance. Jali performances of everyday interactions work in just this spirit. Because jali are also formal performers with a trained eye for genre and style, however, they work their everyday negotiations with a care and skill that sheds some light on the formal requirements that all performers—self-conscious and otherwise—must bring to social interactions. They reproduce the habitus of social distinctions through performance even as they manipulate and stretch individual relationships into forms that their interlocutors may or may not appreciate. But that is their job.

Small lies, then, do not stay neatly in their ethnographic context; they force themselves against scholarly conventions, urging us to rethink working assumptions. My major concerns in this chapter are twofold. On one side are issues of ethnographic method, culture, and experience. Against scholarly conventions that offer life-story interviews as transparent windows into the truth of experience, small lies remind us that self-presentation is always as important as self-reporting. *Presentation* becomes the methodological issue through which we must filter our anthropological concerns about social classification, power, and agency. On the other side are issues of social organization and political economy. Here, too, small lies reassemble the structures we know; they are the mortar of personalism with which social relations are built and rebuilt. Again, issues of presentation take the methodological foreground, for through them the dynamics of personalism can be studied. As my jali informants told me over and over, a jali's words must move people to action. Small lies create leadership and stimulate accomplishment. They enable both the movement and structure at the heart of social life and history.

Ethnography depends on the ability of researchers to comprehend unfamiliar points of view, and the interview is one of our most important tools for learning new perspectives. As ethnographic researchers, we hope that our interviews, along with participant observation, will draw us into the worlds of the people whose cultures we study. Furthermore, the personal perspectives learned from interviews take theoretical center stage in scholarly approaches that stress "the view from below." Since the 1970s those anthropologists, social historians, feminist scholars, and others working to bring gender, ethnicity, and social class into scholarly portraits of society, have paid special attention to the perspectives of those who did not control the official media of representation—women, the poor, peasants, minorities, etc.—as these could be studied through ethnographic interviews. In this context, interviews with jali women and men seemed a sensible focal point for my project. Indeed, I did learn a great deal about jali perspectives from my interviews, yet these interviews also challenged my notions of perspective, as they showed themselves to be grounded in assumptions about structure and agency.

When I initially designed my research in The Gambia, I hoped to show the mutual importance of culture and political economy in a local-global system of social dynamics. I came from an institutional setting where a few argued that study of both culture and political economy suffered from being studied isolated from each other. On the one hand, I hoped to interrupt static and overly harmonious notions of culture by paying attention to the discordant views of people positioned rather differently in relation to political-economic structures: women and men of different castes, classes, ethnicities, etc. On the other hand, I was convinced that accounts of West African economic systems could be enriched by attention to culture in all its various meanings: interpretive frameworks, the production of music and the arts, and national, ethnic, and communal identities. Within this set of concerns, interviews with different kinds of cultural producers formed an important element in my research to establish distinctive perspectives and to trace their role in social dynamics. My concerns led me toward the hope that my interviews would take place in enough of a context of intimacy and trust to reveal neglected truths of experience learned through structural positions in a system of political-economic inequalities. Yet when I actually began to conduct interviews, this hope quickly fell apart—and with it, slowly, the framework on which it depended. In sharp contrast with the situation that the then-current reflexive literature in anthropology had led me to expect, intimacy and trust were not the key issues at all. Instead, jali used the interviews as a context of performance. After all, they are performers. Why should an encounter with a foreign scholar be so different than an encounter with a tourist or even a local patron?

Jali used the interviews to present themselves not only to Mariama and to me but also to a host of potential listeners and patrons. Rather than a window on experience, what I gained was the opportunity to witness the performance of self. I admit that I was initially taken aback by the amount of self-promotion and negotiation of personal benefits that occurred at the center of every interview. I had been led, after all, to imagine self-revelations. Only in recognizing the importance of presentation, however, was I able to glimpse new aspects of the ethnographic situation. Ironically, I eventually realized that I was learning about the interdependence of culture and political economy, although not in the way I had earlier imagined. In chapter 4, I argued that personalistic self-presentations, by jali as well as nonjali, are key to the networking at the center of Gambian politics and economics. Posing was not just what Westerners tend to think of as a fraud or an empty show; it was the essential ingredient of social mobility and influence. It was the most important skill of jali self-making. And it came to offer me a new view of self-making and social mobility not just in The Gambia but elsewhere—although a view often concealed by the shadow of popular and scholarly assumptions.

Culture as Commodity

M any contemporary social analysts have suggested that the distinctive feature of late capitalism is consumption. These analysts have traced how consumerism surrounds us, marketing our identities, lifestyles, and sense of belonging through consumption. One key feature of this globalized consumption is tourism: tourists, particularly from the global North, want to travel everywhere to consume the heterogeneity and richness of culture. In The Gambia, tourism is important; it shapes local articulations of culture both within and beyond the practices of jali.

This third part consists of two chapters that revisit the salient themes of the book: the circulation of Africa through ideas of both performance and representation. This part takes us through a consideration of The Gambia in the context of journeys made by European and North American tourists to "experience" The Gambia and Senegal. In contrast with the previous chapters, jali are not explicitly present. Certainly jali have helped create an interest in The Gambia. The jali I knew who traveled with the Gambian minister of tourism to Jamaica in the 1970s to learn about tourism has since devoted himself to promoting jaliya and The Gambia abroad. The skills of jali are made into a valuable cultural artifact, above and beyond their responsibilities to Gambian patrons, as they are used in the country's promotion of tourism.

Yet the question of culture as commodity, to which jali lead us, extends beyond jaliya. In a place where tourism is the nation's most valuable industry, culture more generally becomes an object of economic attraction and is fashioned to draw the attention of foreign consumers. How are we to understand ethnic, regional, and national cultures in the global tourist economy? Analysts are just beginning to develop signposts and guidelines that help us see the newness as well as the sustained legacies of global culture-making. I find these models provocative. I also insist that they must themselves be regionalized and historicized to be useful.

Contemporary Gambian inflections of international tourism both draw upon and transform global fantasies of difference and movement. Many of the citizens of The Gambia barely eke out a living above the poverty level. Under the regime of President Jawara, the country was ranked 166 out of 173 countries in the United Nations Development Programme's Human Development Index (Saine 2000). President Jawara initiated The Gambia's involvement in tourism in the early 1970s as a response to the country's poverty. An ever-expanding culture industry in search of entertainment that will amuse leisured consumers, mainly of First World countries, seemed a rich resource. Now Gambians vie for the attention of foreign tourists and craft themselves to their desires.[1] Yet in the dialogue, those desires are remade. Something new and regionally and historically particular is generated. Models of global cultural production must similarly be transformed to illuminate both the force of transnational desires and their regional transformations.

One model for analysis of the global cultural economy is Arjun Appadurai's (1996) set of global "scapes." Key for Appadurai is the notion of global flow—the movement of people, ideas, and capital. This global flow creates five overlapping yet disjunctive scapes. Ethnoscapes are made by communities in motion; they are identity processes of travelers of all kinds—refugees, exiles, guest workers, and tourists. Technoscapes are mechanical and informational worlds that move beyond national borders. Mediascapes are formed by information that is electronically produced and circulated in various kinds of media forms. By ideoscapes, Appadurai means the spread of ideas and images associated with European Enlightenment values, such as freedom, democracy, and rights. Financescapes chart the rapid movement of capital.

Models are best used to open up our analyses to new ideas. Global scapes can shed light on travel and tourism in The Gambia, pointing to their disjunctive yet intertwined imaginative terrains. For this model to be useful, however, I must reformulate it. New scapes emerge, not hegemonically, but in relation to particular cultural configurations: history and memory scapes, and gender and sexuality scapes. These, in turn, are in continual dialogic movement as culturally diverse participants negotiate their misunderstandings and arrive at new collaborations. Culture as commodity emerges from this unequal but still invigorating negotiation.

Another model, developed by the Birmingham Centre for the Study of Contemporary Culture, uses the idea of "circuits of culture." This model works to put culture in the center of a still-determinedly materialist analysis that does not ignore production. It reacts to earlier Marxist model-building, in which culture is epiphenomenal; yet it also draws on Marxist ideas of the importance of the making of the material world for power and class status. Instead of offering production as a base and culture as a superstructure, it offers a "circuit" in which symbolic and material elements of the social order are in constant interaction. Thus, it identifies five elements, each on an equal analytic plane of importance: representation, identity, regulation, consumption, and production. Each of these processes, according to the model, contributes to culture-making under contemporary capitalism. Each process is linked to the others in contingent relations of "articulation," which implies that the process of linking is in itself a meaning-making activity at the same time that it is a social and material activity (du Gay et al. 1997, 3).

This model usefully draws us back to relations of power, as these pervade culture-making on every scale. Powerful media amplify the representations that reproduce their power, and this power is grounded in their control of the production of information. Unlike Appadurai's global scapes, which bring us directly to the imagination, "circuits of culture" remind us that some kinds of imaginative projects will be broadcast more loudly than others. This is a useful beginning point for understanding tourism in The Gambia. Tourist desires are not just any circulating dreams; they are backed up with the economic and political power of tourists, the companies that bring them, house them, and entertain them, and the governments that regulate and privilege them. Gambians must come to terms with their representations of identity and difference asymmetrically; tourists may or may not choose to engage with Gambian perspectives on tourism.

The model, however, also must be drawn into the richness and particularity of Gambian culture-making. Appadurai's scapes are useful here because they remind us of the breadth of the globe and its terrain of disjunction. Not all kinds of representations are alike. The imaginative worlds created by Northern tourists in the global South have distinctive material and symbolic features. They rely particularly on geopolitical fantasies: the smug sense of Northern privilege, and the Southern dream of opportunity and wealth in the North; the Northern search for "something missing" that might be found in the South, and the Southern pride in heritage. Key "circuits" here, then, are wider than the tightly communicative inside of postindustrial capitalism; global regionality forms the ground for the cultural and political articulations of Gambian tourism.

Gambian tourism is an economic process that comes into being through performing "Africa" for tourists. Gambians have been busy developing local traditions and crafts into "African" artifacts for tourist consumption; in The Gambia these items include such tangible objects as cloth, leather, and woodworking, but also include the marketing of an aura not particularly tied to the physicality of an object. To refer to culture as commodity, then, extends beyond material objects and yet is in keeping with Marx's idea of the commodity as fetish. Like fetishes, names and genealogies tied to places develop that aura that makes them salable as sites of desire.

The power of institutions shapes this process at multiple levels. Development agencies, international regulatory bodies, and philanthropic foundations have promoted tourism and guided its forms. Working together with the national government, they have introduced the mission of commodifying culture, and they have suggested strategies—ranging from the rehabilitation of historical sites to the internationalization of concert standards—through which this can be done. International tour agencies and hotel entrepreneurs have gained huge concessions from the state, using the rhetoric of privatization to make use of national resources. Marketing agents and journalists in Northern countries have felt free to exoticize The Gambia to make it the "right" kind of travel destination.

Yet the success of tourism also involves imaginative investments and negotiations from multiple parties, including tourists, marketers, and Gambian cultural producers. The scapes they produce are creative dialogues and interventions. They thrive through misunderstandings and bad translations. (Why might African American tourists resent hearing about West African politics?) They produce unexpected dreams. (Why might young Gambian men imagine that they could make their fortune as sexual dependents on the tourist industry?) The next chapters visit two of these local/global worlds.

CHAPTER SIX

Travel Stories

You don't ask for sex, but the men seem to know you want
it. They say things like, "Would you like to see the real Africa?" It's all very discreet. I had four different boys that holiday and the best sex I have ever had. I came back a new
woman.
—Mary, English tourist (to Christine Aziz)

In July of 1994, the thirty-year reign of Sir Dawada Jawara came to an
end as a new political regime rose to power: the Armed Forces Provisional
Ruling Council (AFPRC). During this transition, installed as president
was Lieutenant Yahya Jammeh, elected through a peaceful, although not
invited, shift in power. The former president, Jawara, had been elected
head of state since the end of colonial rule, but the democratic elections
that periodically marked the postcolonial political era did not create a
shift in political leadership. Many felt it was time for a change.

One of the first agenda items that President Jammeh called for was
an end to the government corruption that had come to characterize, in
the minds of some, the problem with the former administration. In addition to his concern about corruption, another of his initial concerns was
to end "moral decay," a reference to what Jammeh saw as immorality
associated with the tourist industry. Tourism had gained in prominence
since the end of colonial rule as it captured the imagination of economic
planners as well as service workers, who knew it as one of the few sectors
of employment, outside of the government, that provided steady work.
But this sector had gained in notoriety in recent years as The Gambia
became known as a place where vacationing European women might
come to seek male "friends." Directing attention to all of the associated
activities related to tourism in The Gambia, including prostitution and the
drug trade, President Jammeh demanded a rigorous attack on activities
perceived by some Gambians as having gone far beyond the bounds of
acceptable behavior. These sentiments were articulated in a press release
in which Jammeh made it clear that he would not allow women tourists
to visit his country in search of sex.

> We are Africans and we have our own moral values. . . . Prostitu-
> tion and drugs, those are all moral woes that we don't want in an
> African country because those are ideas which are alien to the Afri-

can people. . . . We are not sex machines. I want that to be clear to
whoever comes here purposely for sex. (Reuters August 20, 1994)

The phenomenon of European women in search of male Gambian
partners has garnered a great deal of international attention. Travel agents
regularly book flights for women visitors, some of them returnees; journalists of women's magazines interview women travelers and write tantaliz-
ing stories of emancipated women on holiday in The Gambia (Aziz 1994);
social scientists in Europe track the migrations of Gambians to European
countries and follow their romantic connections (Wagner and Yamba
1986; Mansson 1993); international health agencies, concerned about the
health of tourists and the potential spread of HIV, study the impact of
sexual encounters on holiday tourists (Pickering et al. 1992). This inces-
sant interest in sex tourism in The Gambia has helped codify aspects of a
sociological phenomenon. Yet the significance of European women and
Gambian men is not just in the sexual partnerships—with their implications for emigration, AIDS, or local incomes—but also in the formation
of allegorical narratives of personal and national mobility and morality.

This chapter explores the wider significance of these sociological studies as they intersect with tales I heard in The Gambia about men, women,
and tourism. The discussion is wide reaching, drawing on a number of
debates as they intersect with feminist theory and travel literatures. The
best aspects of our work as anthropologists lie in the move back and
forth between case materials and theoretical propositions whose limits
are highlighted as they are bound into conversation with locale. During
my fieldwork, the repetitive telling of a few almost stereotypical anecdotes drew my attention. These narratives, related to me by Gambian
men, reiterated the sociological "facts" of tourist relationships but also
gave them a wider cultural and political significance. I began to recognize
a recurring set of themes in many of the narratives, and I started to hear
these as more than a series of anecdotes. Their repetition, frequency, and
accompanying commentary suggested that these stories could be appreciated outside the bounds of the tourist industry as parables that expressed
national anxieties over power differences between Africa and Europe, and
between men and women.

The stories were regularly marked by ambivalence about tourism as
well as a sense of the excitement created by anticipated possibilities. In
villages and urban neighborhoods near the tourist areas, I repeatedly
heard comments that echoed President Jammeh's fear of national moral
decay. Stories that centered around sex and the transgressive behavior of
Gambian male youth and *toubob* (European) women friends became a
regular part of public discussion. In informal performance events, where
stories were exchanged to pass the time, my Gambian male associates

entertained me with the adventures of their friends and acquaintances who had traveled to Europe. Initially, these men appeared as successful winners in a game of chance, but soon enough—inevitably, they would say—these men fell into desperate circumstances. Clearly, the tellers saw these stories as portraying more than the plight of an individual; these men enacted nationally recognized anxieties. Even for those who had themselves never traveled beyond urban areas, such tales took on the aura of a national trajectory.

Immediately, too, I noticed striking differences in how these Gambian storytellers described the travels of men and of women. Women's travels were never described in a complimentary way; women can never carry national hopes and dreams in their travels. The Gambian men I knew often portrayed European women as engaged in a morally distasteful, single-minded search for attractive Gambian men. The Northern women in these stories were uncontrolled sex zealots. In contrast, the Southern men were adroit businessmen ready to design their success by capturing raw European passions. The stories told, then, of Gambian men crafting a masculine national trajectory in which political and cultural agency depended upon African male abilities to fashion themselves as entrepreneurs who could shape themselves to suit Europeans desires. In this nexus of dreams, the power and charisma of Europe was imagined as that of sexually promiscuous women, while Gambian men were desperate catchers of an opportunity.

Much of the success of these tales took place at the level of storytelling. Someone knew someone or had heard about someone who was part of the adventure. The trials and misfortunes of men were then aired with an engaging twist. Gambian "traffic-in-men" narratives disrupt our taken-for-granted axioms about the gendered locations of sexual agency. In these stories, women are not merely targets of male sexual opportunities. European women, empowered by national status, comparative wealth, and racially defined mobility, are imagined as the controllers of sexual opportunity. Furthermore, Gambian men's stories seem plausible and "true" because they overlap just enough with the stories European women tourists tell about themselves. In one magazine article, English women tourists pronounce themselves enchanted by the prospect of having their pick of "beautiful men" (Aziz 1994, 12). Still, the women appear unable to completely invert European hierarchies of gender dominance; their sexual vacations are empowering precisely because they tell their narratives as temporary emancipation from the male dominance of their ordinary lives.

In other ways, too, their stories are no simple inversion of European men's travel tales. The women do not imagine Gambian men as easy victims, and Gambian men's stories are certainly not tales of their victimization. Men imagine these connections as the means to wealth, status, and transnational mobility. Thus the sets of stories woven around romantic travel between The Gambia and Europe upset conventional parables about male sexual subjects and female sexual objects—though not in any simple ways. They refuse universal assumptions to demand specification of the transnational content of these erotic fantasies as well as the erotic charge of these transnational interconnections.

This chapter explores the construction of gender, desire, and social location across geographic boundaries and the ways these ideas figure into Gambian commentaries about tourism. Integral to the discussion are the continual refigurings of gender and power differences at the intersection of North-South relations. I begin with a discussion of the development of tourism in The Gambia to offer background to the allegorical aspects of the stories people tell about tourism. Particularly important is the context of the national vulnerability of The Gambia in the global economy. Another section of the chapter engages feminist theories that draw attention to the significance of political status in the negotiation of gender. Writing against popular and scholarly frameworks that assume gender as a universalized category of women's subordination, I argue that theorists who ignore the specificity through which gender is configured overlook a critical transnational aspect of the social construction of gender. This section is followed by a focus on the fashioning of charismatic style by Gambian male participants in transnational tourist adventures and the development of what I have been referring to as the "personalistic economy." I then turn to specifically address a few genre pieces that typify the narratives I heard during my fieldwork, analyzing the ways these stories rhetorically help refigure theories of gender and the nation. Finally, I revisit the literature on transnational sexuality as I position my work within these debates and attempt a reformulation of the relation between gender and transnational travel.

Women Tourists and Their Hosts

Relations between Western women visitors and Gambian men fit into an emerging body of literature on the sexual encounters of "Third World" men and Northern women tourists. These encounters have become a way of discussing the political relationships of world regions. Glenn Bowman (1989) describes Arab shopkeepers' use of sexual stories as a means of challenging the political and economic discrepancies between their lives as tourist merchants and the privilege and economic power of tourists. The stories are vehicles for expressing what Bowman refers to as a vengeance towards the tourists; the stories are also a means of creating status distinctions between themselves and their fellow merchants as they try to one-up their friends. As Bowman suggests, the currency of the stories is created in the telling of successful seductions; the telling of sexual conquest of Northern women became a means for redressing power imbalances.

A similar discussion of Northern women and Southern men in an earlier article by Erik Cohen (1971) describes the vulnerabilities of Palestinian men who long for the favors of Israeli women tourists. Their pursuit of these women becomes a means of escaping the conditions of local life. Palestinian men, according to Cohen, construct a "mythology of emigration" that will transport them beyond the strains and moral confines of everyday life. Both Bowman's and Cohen's essays begin the process of specifying local interpretations of travel and lives caught in complex power imbalances between Northern visitors and Southern hosts. Yet much is left to be explored. How is the construction of men's agency as sexual and national subjects always refigured in transnational interactions? How do the narratives of Southern men with Northern women speak past and to each other? How does the formation of sexual national Others offer insight for understanding gender globally?

A set of issues converges in the case of The Gambia. The historical conjunction between the development of tourism in The Gambia and the national allegorical thread indicting moral decay in contemporary commentary are intimately intertwined. Former President Jawara joined with international development agencies and set the course for the country's economic future with tourism as the cornerstone of that development. In desperate need to suggest alternatives for economic growth, he hoped that as a nation The Gambia would find its ability to move forward through enticing European visitors. Yet it was precisely this strategy of national enticement that many found distasteful. This would lead, almost thirty years after the end of the British colonial presence, to current moralist efforts to reclaim the nation. According to Jawara's critics, placing the nation in the position of catering to European guests reinscribed The Gambia's peripheral status.

Indeed, from the start, Gambians controlled few of the terms of the tourism business. Furthermore, tourism produced the kind of social relations that President Jammeh and others considered immoral. As he stated in his press release, echoing the rumblings of leaders in other countries concerned about the presence of sex tourism, "Africans are not sex machines." The "Africans" he refers to are almost certainly not women; rather, the objectification of the nation's men and their reduction to mechanical parts without agency brings the president so close to abjection. Once again, gender becomes the terrain for an imagined rearticulation of "traditional" values. When powerful Northern women are thought to be stalking junior and Southern men, a disturbing gender inversion has occurred. Gambian men are feminized. National honor and masculinity are at stake.

The historical specificity of this Gambian allegory of national revitalization intersects with specific changes in Europe as well. In the 1970s, European and North American women began to discover travel as a form of self-making. The travel industry created a niche for women travelers, as women were promised the freedom and power they could not experience at home. If such women could travel, perhaps they might "find themselves" abroad. Women's travel memoirs became particularly popular, and travel advertising increasingly targeted women.[1] Women's magazines featured articles not only of female travel but of its erotic and romantic possibilities. The Gambia became one site within the new female travel trajectory for Europeans. Women travelers rushed to see "The Africa" of Jawara's tourism plans. They also found the possibility of more informal encounters with local men.

Most literature on culture and travel assumes that travel traffic is a disruption of the cultural assumptions of ordinary life. Here, however, I begin with the idea that global traffic is one aspect of culture-making. It offers a way of understanding the spatial intermeshing of relationships. Culture is a dynamic process; there is no "once upon a time" when places were enclosed and bounded systems. Renato Rosaldo's (1989) image of a busy intersection is suggestive of the kinds of overlapping, crosscutting connections and agendas that help frame social life. The notion of "intersection" allows an appreciation of the fluidity in which culture is formed and the ways that a diverse set of discussions—in this instance, conversations that surround global traffic and the configuration of transnational zones of desire—get formed and reformed.

Travel, Status, and Desire: Trajectories in Feminist Theory

In a classic essay, "The Traffic in Women," anthropologist Gayle Rubin (1975) explores the implications of women's "travel" as objects of male-dominated sexual exchange. Rubin refers to an earlier essay in which Emma Goldman expresses concern about the trafficking of white women in prostitution. Many feminist theorists have pursued an interest in prostitution, but it is Rubin's contribution that brought the discussion of women's subordination back home. She moves from the existence of transnational sexual procurement to a theory of gender and desire. Where common morality condemns the long-distance circulation of prostitutes as unfortunate for women, Rubin argues instead that objectionable power asymmetries are crucial to every local context—in marriage as well as prostitution.

Rubin argues that gender asymmetries are formulated in particular *systems*, non-universal configurations of power and meaning. Rubin's work inspired a generation of feminist scholarship that analyzes the gender asymmetries of the local (e.g., Ortner and Whitehead 1981; MacCormack and Strathern 1980). At this point, feminists have returned to global questions; it makes sense to reconsider the wider reach of the original meaning of the "traffic in women." Rather than return to the assumption of universal gender hierarchies that Rubin disrupted, however, we must study both local and translocal elements of gender. The analysis must include simultaneous attention both to local contexts of power and meaning and to the translocal interchanges that both reaffirm and challenge locality. In this chapter I argue that this double focus can be achieved by specifying travel trajectories. This specification involves attention to their possibilities as well as their constraints; it highlights how power is shaped in relation to travel. In this we are able to see that the world is always localized at the same time as never closed.

Cultural theorist Janet Wolff (1995) suggests that travel is the key trope of many current theories of culture-making. Travel creates cosmopolitan subjects, subjects whose agency takes cultural difference in stride. This is the kind of agency intended to inhabit a culturally diverse world—that is, a world of divergent cultural positions as well as social locations. Cultural and social boundaries—and their crossings—are at the heart of the psychic formation of traveling subjects. These subjects cannot be imagined as coming into being in a closed cultural enclave—whether "Europe" or its Other, imagined as parallel universes. Any desires and fantasies that the traveling subject has are fundamentally patterned by social and cultural difference.

As Wolff further argues, traveling is imagined through a gendered history in which traveling and masculine agency are intertwined. In this formation, cultural stability is the imagined female to the traveling male. And even as this history is twisted and transformed to allow us to imagine women finding themselves through travel, these traveling women, like traveling men, must deal with the gendered history of travel. Wolff does not point out the ways that our imagination of travel assumes the mobility of a European passport. Yet the point is similar. African and European travelers alike must measure their different kinds of mobility against that historical standard. If agency and the ability to be a subject of desire are understood through mobility, then Africans and Europeans, and women and men, are each shaped within the forms of agency and desire developed in relationship to the kinds of mobility to which they can socially aspire. If desire involves traveling, it is always asymmetrical and social in relation to the social construction of travel.

Gayle Rubin's article continues to offer useful clues about how to approach this analysis. In an insightful reading within and across theoretical frameworks, the works of Levi-Strauss, Engels, and Lacan become central to her engagement with two major strands of feminist theory in the 1970s: structural Marxism and psychoanalysis. Levi-Strauss maintains that the exchange of women is central in the formation of culture. Where he naturalizes this exchange, however, Rubin pushes his ideas to show that the exchange of women is at the heart of specific forms of inequality. She argues that to understand male dominance, it is necessary to understand how women are traded as pawns in sex and marriage.

Drawing on Engels's emphasis on social location and on Lacan's emphasis on the centrality of a psychoanalytic approach to notions of psychic formation, Rubin's analysis moves in two important directions: first to show that the inequality involved in the exchange of women is linked to all other kinds of inequality, including class and rank, and second, that this inequality helps constitute the psyche in relationship to desire through the asymmetrical creation of men as the subjects of desire and women as the objects of men's desire. In Rubin's formulation, the "traffic in women" is at the heart of both social inequalities and the bodies and psyches through which we engage in them.

Although she links the social and the psyche in her analysis, Gayle Rubin stands at a bifurcation of positions within feminist theory that persisted through the end of the century. I frame these positions as those in which female agency is defined through status and social location on the one hand, and through fantasy and desire on the other. Theorists of these two directions often appear not to communicate with each other. Feminists interested in social location rarely pay adequate attention to either sexuality or fantasy, while theorists of desire, in their allegiance to psychoanalytic theory, have often had a limited appreciation of social difference beyond gender. Yet social location is constitutive of psychic subjectivity, and vice versa. Furthermore, attention to the gendered nature of geopolitical difference might reshape our theoretical insights concerning both social positioning and psychoanalysis.

In understanding Northern women and their Gambian male friends, Rubin's methodological approach is suggestive of how these theoretical dichotomies might be bridged. While the power relations between Africa and the West can be understood as an eroticized asymmetry, it is necessary that theories of desire take account of real men and women and their relationship to the discourses and institutions that shape attractiveness and availability. Theories of the intersection of race, class, and gender are notably weak in showing how sexuality is constructed and how sexual agency is created. Yet theories of desire have tended to ignore the specificities of culture, race, and class in favor of a universalized notion of the subject. In this formulation, fantasy is marked primarily through universalized notions of gender. The sexual adventures of Western women in

Africa are linked in part with the power asymmetries between Africa and the West as these reformulate male and female in significant distortions of European and American myths.

Efforts at joining psychoanalytic perspectives with materialist theories of identity have in recent years revitalized social theory. Two examples are worth noting. Ann McClintock's (1995) study of colonial Africa points to the centrality of the intersection of multiple social categories— race, class, gender and sexuality—in making colonial culture. Her analysis refuses the privileging of a single category of social location that can be read in any way other than complicated. She proposes the notion of situated psychoanalysis that can address what many perceive as the ahistoricity of psychoanalysis(McClintock 1995, 72). Kobena Mercer (1994) considers the meaning of sexual representation and the fetishization of the black male body in the photographic work of Robert Mapplethorpe. The presence of black men as objects of the gaze revises many early theories that naturalized a binary between men as gazers and women as objects of the gaze. Our early theoretical propositions can now be understood as more than parallel categories that can be added to in any simple manner. Rather, they shake the fundamental principles embedded in our social theories.

Fashioning Charismatic Style

The development of tourism in The Gambia is intimately linked to the end of a particular form of colonial presence. In the mid-1960s, Scandinavian charter companies began marketing The Gambia as an ideal vacation spot for Europeans during the winter months. Hotels were soon built to accommodate tourists, and by the early 1970s holiday visitors began arriving, particularly during the peak months of December to April (Wagner 1981, 1987, 1982; Brown 1992). Initially, much of the control of the tourist industry was in the hands of foreign companies. Lacking the resources and the infrastructure to control the industry placed The Gambia in a vulnerable position, and charter tours organized and facilitated by European nationals continue to jeopardize Gambian control of financial revenue and employment opportunities. Upper-level management positions are usually reserved for expatriates, while Gambians, primarily men, work in restaurants and hotels as service staff, hotel security guards, and taxi drivers. Perhaps a more inclusive sector for women is the tourist markets adjacent to villages such as Bakau where textiles and garden vegetables produced by women's cooperatives are marketed to tourists (Wagner 1982; Schroeder 1999).

Tourism, however, provides a measure of employment in a job market that is otherwise tenuous. Even as the largest employer, the Gambian government cannot support the burden of the population needing jobs. Most people are relegated to the non-self-sustaining agricultural economy; few regularized employment opportunities exist. Increasingly, youth migrate to urban areas in search of alternatives to farming. An outgrowth of the service industry is the presence of what Wagner (1982) refers to as "professional friends" who move alongside tourism yet outside many of the formal aspects of the system. These "friends" are not paid wages, their services are multiple, and they can be compensated in a number of ways.

Many male youths, generally between the ages of sixteen and twenty-five, are part of a "professional friend" circuit. (The sociological literature also refers to them as "bumpsters"[Brown 1992].) These young men comb the beaches and hang around hotels in search of potential "friends." They are often prohibited from entering hotels. Thus they stand outside hotel entrances waiting for tourists who, upon exiting, encounter a number of boys and men approaching with such welcoming phrases as "Hello, I want to be your friend; I want to show you around The Gambia. I can make your stay very nice." Relationships formed between tourists and bumpsters can include a number of activities. They act as tour guides to both men and women, as interpreters and negotiators between local people and tourists, as facilitators of sexual liaisons for male travelers who seek female companions, and as escorts for tourist women to the night life in The Gambia.

Some bumpsters also seek involvement in romantic affairs with women tourists who potentially have the resources to help them travel. Indeed, with the arrival of each tour group, bumpsters scan the scene for prospective patrons. Two brothers interviewed in one magazine article spoke of surveying the possibilities in a recently arrived group of tourists. With a sense of confidence, they walked up and down the beach and commented on two middle-aged women guests. One said, "She's a new arrival—she's still white—and she's ready for it. . . . She's been here before. I bet she hasn't unpacked yet, she's so eager to be picked up by one of us." The second commented, "She's a first timer, but she's up to it. You can tell by looking at her. I'll know more when I speak to her. You always know if they want sex when you look into their eyes—there's an invitation" (Simon and John, quoted in Aziz 1994, 12). From the perspective of these professional friends, all tourist women are potential sexual partners.[2]

Most Gambians respond to bumpster activity with ambivalence. Male elders are often urged to enforce sanctions against them, and they are disparaged by the state as well as the ministry of tourism. In 1989, after increasing reports by tourists of being harassed, bumpsters were targeted and a few were detained for hours by the police. The police officers were soon deployed to patrol the beaches. In addition, the ministry of tourism attempted a registry of guides to make the status of bumpsters official by providing identity badges and uniforms. But bumpsters soon rejected the ministry's efforts. After all, such policies could not accommodate their crafted efforts of individual style and the appeal of both pleasure and danger. The threat bumpsters pose appears formidable to Gambian officials. The 1989 conflict mobilized some of the bumpsters' mothers who supported their sons' activities by staging a protest at a major hotel.[3] In a more recent sweep that was part of one of the government's clean-up campaigns, prostitutes and cannabis smokers—that is, men with long dreadlocks—were targeted and their heads were shaved (Reuters Aug. 16,1994). These men became a visible sign of what was responsible for the crisis in the national consciousness.[4]

Bumpsters are symbols in another sense as well. The young Gambian men I knew were not bumpsters, but they identified deeply with the dilemmas of bumpsters. Like bumpsters, they saw available forms of employment as unstable and inadequate. They hoped for a lucky break, usually imagined as a tie with a foreign acquaintance, that would make it possible for them to either gather some capital or, better yet, leave the country for employment in the North. They told stories of possible romances or marriages with Northern women as a way to make a new life. And at the same time they also laughed and scoffed at Northern women, whom they considered dissolute and morally decadent. The stories of these men—not bumpsters themselves but rather those who shared the bumpsters' dilemmas—are the subject of my analysis.

The men themselves pointed me toward the national significance of their stories. One friend joked about the long line of Gambians that formed early in the morning outside the American embassy as people hoped for the miraculous charisma to convince embassy officials to offer them a trip to the United States. Romantic hope in the Gambia, he argued, was caught up in leaving—or forming ties with powerful foreigners. His comment brings the representation and performance of "Africa" back to the surface—at the beach, at hotel entrances, and in front of the embassy.

Crossing Conversations of Desiring Subjects

My inclusion of stories as a critical point of negotiation between social science "facts" and literary "allegory" owes a great deal to the work of Tsing (1993), whose use of stories effectively illustrates the importance of crosstalk and overlapping agendas in the ways that social worlds are constructed by those we interview, as well as by the anthropologists themselves. Within the space of structural figurings, Tsing urges us to appreciate how subjects actively contest, talk back, refigure, or just comment on the social worlds they inhabit. In the following sections I present four stories, each representative of a genre that I heard a number of times. I recount them here in parable form to protect the identity of my informants. More important than details of identity is how the narratives become national and continental allegories that express much larger concerns than the dilemmas of individuals. As I mentioned previously, deep distinctions separate the stories Gambian men told me about men and those told about women. The storytellers recounted men's travels as stories of masculine agency and national dilemmas. Men's liaisons were presented as entrepreneurial strategies and career moves, with contradictory aspects and feminizing qualities. (This feminization is created in the unequal relations between the North and South.) Despite nationalist claims like those of President Jammeh that men should not be a part of these encounters, young men were drawn to this activity. In contrast, the stories of women travelers were commonly relayed by Gambian men and women as if the women were moral transgressors. The stories emphasized the inappropriateness of female travelers and the problem of their lack of containability, understood simply as promiscuity.

Significantly, these stories crosscut or reinterpret stories that Northern women travelers tell of the search for self-fulfillment, knowledge, and power. The tourist gaze becomes the medium for creating contradictory stories of national agency. For men, the crucial skill is the ability to fashion oneself as the bearer of natural charisma.

Intimate stories of the adventures of women travelers to The Gambia were somewhat more difficult for me to come by than those of Gambian men. My research required close work with Gambian men, which was disturbed by my occasional attempt to interview tourist women. Indeed, it became essential to my research rapport to separate myself from tourist women. And yet I, too, as an anthropologist traveling without the guardianship of a male protector, was implicated in many of the same ways as other women travelers.

One particularly useful source in constructing the story of women as travelers presented itself in an article in *Marie Claire*, a monthly women's magazine marketed as being about "real fashions, real stories, real women." The article, "Seeking Sex in the Gambia," offers possibilities for understanding these transnational connections from the point of view of women travelers (Aziz 1994). The "reportage," as *Marie Claire* calls it, fits into a genre of popular-magazine storytelling much like that of *Cosmopolitan*, where the agency of women is supported and encouraged through a certain bravery, badness, and more blatant eroticism than what is allowed in "conventional" ideals of femininity.

The women tourists interviewed in *Marie Claire* appear as allegorical figures of female travel, nomadic subjects who challenge the confining boundaries of marriage and home. The article is surrounded by a number of photos of European women informants and their Gambian friends. The women speak frankly about their sexual desires. The quotation that opened this essay is that of Mary, a fifty-eight-year-old art dealer who travels to Gambia twice a year in search of Gambian men. Mary initially traveled with her husband, and she and her spouse once accepted an offer to be escorted by a young Gambian man. After her husband grew tired of sightseeing, Mary desired to travel with their guide on her own.

> Towards the end of our holiday my husband just wanted to lie on the beach, so I went out with Mace on my own. He offered to take me to less touristy beaches and I agreed. Once we were alone it all happened quickly, on the beach, under the palm trees. Afterwards I was shocked but I wanted more. My husband lost interest in sex a long time ago, and after my encounter with Mace I realized how much I missed it and how important it was to me. (Aziz 1994, 12).

Initially, Mary was reluctant to tell friends about her adventures, but once she confided in a few friends, they cheered her on. One of her friends expressed a desire to join her on a future trip to The Gambia. She, too, found the prospect of having a Gambian friend inviting, for her husband too had long tired of sex. Mary insists that she is committed to her marriage and in fact her travels to The Gambia strengthen their marriage (Aziz 1994, 12).

Other stories, however, suggest that there is more to women's travel than new sexual encounters. "I didn't come with the intention of picking up someone," one woman tries to explain (Aziz 1994, 16). But the reporter is mainly interested in their sexual bravery. Their vulnerabilities and dreams of romance and self-fulfillment must slip through the lines of the "reportage." Women speak, for example, of being left by husbands after several years of marriage for younger women. The Gambian men, at least initially, seemed devoted to them. So captivated by the attention are they that some of the women go to great lengths to keep their connections alive. They speak of working three jobs—even five— to bring their Gambian friends to Europe. They mention public disapproval, the rejection of their families, and their hopes for an alternative to the loneliness of their ordinary lives. Unlike male sex tourists, at least in stereotype, many are hoping that their Gambian lovers will really turn out to be the loves of their lives. They are willing to work hard to fulfill their boyfriends' desires to return with them to Europe—even though they know the men might leave them for someone younger and more desirable once there.

Strategies of Entrepreneurial Romance

I return to Gambian men's stories. One of the narratives I heard during my fieldwork was of a man I will refer to as Lamin Sane, who was eager to go to Sweden to find a wife, that is, as my associates told me, a patron.[5] Unlike many men his age, he could pay for the trip on his own because he had recently inherited control of the family assets. As with an investment, he tried to increase his possibilities through finding a wealthy donor. This story was whispered about since, in order for Lamin Sane to pursue his marriage dreams and schemes in Sweden, he had to divorce his Gambian wife. He did divorce her, although everyone said that his wife was unaware of his action. (Yet one wonders how much a story can circulate before it comes back to haunt. After all, I heard the story from more than a few people). Should he need to present divorce papers to prove he was able to marry while in Sweden, he could do so. His wife, thinking this was a business trip—and perhaps in a way it was—went to the airport with all of his well-wishers. Like those who went by invitation to Europe, Lamin Sane had the same dreams of catching a woman and marrying her. He was at a disadvantage, however, because he did not come with the necessary contacts to provide him with an entree into the society. An important facilitator for many of the travelers is a host, and without this Lamin Sane's journey was made more difficult. He traveled on a three-month tourist visa to Sweden where he stayed with friends and distant relatives, but he was unsuccessful in his marriage attempts and at the end of the three months, he returned to The Gambia to resume his regular routine—and his marriage.

   In stories such as this one, men are smart enough to outmaneuver Gambian wives but not always successful in netting foreign patrons. Stories of men and their dreams of travel and attachment tell us about the ways that men are vulnerable as well as tricky in these encounters. Subordination is created in part through the marginal and dependent status of the Gambian economy. Gambia remains a neocolonial outpost with no industry and no sustaining means of support other than a personalistic economy. Catching women is one option within a niche of desperate strategies to make ends meet. Yet I would caution that we not reduce these relationships to mere utility. Worth considering is the integral part a fashioned identity plays; men imaginatively create themselves as cultural ambassadors, crafting Africa as well as their own Africanness. Complicated constructions of masculinity are operating as masculine identity is often constituted through travel. Again, however, we are reminded of the difference between these travelers and the relative ease we have come to associate with European men's ability to travel.

Dilemmas of a Kept Man

"It is really tragic," Malimin Keita, one of my associates, said to me one day as he told me of a friend who had traveled to Denmark to be with a woman he had met while she was vacationing in The Gambia. "He has to stay at home all day while his wife goes out to work. And she expects him to sweep the floors and do the housework and watch television all day. And when the lady comes home, he says, all she wants to do is have sex. She won't stop even if he tells her he is tired. The only time he is let out of the house is to go to language class twice a week."

I tried to express my sympathy for Malimin's friend's predicament as a "kept man," while at the same time I was exploring further the meaning of this gender-inverted image of domestic constraint. Over the next few months, I frequently heard this kind of story. Curious, I asked about the experiences of others and how such encounters were made. Malimin explained, "Often white ladies come on holiday and meet up with men here. While a lady is in The Gambia before she leaves for home the man will try to get her address and he will write to her. He may write many letters, and they will correspond for a time, and then hopefully he will be invited to come to where she is. Then if he is really lucky he can stay long enough to get a resident's permit, and then he can stay. Sometimes people get married."

Other accounts of Gambian men traveling to Europe and the difficult life they lead there are offered by Wagner and Yamba (1986). They confirm the vulnerability of Gambian emigrants, who often lack access to social services, suffer from discrimination, and have few legal rights and recourses. Men often express a sense of loneliness and isolation as many of their women hosts work much of the time. Often arriving without appropriate language skills, they find that life is difficult. One fifty-six-year-old woman regularly sent her twenty-five-year-old Gambian partner out on Sunday afternoons when her adult sons came to visit. Thus, her circles of friends and family members were not a source for integrating her Gambian partner.

The clubs frequented by Africans provide a way for Gambians to meet fellow countrymen. Wagner and Yamba explain this as one option to isolation. While this may appear to be the solution to the sense of isolation many men experience because of language and social barriers, these clubs can also become threatening to one's ability to stay in Europe. As one meets other Gambians, often in the same vulnerable position of seeking a resident's permit, one is also meeting men who might vie for the same position with a woman. For example, while one man was at work someone called his partner to say he had been seen with another woman.

This led to his being kicked out by his partner and eventually being deported (Wagner and Yamba 1986, 213). Other men find the company of younger women in the clubs appealing and seek the friendship of these women over that of their older companions. This, too, jeopardizes the relationship and the critical probationary period before a man receives a resident's permit.

The story of Malimin's friend suggests a reversal of sorts: his friend was relegated to doing housework. Malimin commented, "Can you imagine, he's treated like a woman. He was locked in all day with nothing to do but watch television, and upon the friend's return all she wants is sex." Read as an allegory of power and difference and not simply as an account of fact, the powerlessness of the Gambian émigré is expressed in what are familiar categories generally associated with women in both The Gambia and the West. Indeed, while travel affords men agency, as the story is told, this mobility also places them in the position of women.

In considering the allegorical nature of such tales, remember that the European women may have other stories to tell. A tour organizer quoted in the *Marie Claire* article reports, "The British embassy here has loads of letters from women in the UK complaining that the boys have stayed in bed all the time, or disappeared—mostly with someone younger" (Aziz 1994, 16). Domestic imprisonment from the perspective of the men may look like laziness to the women. But these differences are even clearer in relation to the stories Gambian men tell about women.

"True-Life Adventures" of Lovely Laura

As women pursue their goal of self-fulfillment through travel, they are often drawn into stories not always of their own choosing. I heard a number of stories that spoke past each other on the subject of toubobs "Europeans." One example of crosstalk in these narratives is the story of a woman commonly referred to as Lovely Laura. The way her name was used in conversation suggested that she was not considered very lovely. Indeed, she became an exemplar of all of the aspects associated with Western women. New installments were regularly added to the "Lovely Laura stories," comparable to the fascination embodied in *Soap Opera Digest*.

Laura was a comparatively well-off English woman who had been married and divorced. In the settlement her husband had given her enough money to travel. My friends said, with dripping sarcasm, that Lovely Laura came to The Gambia every three months or so to find a new boyfriend. Each time she came she would invite the newest one to visit her in England. "When she tires of them she throws them out and then soon returns to The Gambia to find another friend."

One person telling this story, a man just turning twenty, projected many of his fears onto this symbol of Northern promiscuity. He spoke of his own hesitation in entertaining a Laura fantasy. In his words, "Any woman who has slept with that many men could be passing on disease." With repugnance, he said, "I wouldn't have anything to do with her." Still, while the gossips talked and people found her behavior distasteful, Lovely Laura was treated like a queen by all in her presence, but mouths flew fast about her latest conquest as soon as she left. In this narrative she represents the double edge of power and danger.

Lovely Laura raises a number of questions about what it means for women to travel and to travel alone. Both as a woman of means and a decidedly unruly woman—that is, one whose movements are not confined by the sanction of marriage—she was a woman out of place. She could play at the margins unavailable to most local women and still, at least to her face, be treated as a respectable woman—her national status offering a momentary reprieve. Yet by local standards, any woman unattached to a man was suspect; for respectable, local women, having multiple male partners was out of the question. Fortunately for Lovely Laura, however, there was never a lack of male companionship, and her money continued to allow her to appear to rise above the stories. These stories, however, also spoke of the disdain people felt toward her, particularly the elders and women without the same privilege she had. One commentator described the Western women's attittude as "the rudeness of foreign women who flaunt their naked bodies and love affairs in the face of the people." Though her journey was always described in sexual terms, she, like many women, did not see her travels as simply sexual. Sex was only one part of a larger project of self-discovery.[6] Women such as Lovely Laura are drawn to Africa in part because of their desire to learn about the "real Africa." Thus Lovely Laura was not easy to classify as "culturally insensitive." She occupied the more contradictory position of a "woman out of place."

White women traveling in Africa feel empowered in searching for male lovers because they can expect these men to accompany them on their own terms. These women do not have to feel constrained in the ways they might at home. Similarly, Gambian men find their agency from accessing their situation as dependent entrepreneurs. As allegorical figures, unruly Western women and African trickster men come together to negotiate their attraction. Although these singular constructions of men as tricksters and women as unruly are somewhat reductive, they do challenge the common presumption that power structures allow us to easily separate oppressor and oppressed. Scholars and activists are often better at pointing to victims than seeing complex negotiations. This is true of both the feminist literature and the growing body of literature focused on non-Western men and Western women.

Yet in these transnational relationships, Gambian men and Western women each have a different notion of what is happening. Each imagines himself or herself evading or escaping the worst aspects of domination. In the misunderstandings and overlaps between these two forms of agency, both the pleasure and the danger of the relationship develop. Women believe they are escaping the patriarchy of their homeland just as men believe they are escaping national inequality. While Northern women describe themselves as strong in their beliefs and determination, African men speak of the women as a means to a national, entrepreneurial end.

Hopes, Dreams, and Aspirations

The situation becomes even more complicated once we take into account that not all women from the North in The Gambia are white. One significant group of women travelers in The Gambia are African Americans. Since the publication of *Roots* (Haley 1976) and the airing of its television version (in 1977), African Americans have visited The Gambia as a site in which to envision an African home. In many cases, African American women travel without male escorts; indeed, many hope that this site of "home" will also be a site for kinds of female empowerment not always available in their other, more mundane home across the Atlantic. Yet the travels of these African American women are subject to the same interpretations in the stories of Gambian men as are those of white women. To many Gambians, African American women are just another kind of promiscuous toubob, for the mark of difference is wealth and mobility.

Furaha Salim traveled as an assistant to a Gambian artist-entrepreneur on one of his brief trips home to The Gambia. Like many African Americans who visit Africa in search of their ancestral home and a sense of connection, she too thought this would be an opportunity to reconnect with Africa. Even her Africanized name suggested her pan-Africanist dreams and her efforts to redraw family ties with Africa. Yet her dreams were not those of her hosts.

I first met Furaha Salim during a debate she was having with an distinguished older Gambian man while she was trying to convince him of her thoughts on women's agency. She thought that it was unfair that women could not have as many husbands as men could have wives. Unlike European missionaries, she was uninterested in forcing African men into monogamy. Instead, she endorsed what she thought of as an egalitarian but "African" alternative: multiple spouses all around. She pressed her point through a refrain: "Every woman has the right to her own hopes, dreams, and aspirations." Meanwhile, I sat uncomfortably, caught between her opinion—a version of a womanist perspective—and the Mandinka views with which I had become familiar. Although I understood her position and the intervention she was trying to make, I also sensed that she was quickly beginning to represent what some Gambians perceive as the arrogance of Northern women. Though the older man remained polite, clearly he was not at ease with the conversation.

Furaha Salim was intent on exploring Africa and her own "hopes, dreams, and aspirations" during her brief stay in The Gambia. She had decided to accompany a Gambian artist after meeting him in the United States earlier in the year. Their friendship, at least in her understanding, was platonic. For her, this was a trip home with a distant relative, so to speak. The gap in understanding became clear, however, when I heard of what was seen as her unruly behavior from Boubacar, the artist. He approached me about the problem of her staying out all night, "sleeping with any man she could find." These were not important men, he suggested, but bus drivers and the like. He asked if I could speak to her and tell her to stop. "She is a mother with a husband at home; her husband entrusted her care to me." It was not clear to me that she was the loose woman that he indicated, and when she told me her version, I learned, as I suspected, that she had not been "running about as a prostitute," "dating man after man," as Boubacar had repeatedly suggested. Rather she said she had been "talking" to a man from a different ethnic group—which infuriated her host. Furaha was aware of the tension this created both for her host and for his family. She insisted, however, that Boubacar was not going to control her. "Every woman," she said, "has a right to her own hopes, dreams, and aspirations."

Boubacar was humiliated by a woman he obviously could not control. The public display of her independence, even more than her actual behavior, threatened his stature as head of a household. As he told his friend of her offensive behavior, thinking that I did not understand, he again expressed his disgust. His speech helped me to understand some of the contradictions of the situation. He had used the lure of family and home to get her to come to Africa and had assumed that she understood what his obligations and expectations of her were. Her behavior, however, soon came to seem to him to resemble toubob behavior—just another sign of the West. For him, she showed that sense of European privilege that appears to prioritize individual desire over all others, and that takes advantage of mobility when others are bound by many constraints.

Lovely Laura and Furaha Salim, as women travelers, carried parallel imaginings of Africa—an imagined Africa of free expression and sensuality. Africa is that primordial place where one can transcend the confines of a constricted life in the North. Though they came with different agendas, Laura and Furaha were quickly joined in a set of tales that spoke of their blatant disregard for appropriate feminine behavior. Although aware of the constraints placed on local women, they saw themselves as liberated and even as creating possibilities for other women through their behavior. Yet neither woman could easily befriend Gambian women, for their presence and actions made even more apparent the restrictions on Gambian women's lives.

Anthropologist Anna Tsing (1993) asks a series of questions that illustrate some of the overlapping and contradictory aspects of women travelers and women anthropologists. Where does the woman anthropologist stand in this story as she listens to the construction of Western women since she herself is "out-of-place"? Lovely Laura was more than a passing visitor; she returned many times and tried to incorporate herself—at considerable expense—into the same compound. She, not unlike myself, was trying to develop an understanding of Africa through a process familiar to anthropologists—social immersion. While I listened to the stories of her transgressive behavior, I could not stand outside of this commentary on North-South relations; rather, I was deeply implicated as well. While a man's status and reputation could be made through travel and adventure, and to a certain extent through heroic tales of conquest, a woman's reputation would be drawn through a series of derogatory characterizations and exaggerated tales of bad behavior. Lovely Laura served as a reminder of what happens to the reputation of unruly women. Again, the gendered power dynamics, once shifted, do not simply reverse the effects of the story.

The dilemmas here for the woman anthropologist—and particularly an African American woman anthropologist—appear even more starkly. African American women tourists in The Gambia are engaged in a search for African culture, a culture that will help them alter their own U.S. predicament. How different is the task of anthropology, the discipline that describes cultures by illuminating their differences from a European standard? And what of the African American feminist anthropologist who intervenes in the discipline to show the power and plurality of transnational spaces? These are questions that cannot be avoided as I describe how African American women's attempts to build a bridge of cultural knowledge in The Gambia are insistently and repetitively reinterpreted as promiscuity. These reinterpretations are ones I too must negotiate.

Rethinking Transnational Sex and Desire

Transnational sexual encounters have been considered more frequently in the context of Northern male travelers and Southeast Asian women than in the context of Africa, and this Southeast Asian discussion serves as the basis for much of the literature on international sexual relations. The images of Southeast Asian women traded and claimed by Western as well as Japanese men have become almost cliché: sex tourism, prostitution, and mail-order brides dominate the global representation of international sexual liaisons. In this global imaginary, Asian women become objects of the Western male gaze; they are fashioned as sexual commodities for "white" male desires (Lee 1991; Enloe 1990; Hall 1994; Odzer 1994). In many instances, attention to women as sexual objects in the global economy remind us of the intertwined relationship among travel, national development schemes, and the sexual services of "local" women in easing national debt.

Yet in most of the studies of the international sex industry, many of the authors take as a starting point the parallelism of power differences between men and women on the one hand, and the West and Asia on the other; Asian women are vulnerable in the same ways as Western women, but even more so. The politics of representation is key because women are seen as desirable especially *because* they are imagined as docile and obedient as a result of their Asianness. In this imagined geography, men are seen as active agents and women as passive victims.

Theories of international sexuality and national and class differences have tended to assume that internationalization brings an increasing homogenization of the sexual (Barry 1984). This assumption parallels in many ways what many have come to think about the penetration of the market in relationship to capitalism; the market is a homogenizing force, creating a singular global culture (Jameson 1991). Indeed, the market and sexuality come together in the discussion of international sexuality because most discussions focus on the tourist industry and prostitution, that is, on commercialized sexualities. The international prostitute appears as the sign of a global circulation of sexuality in which local cultural markers seem increasingly archaic. Just as scholars have tended not to look at the localization of capitalism but instead assumed the unified nature of capitalism as a homogeneous cultural and political economy (Gibson-Graham 1996), discussions of the international commodification of sexuality also assume a homogeneous logic. This assumption, however, creates a single and monolithic standard of the sexual. Sexual meanings, forms, and identities are assumed to be constructed through an imagined single logic. My argument, in contrast, calls attention to the specificity of sexualities across national boundaries. Rather than thinking of a homogeneous global sphere of circulation, it is critical to attend to the localizing processes in which particular male and female sexualities are discursively and institutionally created. In The Gambia, international sexualities are not merely commodified reinforcements of Western contrasts between male sexual subjectivity and female sexual objectification.

As Southeast Asian prostitutes and mail-order brides begin to organize, they insist on their own agency. As long as they are considered victims, they can only bemoan their situations, not improve them. Yet despite
the attempts of feminist scholars to participate in this rethinking, our
scholarly tools have not been very helpful. We can think only of "agency"
as erasing "oppression"; where a clear power imbalance exists, we reason-
ably want to show cohesion and vulnerability, not self-fashioning. The
Gambian "traffic" I describe is perhaps different enough to be illuminating. Imagining any of the participants as victims is difficult, for none will
let themselves be described that way. Power differences, instead, are inscribed in different configurations of mobility. And agency involves the
storytelling events in which all participants negotiate contact despite differences in power and perspective.

Rather than beginning with "women" and " men" as universal categories, I have argued that we need to think through different kinds of
travel and their possibilities and limitations. Travel trajectories are trajectories of desire in transnational space, yet they are neither homogeneous
nor stable. The narratives people tell of their own and others' travels are
key to our understandings of these trajectories because narratives help us
see the flow of hopes, dreams, and aspirations, which can make power
asymmetries both livable and intolerable, both reminding us of our constraints and our chances for freedom. The contradictory and unequal narratives I have described here chart out a space worth fighting over—in
coups, love affairs, and, indeed, cultural analysis.

CHAPTER SEVEN

Tourists as Pilgrims

You are on a pilgrimage, not a safari.
—tour guide, Heritage Tours

Africa captures the imagination and travel itineraries of a range of consumers, among which are African American tourists. Several West African countries have attempted to develop an aspect of their tourist ventures by making explicit the connection between African Americans and Africa. Some of these ties are facilitated with the help of multinational sponsorship that rarely leads to sustained interest on the part of the company in participating in the dreams of African national projects. This final chapter describes and analyzes a corporate-sponsored homeland tour for the purposes of exploring both the context and the specificity of contemporary transatlantic imaginings primarily created for and by African Americans. I analyze a "homeland" journey made by African American tourists to Senegambia, the region so critical to the story of *Roots* (Haley 1976). Performance and representation once again frame the significance of an imagined Africa.

Places, histories, and subjectivities are brought alive in this encounter through the convergence of ethnoscapes, finance capital, and crosscutting histories that make for an alluring adventure. Travelers, tour guides, local market people, and transnational corporate sponsors stage and, indeed, perform ideas about Africa and the United States within the frame of the journey. At the center of my discussion are questions about identity formation, global politics, and the culture of capitalism. Not incidental to the ways Africa circulates in wide-ranging contexts are the ties forged between African Americans and people residing on the continent. These alliances and disjunctures are critical sites in which to see the negotiation of "Africa" within the global politics of the Atlantic.[1]

In this chapter, I follow a McDonald's advertising campaign and sponsored tour that successfully gathered together a group of African Americans and created a sense of diasporic identities. The formation of these identities relied on an historical connection of African Americans to Africa. The collective removal of Africans from the continent centuries ago during slavery leaves many African Americans with a sense of longing. The homeland tour was successful in producing deep feelings and a sense of transformed identity because it mobilized familiar images, symbols, narratives, and artifacts to stage events that could function as transformative personal "experience" (Scott 1994; Hall 1990).[2] The commercial campaign began this process by bringing together the group and formulating their common project. Still, this was not enough. The tour itself was carefully crafted as a Turnerian "ritual process" in which stages of separation, liminality, and reintegration with transformation were used to press the participants to rearticulate their identities within particular narratives of family and homeland—narratives that allowed the participants to reaffirm their sense of being successful American consumers but with a culturally privileged difference.[3]

The wealth of familiar and powerful public imagery used during the tour—concerning slavery as well as images of "African culture"—came together with the materiality of the tourist visit to produce a sense of personal involvement. The tourist as pilgrim, produced as a frame of experience, in turn enabled the trope of collective memory, the central trope of African American identity discourse, both as oppositional creed and American affirmation (Fabre and O'Meally 1994; Roach 1996).

The sponsorship of this tour plays a critical part in the story of the event; its very existence had much to do with the McDonald's corporation. Ironically, in many places around the world McDonald's has become a symbol of U.S. imperialist commercial domination. But in tours such as the one described here, McDonald's has become an enabler of minority U.S. cultural identities. Cultural histories and commercialism are here simultaneous figured. Through an explication of the tour, I illustrate the processes of how "culture" becomes a commodified object. I explore how despite the promotional aspects of the tour, deeply felt affirmations of identities also developed. I probe the relationship among multinational capital, local marketing schemes, and African American participation in contemporary global marketing visions, and a world set in motion through the presence of Alex Haley's project, *Roots*.

The heritage tour brought ninety-six U.S. citizens, eighty-nine of whom were African Americans, to Senegal and The Gambia in the summer of 1994. Participants ranged in age from a nine-year-old to a woman in her early nineties, although nearly all were between the ages of thirty and forty-five. The overwhelming majority were women. Visits to a fifteenth-century slave fort, contemporary markets, an orphanage, and villages all framed the experience, inducing for many an emotionally charged moment of reflection and immersion. Travel routes in such contemporary "return" journeys to the continent are maps of collective memory; the visit becomes a "revisit " with aims to attend to the trauma created by the capturing of African bodies taken to the New World as slaves.

Yet it was difficult to ignore our sponsorship by the giant hamburger chain. The most intimate memories of reunion with "Mother Africa" were moments anticipated by clever marketing strategies, moments that helped create what McDonald's has called, in another context, "McMemories™." In the context of the tour, transnational trends and ideas about culture and identity converged with the strategies of multinational capitalists, the dreams of diasporic communities, and the income-generating plans of African national governments to produce Africa as a commodified cultural object of global significance.

Such heritage tours as this one merge stories of remembered slave journeys with the contemporary physicality of Africa, thus creating a subjective sense of newly experienced remembrance. At the same time, the tours provoke varied and complicated responses among participants; the experience can prompt crises and a sense of contradiction even as the journey carries the participants through the rites of passage that allow them to experience Africa as home. In the liminal space created by this particular tour, notions of self and community were called into question and, at least momentarily, sedimented ideas about Africa's meaning emerged and became a site for critical engagement and reassessment of our divergent histories.

Most of the travelers on the tour were winners of a contest sponsored by McDonald's during African American History Month. McDonald's had launched radio campaigns in selected cities, and used a number of strategies to select contest winners. Some contestants were required to answer questions about African American historical figures, while others were asked to explain why they wanted to go to Africa. Still others were randomly chosen as part of a phone queue. Forty-one winners, each of whom could bring a guest, were eventually selected. The winners came from Los Angeles, Chicago, New York, and elsewhere; notably, all of the white participants came from small towns in Mississippi, North Carolina, and Oregon. The selection process provided a cross-section of age, class, and racial group distinctions among the participants.

Not all of the travelers, however, were winners of the contest. Also along on the tour were members of Alex Haley's family, a member of the original *Roots* cast, and a biographer of Alex Haley who was making the trip to meet informants who had assisted Haley with the research for *Roots*. In addition, the group included members of the major Chicago-based African American advertising agency that had helped arrange the contest, who came along to facilitate the logistics of the tour; an editor from a popular African American women's monthly journal; and two academics (including me).[4] For this wide assortment of Americans, the pilgrimage tour offered a number of expected and unexpected connections.

The ten-day trip was facilitated by William Haley, the son of Alex Haley, who undertook the project in his recent turn to tourism. When I inquired how McDonald's had become the sponsor of the trip, Mr. Haley explained that in response to a suggestion made at a McDonald's executive board meeting, a proposal was drafted and accepted that requested the corporation's support in sponsoring a contest during African American History Month. The prize: a trip to West Africa. Haley added that McDonald's had agreed to an initial commitment of sponsorship for three years. The plans and details of the tour were to be handled by a prominent Chicago-based African American advertising agency.

From the perspective of the majority of the tourists, the most striking aspect of the tour was the immediacy of "The Africa." The tour allowed travelers to experience Africa with a sense of awe and wonderment. From my perspective, as I had already spent time in The Gambia, the most striking aspect of the tour was its ability to allow many of the travelers to see exactly what they already believed Africa to be: a poor, struggling, hot, spiritual, creative place, full of sound and color. Some of the responses people expressed as we moved about Senegal reflected this view. "The Africa" that travelers experienced was an Africa of tour brochures, television, films, coffee table books, and African American magazines. The tour created photo opportunities into which travelers could insert themselves, thus reproducing familiar images to enhance the personal intensity of experience.

For most of the travelers this was their first actual experience of being in Africa, but this Africa had already been virtually scripted by media-generated images and stories. Furthermore, the tour itself played an important role in structuring the perspectives of the travelers by shuttling them with care and efficiency from one impressive and vaguely familiar site to another. In my account, I recapitulate the stops along the tour to illustrate how it helped shape the subjectivities of the travelers, including my own. My aim here is to convey this encounter with Africa within a "structure of feeling" that produced a longing for place and identity. At the end of the chapter I look at how the tour aimed to produce a distinctively American longing for place and identity even as it staged encounters in the realm of "African" culture.

The itinerary of the tour was designed by organizers from a company in Senegal, Heritage Tours, in conjunction with the organizers in the United States. Strikingly, however, the organizers seem to have consciously modeled the tour on the classic rites of passage as described by Van Gennep (1960 [1909]) and interpreted in several works of Victor Turner (1969). As I recount aspects of the tour in an effort to suggest the multilayered dimensions of the "return" journey—as in a familiar Turnerian ritual process—framed by tour guides, I also analyze how temporal and spatial disjunctures that we experienced throughout the journey are conjoined at the end of the trip through participation to create a sense of transformation and reintegration, again anticipated by Van Gennep's and Turner's discussions.[5]

The Turnerian structure of ritual as well as its commercialism helps to set the frame for a discussion of diasporic dreams and desires. Yet the tour as ritual would have been less satisfying had it not brought together a rich and sometimes contradictory set of images, expectations, aspirations, and self-making projects. The travel encounters could not be restrained by the plans of the tour guides. My interpretation, then, must consider the participants' conflicting experiences. By including particular participants' activities in my description of the tour, I show how the tour worked—both in and beyond the intentions of its planners.

Separation

The first task of the tour organizers began before we left the United States and offered participants a sense of common purpose: the recovery of our historical ties to Africa. An orientation session offered contestants ideas about the proper way to approach Africa. This was not the imagined Africa of wild jungles; rather, it was an Africa that was the site of a great civilization. As students of African heritage, we were encouraged to be respectful of the legacy of great kingdoms, "queendoms," and royal lineages that framed this vision. There was no better place to convince the travelers of this splendid heritage than the Schomberg Museum in Harlem, New York, the site of one of the major archives of African American culture and history, a place where culture, at least for some, can be considered in a context of high reverence, a fitting place for the trip's beginning.

The evening before our scheduled departure to Dakar, a reception was held at the Schomberg for the travelers. This send-off reception was the first time the tourists had met, and provided a chance for members of the group, with their diverse individual experiences, to receive an initial tutoring session in the shared meaning of Africa. The reception was an elaborate affair, with musical performances and speeches and invited guests to wish us a safe journey. This event was designed to set a tone for the journey as a whole; Africa, in this imagined space, was a place to be revered. To chronicle their impressions and personal experiences of "home," winners were presented with imitation African kente-cloth-covered travel journals.

The travelers I spoke to were impressed by this elaborate send-off party, although some also found the event uncomfortable. Although it provided an initial cohort-forming moment, the opening ceremony left

many of the participants with mixed feelings about what they were supposed to do during the reception. Some of the people I spoke to after the
gala said that they felt intimidated; some even felt alienated. One contest
winner compared the event to a gallery opening for an exclusive art show,
and she wondered why she had been asked to attend. "It seemed like just
another high art event, at an exclusive club that I wasn't a member of."
Even as a unifying event, the reception thus highlighted differences, "distinctions" reminiscent of Bourdieu's (1984) discussion about class and
cultural capital. Cultural capital, exposed through class and regional differences, would surface repeatedly for members throughout the trip despite the organizers' best intentions to create a unified community. At this
early point, however, much deeper displacements were required for the
group to begin to feel the unity of the pilgrimage.

The following morning we boarded an *Air Afrique* plane in New York
City and by afternoon arrived at Joof International Airport in Dakar,
Senegal. When we disembarked in Senegal, most of the tourists stood at
a distance from each other. For many, this was a first trip to Africa, and
few of those who had traveled to Africa previously had visited Senegal.
Indeed, the seasoned travelers' comments such as "I've been to Africa"
lacked national specificity or the distinction of place. The range of particular travel sites, including Kenya, South Africa, Ghana, and Egypt, melded
into a single representative site: "The Africa." Being a tourist was a new
experience for others of the travelers. The event drew us together, although at times in bizarre and ironic ways.

We skimmed through immigration with the privilege of an organized
tour group from a powerful country. Then, however, we found ourselves
stranded together, waiting for our luggage in the dim light of the airport
lobby. Pensively, we wondered what would happen next. Soon an enormous mass of suitcases began to arrive suitcase after suitcase, forming a
daunting pile to our travel hosts; the sight of so many bags certainly implied a stay much longer than ten days. Later the bags upon being opened
and their contents revealed seemed like magic trunks, containing an amazing collection of objects: wide-brimmed straw hats, clothes for every occasion, however casual or formal, full-size irons, accouterments and acces-
sories to dress up ordinary wear, presents to exchange and supplies to
give, and much more—even food prepared by one of the travelers just in
case the meals did not measure up to her familiar standards. This could
only seem like heavy freight to the baggage handlers, yet the comforts of
home were not to be left behind by these tourists. The weight and contents
of the luggage would later become the source of laughter as we were
struck by the convergence of packing styles that had led to this oversized
heap. Obviously, no one wanted to be underdressed. Someone quipped,
"Is this our African heritage?"

Two Senegalese guides from a tour company met us at the airport. Video-cameramen paced around, eagerly stalking the McDonald's winners to record their first impressions of what it felt like to be "home." One person seemed especially unprepared for these questions, and perhaps understandably since for most people an airport waiting area is hardly the place to conjure up images of home. Soon the guides offered their official welcome: "You are on a pilgrimage, not a safari." The reminder was first a subtle suggestion; as it was repeated each day, it became like an advertising jingle, a collective prayer, as well as our hosts' desperate plea that we remember the distinction between this tour and an ordinary tourist jaunt in which privileged and culturally insensitive behavior could get utterly out of control. Even in the moment of becoming tourists with our bodies and baggage, we were called upon to be more than tourists; we were to be pilgrims. The image of the "pilgrimage" was an effort to carve a distinctive regional niche in the more common representation of travel to Africa, which often takes the form in imagination and in practice of a safari venture.[6] But this introductory greeting would come to assume a deeper significance; repeated almost like a chant over the ten-day period, it prompted us to be mindful of the proper perspective to maintain on this tour and the difference between this trip and other journeys. This phrase would come to embody the exasperated sentiments of our tour guides, particularly when they had reached their limits with the group's behavior.

After the welcoming speech that the guides offered, a bus took us to the hotel. As the tour bus approached the hotel entrance, a glance at the building again reminded us of our sponsor: a large banner flying overhead read, "McDonald's and Novetel welcome the Alex Haley family." This was not the only reminder of the commercialization of homecoming. As we exited the bus, we could hardly emerge beyond the door without meeting other welcomers. "Hello, my brother, my sister, welcome home," offered the vendors, showing us a full display of trinkets and souvenirs. These "instant kin" appeared to see little difference between building ties of kinship and making good deals. At this first welcome, we did not know how to receive either; most of the travelers were uninterested in such deals after the long journey from New York. Within a few days, however, many had learned to participate in bargaining more fully.

Once we were registered, the hotel representatives offered a small welcoming reception. Much of this moment of hospitality was familiar and standard fare for tourists who arrive as part of a group; yet the constant references to home and family reinscribed the importance of this tour as a special kind of journey. Later in the day, standing high above the streets of Dakar and gazing out the hotel window, a few of us noticed the island of Goree, known to some of us because of its significance in slave-trading history. At a distance, its appearance through the mist conjured the eerie first soundings of what we came to experience as collective "memory."

Our tour of Senegal began the next day with an early visit to the U.S. embassy. To the people on the tour, with whom by now I had made a brief acquaintance, this embassy visit appeared curious. What reason would we have to visit the U.S. embassy? There was, after all, "so much of Africa to see!" Another wondered, "Why would we waste our time visiting Americans?" This visit, however, helped illuminate some of the cross-purposes and assumptions intimately wrapped up with the tour. Our tour guides thought it only fitting that we be introduced to representatives from the United States; they brought us to be greeted by our countrymen as any proper host might do. In contrast, for many of the pilgrims, this journey represented an opportunity to distance oneself from the United States, to find a more significant home.

The cultural misunderstanding that plagued this event only deepened as the embassy visit unfolded. Our African tour guides assumed that the American hosts would certainly provide refreshments for their American visitors. Yet the foreign service staff did not provide what the tour guides viewed as a proper welcome. "Not even drinks," one of the guides commented, marveling at the poor hospitality offered by our hosts as they navigated through their sense of race relations in the United States. Was this intended as an affront? From the perspective of many of the tourists, however, this was the least significant issue raised by the visit.

Many of the American guests, troubled by having to visit a U.S. office while in Africa, wondered what American officials could possibly contribute to an understanding of African heritage. We were ushered into a small and soon over-crowded room and were asked to listen to another welcoming speech. This speech, however, did not emphasize the uniqueness of the tour group and the meaning of the "homecoming"; instead, the American hosts explained the conventions of proper behavior in Senegal. The expressions on the faces of the tourists hinted at the lack of enthusiasm for this lecture. Several of the tourists sat with a bored affect, appearing much like they were attending a junior high school event in which the teachers were explaining some of the basic rules to follow while on the class trip.

The age and race of the welcomers was not inconsequential to the group's reception of their lessons. Many of the tourists found it disconcerting to have to listen to two young white men introduce Africa to a primarily African American audience. In the context of race relations in the United States, it was not an easy leap to assume that the embassy representatives' introduction to cultural conventions in West Africa was intended as a helpful gesture. The collision of worlds, one made up of practical suggestions and the other filled with the emotions of history, provided a fertile example of the tensions created when actual worlds and imaginary social worlds collide. The group grew restless and appeared exasperated by the appearance of the white men as authorities on Africa. That annoyance peaked as one of the men began to explain the current political situation on the streets of Dakar: "Today, around noon, there is going to be a political rally, and there will be soldiers around the streets. If you see a crowd, just go in the opposite direction." With this cautionary advice, one elderly man rose from his seat and assertively asked, with indignation in his voice and yet with a middle-class African American sense of entitlement, "Why do we care about this? We are here on a home-land tour. We are not here to listen to you tell us about political problems. What has this got to do with a homeland tour!" Some of the tourists seemed embarrassed by the directness of the confrontation, but, for many, he had verbalized what had caused their restlessness during the entire presentation. The details of contemporary Senegalese politics seemed ir-relevant, even antithetical, to a voyage of self-discovery and nurturance.

This encounter lasted less than an hour, yet it brought to the surface several moments of crossed expectations. The guides had carried a set of assumptions about guest-receiving hospitality and generosity that the U.S. representatives had not fulfilled. Even though this was a tour that targeted African Americans and their particular relationship to Africa, the expres-sion of our differences as Americans, black and white, seemed odd to one of the guides. One guide appeared somewhat perplexed by the hostility of the group toward the embassy representatives because much of what was conveyed to us were points of etiquette for traveling in Senegambia. To this Senegalese citizen, the embassy representatives were playing a helpful role in mediating between Senegalese culture and the American tourists. At least the representatives were knowledgeable and respectful of local conventions, while we, as tourists, appeared to be Americans without much sensitivity to cultural decorum. In turn, the embassy repre-sentatives at first seemed excited by the presence of the group but soon appeared overwhelmed and nervous at the reception they were given by the audience.

Finally, the African American travelers were participants in a different discussion. As the elderly gentleman's point suggested, we were on a pil-grimage to Africa. Such a journey takes place in mythical time; in this case, it involved a temporal displacement of the current moment in which the international representation of contemporary African political culture was at worst a Eurocentric distortion and at best an irrelevant waste of time.

There are important ironies here. News of current events in Senegal were delivered to us from within a U.S. racial politics in which white men, once again, became the experts, thereby sealing the erasure of those events. The African American tourists thus re-imagined themselves to know less about cultural propriety in Senegal than they might have known before or under difference circumstances wished to know. And yet even within a matrix of erasures and over-determined insensitivities, African American efforts to create cultural ties with Africans do still sometimes succeed—if not always in the ways the pilgrims imagine—at bearing significant fruit in the form of culturally rich and innovative entrepreneurial alliances, such as this tour.

Liminality

The trip to Goree Island was the first symbolic marking of the difference in this part of the journey from the arrival day. This segment provided the first inkling of the distinction between tourist and pilgrim, the deeper meaning of the tour. It was our first stop of "homeland" significance: a trip on the ferry to the renowned site of the slave fort on the island. And Goree Island was a name already well known to some. Poet Nikki Giovanni writes,

> It is all but impossible to be a Black American and not know Senegal. So many of us made our way to the New World through Gori Island. Through a fort and a hole in the ground where even yet one hears the moaning of the captives. What made those people survive, to replicate themselves—to live? It had to be indomitable spirit that would not be cowed by the cold from the ocean journey or the cold in the hearts of their captors. What warmth they would find together, not as members of different communities, not as members of different religions, but as people of the same color from the same continent with, admittedly, the same problems—and more significantly the same possibilities. (quoted in Bugul 1991, v)

Historically, Goree's importance lies in its critical place in maritime history. Spice traders, explorers, and missionaries found the island a convenient transit lounge while en route to the Orient. The island, first called Palma by the Portuguese, changed stewardship several times; the sixteenth century found the Dutch in control (Barry 1998). They renamed the island "Goree," and made it into a strategically located military base. Later, the French took over the stewardship of the island. As a point of transit and later as a military post, the island also played a role in transferring slaves to vessels traveling to Portugal. This paralleled the development of sugarcane as a lucrative crop in the Americas (Haardt 1992). Historians have pointed out that the fort at Goree played little more than a minor part in the slave trade. Yet this site, like several other forts, has become symbolically significant for African Americans, as well as tour company ventures.[7]

The symbolic charge has more to do with recent developments in the island's history. In the nineteenth century, Goree Island became an administrative and educational center for West African students; it was a place spatially set apart. In the twentieth century, those interested in preserving the island sought and received commemorative status for it. As a result, Goree Island is now included on UNESCO's list of historical monuments set aside as restored and preserved sites. The island's slave-trading history is invoked in the recent literature on the site: "Goree holds memories of the infamous trade that once condemned thousands of the sons and daughters of Africa, if not to death, then to an exile from which none returns" (M'Bow 1985, 11).

Yet we did return. The short distance we traveled by ferry began the process of homecoming. A dual process was at work: one of distancing and simultaneously coming together in an effort to frame a collective identity. Many on the tour had already started to feel a sense of distance from our "arrival" the day before. This sojourn also offered a closer sense of "home," the place where all the imagined fear about the past, as well as the hope about its renewal, were invested. In reading about the island later, I discovered a statement that echoed my experience of the island: "A visit to Goree is a journey through space and time" (M'Bow 1985, 55).

The walk from the ferry provided several apprehensive moments and perhaps awe brought about by the joining of the myths of our African home with the material site, the slave fort, the place where it all began. The group solemnly proceeded through the town passageways. Soon we entered the great doors of the Maison des Esclaves, the House of Slaves. Once inside, the doors closed behind us, keeping all those who were not a part of our newly forming community outside in the courtyard. Our group wandered about the two levels of the imposing structure.

The ground floor had several small rooms that fanned around a stair case leading to the upper rooms. The heat of the day drove many to seek respite on the top floor, where the large paneless windows overlooked the Atlantic Ocean and offered a comforting reprieve from the tropical heat. The circular stairs ascended to the entrances of rooms big enough to accommodate several large pieces of European furniture. We were quickly reminded that this top floor would not have been our place in history. These rooms were reserved for merchants as well as traffickers in slaves. The spatial expanse of the rooms drastically contrasted with the small cubicles on the bottom floor where, we were told, numerous African men and women had been housed for several weeks at a time, chained to one another while they were held as captive "cargo" to be shipped to parts of the Caribbean and the United States.

After some time during which we wandered about in this contained space gathering first impressions, the curator, Mr. Ndiaye, appeared at the top of the imposing staircase and began narrating the history of the fort in French, which our tour guide translated into English. In contrast to the earlier encounter at the embassy, the group listened attentively while the curator told about the organization of the fort. In a dramatic rendering that evoked the heaviness of the moment, Mr. Ndiaye spoke of the capturing of people to be taken to the New World. Many of the "pilgrims" were sobered by the telling of this story, silenced by the realization of the significance of this site. Distress settled in as present time compressed to meet the past, to recreate the horrors of the slave trade. Many group members, both men and women, were moved to tears by what was becoming our "remembered" history. A historical account from UNESCO offers a sense of representations of Goree.

> In damp, dark cellars, or torture cells for any who rebelled, the importees languished for weeks, waiting for the voyage from which there could be no return. And here, when they were put on board, each slave was branded with the mark of his owner. Then the slaves were crowded into the holds, where many were doomed to perish before they reached their destination. (M'Bow 1985, 1)

The curator's narrative of the history of Goree Island confirmed a sense of collective history for those participants whose ancestors had been taken to America: we were once again "home." Many members of our group wandered around the building a second time now, again entering the small rooms on the ground floor. Something had changed after hearing the presentation. Although we were a large crowd in a small space, we were hushed. Many people took photographs to capture the moment and hold the memory. But a freelance photographer was also present in case any of the many cameras brought by the pilgrims failed to capture any significant scenes. Others filled empty film canisters and small bags with sand from inside the fort as a material memento of the journey. Bill Haley offered a prayer and poured libations for those who had come before, and included a tribute to the memory of Alex Haley, who died in 1992. We were then urged by the museum curator to enter a small room where the walls displayed the chain irons that had been used to imprison humans. Logbooks of the slavers, cataloging the movement of thousands of people, were also on display in a dark room. Certificates, written verification of our visit to Goree, were also available for purchase.

The mood, now dreadfully solemn, remained subdued for several hours after our visit. After exiting the fort we approached a church, and a few pilgrims prayed. We stayed on the island for several hours afterwards, and many of us were now moved to speak more freely with each other than we had before. This bonding experience proved exceptionally potent in creating a deeper sense of connection. Yet the pensive and reflexive moment was disrupted by the swarm of peddlers that surrounded the group once we were no longer protected by the walls of the fort. The historical return met present time and we were urged back into our tourist status: "Hello, my brother, hello, my sister, won't you buy this; it is cheap." The parade of entrepreneurs offering the same items was for many overpowering, yet the offhanded glances of several tourists made a seller's edge seem a likely possibility.[8] We were expecting a performance that was eventually cancelled; it was billed as a tribute to slaves. Crossed disjunctions and connections filled the long wait.

As "pilgrims" we had now taken our first step in the collective experience of regenerating an emotional connection to what had previously been only a distant set of fragmentary semblances. Images of ship hulls packed with Africans form part of African American memories because artists and filmmakers have rendered these images for us so concretely. At Goree we were transported back through time; through our ancestral connection, we were once again there.

One critical backdrop to the framing of the "African" experience in discourses of U.S. African American culture and history is the Middle Passage, an event that signifies the moment of severed ties, the voyage that transported Africans-made-into-commodities to the New World. Pictures of rows of African bodies chained together without room to move for weeks at a time have helped shape an image-laden version of that voyage. The horrors of the Atlantic slave trade have allowed some African Americans to claim this as our holocaust.[9] It is a travel image that repetitively figures difference between Africans and other immigrants, impressing upon us the uniqueness of the status of Africans. They arrived in the New World not as immigrants, migrants, or explorers, but as captured bodies. The Middle Passage also creates the point of origin for African American history as a collective project of memory, trauma, and healing. It serves as a reminder of the physical and psychic separation from "home."

The "return" to Goree Island, then, called up images of the Middle Passage that were readily available for many of the people on the tour. It invoked the imagined horror, the trauma of that experience that had everything to do with the ways people understood their relationship to self and community. The journey to the slave fort filled the abyss of memory and tied it to the narrative of history; it captured an already strong African American "structure of feeling" (Williams 1966). The tour and the rendering of the slave experience into narrative conspired with the heat of the day, the small windowless rooms, and the chains on the walls to convey a sense of experience, a filling-in of "memory." Because of the strength of already cogent images of the Middle Passage, the trip to Goree Island seemed to prick the unconscious, (re)calling the trauma of slavery and the reuniting with "Mother Africa," the mother lost centuries ago and longed for since. The gathering of sand as a memento was an effort to tangibly hold on to the experience once we departed. Much could serve as a token of remembrance.

The participants' sense of self could not go unaffected by this experience; we were transformed by the experience of "being there." A sense of the past was created by the interplay of already-familiar images of slavery and those material objects, views, and stories that bring these to life as "memory." The power of a visit to Goree Island, then, relies on the senses: the material feel of the visit, the sensory experience of public discourses of slave history. Taken together, these sensory provocations allow pilgrims to imagine the possibility of a curative for community ills. At once the multiple spheres of significance come to the fore. The textual figuring of Goree Island as a place of significance in African American stories can be seen in the following exchange between novelist Alice Walker and musician Tracy Chapman, who use their "memories" of slavery and the power of that site to inspire their campaign against violence against women.[10]

> AW: Here we are, sitting on the steps of what is called the House of Slaves, and I wondered what you have been thinking about and what you've been feeling about genital mutilation?
>
> TC: Coming to this place probably felt like the end for so many people; there must have been so much uncertainty and fear. It just makes me think about what's been done to women and that they're being mutilated. . . . I stand here as a free person as much as it's possible in this world, and it's possible that things can change. (Walker and Pratibha Parma 1993, 346)

Horrors remembered so close to the body can lead to a collective rededication.

Reincorporation

Although this tour was a *Roots*-like homeland journey, it did not start at Kunte Kinte's village, Alex Haley's destination. We visited the village of Juffrey after the site of the departure of African slaves for the New World. Much of the tour took place in Senegal, and in retrospect perhaps this reversed order served a critical symbolic purpose: to begin at the place of the dispersion of Africans to America centuries ago and then to work one's way back "home." This explanation serves the logic of tour as rite of passage, but other explanations are equally plausible. As Senegalese, the tour organizers were able to make use of the competition for tourist attention between Senegal and The Gambia and, in the process, to construct a border-hopping evocation of our history as Africans, without loyalties to a single modern nation but with responsibilities as continental citizens. This was nationalism of a different sort, a cultural nationalism familiar to African Americans, one in which nation as a geographically localized space was not the way they framed the world. In this spirit, the tour brought us through ceremonies of kinship and maturation, and blurred present-day distinctions of African ethnicity, nationality, and regionalism.

After the excursion to Goree Island, our tour group continued its introduction to our newly reclaimed African kin. We visited markets and artisan cooperatives, and we were entertained at an evening banquet. Many moments were deeply felt even as they were punctuated with commercial engagement. Everywhere we were accosted by the "kinship" invocations of the ever-present street vendors: "My brother, my sister . . ." Without a sense of national difference, we traveled from Senegal to The Gambia, an eight-hour bus trip many travelers found difficult.[11] Some of the travelers also found the commentary offered by our tour guide an annoying interruption of their own conversations. One young woman on my bus wondered aloud why the tour guide wouldn't stop talking since his description during the long excursion did not hold much for the conversation she wanted to have with her friends. His running commentary, delivered over an amplified system, left little space for interactive, competitive storytelling. Others around me in the back of the bus were regretting that they had chosen a seat in the back. Many cringed at the bus driver's fast driving and vehicular gymnastics around roads familiar to him but not to the rest of us.

We arrived in Banjul, the capital of The Gambia, with barely enough time to prepare for the evening's events; a banquet followed by a "naming ceremony" became a moment in the context of this tour of symbolic regeneration. After a meal of nondescript tourist food, a jali welcomed us and told us of the significance of naming. "When a child is born, he is not named for seven days and then a name is given to the griot, who announces the name to the crowd." African adults are not ordinarily celebrated in naming ceremonies by being given names, but we were not (yet) African adults. Thus we were each offered an "African name." The name was given in a whisper and then announced to the group at large. Mumblings from those who had already taken an "African" name enlivened the conversation at various tables. The idea that every one of the travelers was a neophyte when it came to reclaiming Africa and "African" history and culture, was upsetting to those who had long ago changed their names; this ceremony allowed little room for mutual reception and appreciation. While some of the tourists saw this meeting as a mutual bond that bridged the gulf between Africans and African Americans, to the tour organizers this was an itinerary they provided for many other tour groups, not just African Americans.[12] To those in charge, the distinctions among tourists seemed irrelevant. We were constructed as a mass, and American at that.

The naming ritual made sense in the context of a rite of passage frame, signifying a rebirth that conferred our new identities as changed beings. What seemed less clear to those immediately taken aback by this new naming process was our place as initiates. As perceived by tour organizers, we were—as Turner suggests—in the liminal phase, tabulae rasae. Still, for most participants the process of transformation had begun: We had faced the trauma of departure, and we were ready to receive once again our birthright and place. By shedding our former identities, we continued the process of returning "home." Also present at this evening event was an elderly woman, a great-great-relative of Kunte Kinte, and by extension, of Alex Haley. We were told that she would travel along with us the next day to her village, Juffrey, the village made famous by Alex Haley's search for his roots.

Before we proceeded to Juffrey, however, another important stop was scheduled. The day following the naming ceremony included a visit to the S.O.S. children's orphanage. Group members had been instructed before coming on the tour to bring old magazines and school supplies for the orphanage children. Here again lay a moment of disjunction between story and reality. The idea of African *orphans* seemed unreal to many of us, who had grown up with the notion that African people were never without family because, it was said, "All Africans are part of an extended family."[13] And indeed, this was one of the explanations used to distinguish slavery in Africa from slavery in the New World. The notion that we were going to visit children who were in the institutionalized setting of an orphanage also seemed arresting because, in the mythic time of the tour, the current political realities of people dispersed throughout Africa—refugees without a home—seemed to lie outside of the frame. Yet it was precisely within this imagined reach that the orphanage stop on the tour was experienced as moving. Who were the real orphans: we African Americans with no family to remember us here or these children? As group members brought out the school supplies that we had carried across the Atlantic for the children, including Ronald McDonald's school packages, we rededicated ourselves to our "African families." We could now become family members by taking on a sense of being reincorporated; with reincorporation comes responsibilities. This invitation offered an instructive moment, one that sought to teach those of us estranged from our "African family" what the expectations and responsibilities of family members included. As we toured the children's dormitories, we were told of the disciplinary regime of order and religious instruction, no doubt included to impress Western tourists who might want to know how their donations were being spent. This account seemed designed to prove that the efforts of the orphanage would build strong moral character and a sense of responsibility in the children of the village home.[14]

We traveled upcountry at last to the village of Juffrey. During this portion of the trip, T-shirts with pictures of Alex Haley on them and copies of *Roots* were distributed to the travelers by the U.S tour organizers, adding to the other tokens of the tour. Once we arrived in Juffrey, children met the bus with a chorus of calls: "Toubob, toubob." (No one translated toubob into English, and thus most of the tourists remained blissfully ignorant of what might have been a point of deep confusion and alienation: that they as African Americans were being called "white person" or "European.") We were then brought into the village, where the jali told the story of the kin of Alex Haley. Drummers and town dignitaries greeted us and ushered us to the *bantaba*, the town meeting place. There Binta Kinte, the imam, and the *akaloo* (village head) delivered prayers and speeches welcoming us home and offering thanks for our safe arrival and kind thoughts for our future journey.

Juffrey, like the orphanage, provided another moment for us as tourists/pilgrims to be instructed on the meaning of kinship—specifically, on how to stay connected to our newly found relatives. In a message delivered in Mandinka and relayed through an interpreter, a village official said: "It is very nice of you to visit us here and to travel this far to get here. We want to welcome you home. We hope your stay will be very pleasant. But you must remember that we would like to visit you, too. You must make it possible for us to travel to the United States to visit you." This was another momentary reminder of present-day time: belonging to family brings with it certain responsibilities. In this small way, we were told very explicitly of our responsibility, including making it possible for our relatives in The Gambia to be able to come to the United States. Yet how would one actively challenge the details implicit in this plea: U.S. immigration policy greatly hampers the easy "family" visits one might want to initiate. This was another intervention of contemporary realities into the mythic frame of the retreat. But the gradual process of moving from the slave fort and the historical departure of Africans to this place of receiving present-day responsibilities fit within a context of the neophyte moving toward responsible adulthood.

The trip to Juffrey was another moment of deeply felt emotion, again filling the place in our memory reserved for an African home with the details of an actual site—a village, an event—from which all this memory and meaning could blossom. As in the case of Goree Island, some pilgrims found a cathartic release in this visit, in the thought of being home; others listened attentively as the dignitaries told of the importance of this return journey.

As we walked to an adjoining town, Alberta, not unencumbered by numerous children pressing for our addresses (a familiar part of the ordinary tourist experience), we touched a well-worn stump, part of a tree referred to as the "freedom tree." We were told this was the place of freedom. If someone managed to escape while being taken on board the ships bound for the New World, and could swim to shore and touch this tree, that person would have gained his or her freedom. Somehow the idea that there were rules in this contest between life and death, family and expropriation, offered a strange moment of reflection. In the background were old, deteriorated colonial buildings that had once served as quarters for colonial officers. Historically laden, the setting was very powerful. We had moved from the horror of captivity to an appreciation of freedom in the context of broken kinship ties, now rekindled. As Tracy Chapman suggested after her visit to Goree, "things can change." We were offered the hope of new, responsibly connected lives.

Yet even the most moving moments of deep immersion in the pilgrimage tour seemed to be followed by a break; moments of high emotion were tempered by opportunities to shop for souvenirs. Soon after the trip to Juffrey, we were back in Senegal, staying at a resort for the final days of our trip. We went unrecognized by the resort employees; there was no welcoming of kin here. (Some travelers felt that some of the hotel employees courted the white guests, treating them more cordially than the African Americans.) And once we were back in Dakar, the vendors followed us everywhere: "My brother, my sister . . ."

Again, the effort to sell and buy "culture" framed the journey as a constant companion; no experience was exempt from marketing. In moments that I experienced with extreme embarrassment, the instant kinship was reciprocated in the crudest of "American tourist" ways; one of our travelers, for example, offered the sweaty shirt off his back in exchange for local crafts—a bargain is a bargain after all. Shortly after this, as we waited for the ferry, one of the tour guides lost *his* shirt as he intervened in an altercation between a tourist and seller—it was torn in the altercation. After the tourists recovered from the jet lag of the first day, the tour was plagued with entrepreneurial contests between buyers and sellers, and an endless competition ensued over who could get the best deal. I wondered how far this competitive strategy might have gone if the bargainers had converted their C.F.A. to U.S. equivalencies and realized the meager sums of traders' prices they, the tourists, had worked so hard to reduce. Additionally disturbing were assumptions made on the basis of images of Africa generated by the U.S. media. Misconceptions about Africa were framed within a narrative of underdevelopment; the idea that Africans lacked business sense was used to explain the poverty of the continent. Once again abstracting Africa out of contemporary geopolitical realities, the mythic space of recuperation and rebuilding failed to provide a broad enough frame to understand the conditions of life in Africa.

The guides were well accustomed to travelling with tourists from the United States and Europe, as well as from other countries within Africa. Yet managing ninety-six people under any circumstances is a challenge, and this tour was marked by moments when many of us revealed how much of an "American tourist" we were capable of being. Many of the travelers experienced an overwhelming sense of dissatisfaction when things did not go as expected. In addition to supplying a constant undercurrent of tension, this resulted in the tour officials offering meals not part of the package as gifts to appease disgruntled customers. The tour guides quickly grew agitated by the rumblings of what appeared to them to be a group of privileged Americans.

On the final day a banquet was held, and the tourists/pilgrims were urged to wear their newly tailored African clothes to the final festivities. This was also the evening of our departure, and the celebration was much like a graduation ceremony, with musicians playing and people making speeches. We were each individually invited to the stage and congratulated on completing a difficult journey. We could now return to our homes with the ritually affirmed knowledge that we could carry the strength of this process of rebirth with us for the rest of our lives. Clearly, this tour was meant to be a life-changing experience. We were given a certificate by the tour convener, William Haley, attesting that we had completed the homeland journey. People exchanged addresses and said goodbyes as if we would not be traveling together back to New York later that evening. Yet this too was a process already figured in Turner's analytic frame: reincorporation.

At the end, everything seemed possible: memory, solidarity, regeneration. All of the cultural misunderstandings that framed the ironies of the trip seemed full of productive potential: stories of reuniting that blurred distinction, a moment of growth for both African and African American makers of selves and livelihoods. On the one hand, so much of what was present at that final ceremony was what we had brought with us—even our African clothes. Many of the travelers had brought with them African clothes made in New York; remember those voluminous suitcases? Thus much of the "Africa" we had managed to appreciate was not so different from the U.S.-made Africa already present in many people's lives through the West African tailors and hairdressers of U.S. urban centers. On the other hand, we had tapped a vein of West African entrepreneurship eager to present to us this "Africa." No more inauthentic than any other form of tourism, our experience at least had the advantages of reverent attention and heartfelt—if transient, privileged, and awkward—solidarity. Perhaps something would come of it. And yet one is still forced to ask about the visions we pilgrims carried with us.

The Domestication of Dreams

What can be said about identity formation and the specificity of the current moment in shaping identity and political culture? What about these "sponsored identities" (Davila 1997) that generate a particular relationship to concepts of self and community within globalization? The transatlantic "reunion" sponsored by the McDonald's homeland tour united places and peoples normally spatially dispersed and helped create what was for many of the U.S. participants a deeply moving experience. At the same time it is important to ask about the limits of this vision. The corporate sponsorship fostered a view that, as my informant responses indicated, helped contain and frame those encounters in specific ways. Informal conversations with a few of the travellers suggested that what Africa needed was economic development to bolster the economy. Such assumptions mirror the dreams of modernization. And yet some of these same people noted the failure of their own communities in the U.S. to develop. Less clear in what they said was an analysis of the historical and larger structural relationships that kept Africa in a precarious positions in relation to the world economy. And yet some of the responses of the tourists seemed to indicate a willingness to approach the problem from a understanding of global capitalism. This localized view of causes of sub-continental poverty seemed tied to a particular historical moment when self-improvement and atonement fill the gap between poverty and success.

We can look to an earlier historical period, the 1960s and early 1970s, to see a different critique of global economic relations that in many instances gave a different meaning to cultural nationalism and the politics of identity. In this section I briefly explore this history and also look at how present-day visions are curtailed by a regime that places its main emphasis on the pleasure of consumption. This historical moment is relevant in showing how subject formation was created at one time and has since shifted. Indeed, this history created the context for many of the tourists' experiences.

A comment I quoted earlier in the chapter provides a point of entry. A tourist/pilgrim asked, "What does this homeland tour have to do with the contemporary problems of Africa?" Consider the contrast with African American nationalist disucssions of the 1960s and 1970s.[15] Postcolonial nations still seemed a landscape of promise. Socialist and communist societies formed a competitive force in geopolitics; post–World War II China, Cuba, and the Soviet Union were active political alternatives to North American capitalism. Newly emergent postcolonial nations— among them Guinea Bissau, Mozambique, Angola, and Tanzania—offered different imaginings of what was possible in these newly emergent global transformations. Not unrelated to these international states of difference, domestic social movements advocating civil and social rights revealed an interest in the transformation of "local" society, and actively cultivated visions tied to reframing a global political imagination. Contemporary politics offer a striking contrast. At a moment when capitalism and the magic of the market engulf the world's imagination, social activism is sponsored by the very corporations that benefit from free trade zones and liberal economic policies; they leave little room, on the face of this, to critique the limits of this vision.[16]

A denunciation of commodity culture was central to the critique of capitalism attributed by some groups mobilized during the 1960s and early 1970s, although I should add that there was a range of socially active groups. The Situationists (Debord 1977), for example, exposed the spectacular nature of post–World War II capitalism and argued that it aimed to create docile subjects, that is, consumers. Radical feminists denounced commercial femininity. Anti-imperialists mobilized against the commercial penetration of the Third World. There was an imagined chasm between oppositional political identity and commodity culture.[17] A number of social reformist groups—whether feminists, African American cultural nationalists, or countercultural "radicals" of the 1960s and early 1970s—each imagined that identities could be remade, redefined, purified. This utopic vision held that one could go back to some place outside the economic system, and that commodities were, by their very existence, tainted by their association with the world they had helped create. Indeed, for many North American and European activists, these social movements gained their effectiveness in part *because* they defined themselves outside of the regime of the market—outside of the system, the military industrial complex, and the police state. This space beyond the market reminds one of the dichotomy spoken about earlier in the chapter—sacred and secular—a space beyond the reach of crass commercialism.[18]

Many of the ideals of this period were tied to a different transnational vision—not one of ever-increasing, expanding markets but one in which the possibilities of once-colonial new nations would flourish. These visions may now seem utopian, yet they were tied to major social projects, which shifted the geopolitical landscape of colonialism. The national liberation struggles of Third World countries helped inspire student mobilization and fueled a vision of possibilities beyond a world of Western domination and beyond the endorsement of capitalist hopes, dreams, and aspirations.

Not only were student movements shaped by these interactions, but particular kinds of identification groups—feminist and civil rights groups as well as various Pan-Africanist moments—emerged with a real presence. Ethnic and women's studies programs were developing in universities, and their existence helped form a critical consciousness about politics about Africa. Linked to the interests of social movements were a variety of influential texts, including underground texts. The ground of publishing had not yet been conceded to academic intellectuals and successful journalists but included a number of texts of "organic" intellectuals. Many of these works formed the corpus of an Afrocentric philosophy; these texts are still read and referred to in contemporary discussion.[19]

Along with these texts, the Black Arts Movement, by bringing to communities performances that contained social commentary and critique, was active in shaping consciousness.[20] These sources suggest that it was not just commercial popular culture that shaped African American consciousness; a self-consciously anti-commercial parallel also helped figure "black" identity. One ongoing process of consciousness-making was through these foundational publications that were sold on African American nationalist tables on urban street corners, along with incense, "African chew sticks", and jewelry. These anti-commercial texts helped create and sustain an interest in Africa in the minds of many African Americans. They spoke to a middle level readership, an "informed" constituency between those watching mass-produced pop images and those reading scholarly texts.

Many African American cultural nationalists of the 1960s movements defined their projects as an attempt to build an alternative vision outside of a U.S. politics and logic. Many claimed new identities by rejecting family names—what they referred to as slave names—and by taking on "African" names; many opted for "African" spiritual options alternative to those offered by Christianity. Cultural nationalisms of various forms seemed to suggest some place of opposition outside of the regime of the West —and for many, that place was Africa.

Indeed, there is a deep sense of continuity between these early "alternative" identity makings and contemporary searching for roots. That is why I was not surprised that there were moments of annoyance on the part of some of the tour participants when their efforts to reconnect to Africa before this journey seemed to go unrecognized. Yet the current moment of identity making is also distinctive, and this chapter has worked to define its distinctive traits.

In striking contrast to the existence and effects of these texts and the political organizing of this earlier period, stands the current proliferation of autobiographies and self-help books that now take up a great deal of space in bookstores and within African American book sections. Social organizing around the Million Man March in 1996 and the Million Women's March in 1997 mobilized large numbers of African American men and women in gender-segregated rallies whose explicit focus was on atonement and community development through self-reflection. What was less clear in these events was an understanding of something larger than persoanl self-making. In contrast to the critique of imperial and global expansion that would have been a part of an earlier moment of mobilizing, what we find now is a domestication of dreams—a vision that turns inward rather than challenging corporate strategies and logics. Oppositional identities no longer appear autonomous from global commerce, even to their most radically passionate adherents; instead, they are inescapably intertwined.

Personal transformations are not discovered naturally but need to be seen within a broader context in which a variety of influences help shape one's notion of self. This tour represents, perhaps, an ironic twist in which past and present converge, and culture and economy neatly merge. While seventeenth-century merchant capitalist interests brought Africans to the New World, here at the end of the twentieth century, their journey back is again sponsored by capitalist interests—this time by a multinational corporation seeking to reunite African American tourists with their homeland. This tour illustrates one kind of complex interaction between culture and economy: culture made into commodity for transnational consumption.

In the opening chapter of *The Black Atlantic*, Paul Gilroy notes the centrality of the journey in the formation of African American diasporic identity and cultural history. And the end of this journey allows us to return to the significance of culture and the frame of the Turnerian ritual to identity-making processes in remaking "Africa" home for African Americans. Turner's model of ritual process, particularly as developed in relationship to non-Western societies, places an emphasis on the ways that ritual helps create and sustain group cohesion. Certainly, the tour I have described created a strong sense of unity. Yet perhaps we also need to consider this ritual solidarity in relation to its self-conscious production, that is, in relation to commercial strategy. From this perspective, ritual takes on some of the features of an ideology—one powerful commitment within many. Anthropologist Maurice Bloch's (1989) intervention is relevant; ritual is not the only expression that might come from a given community. Ritual can be repetitive, inward-looking, and celebratory of the powers that be, but other alternatives exist.

My discussion also helps illuminate the relationship between finance and the facilitation of a particular subjective experience. The transatlantic "reunion" sponsored by the McDonald's homeland tour united places and peoples normally spatially dispersed, and helped create what was for many of the U.S. participants a deeply moving experience. Yet this was only one event that has drawn inspiration from Haley's project. The Gambia has also hosted several "Roots" festivals, with a variety of Gambians playing key roles in brokering culture for tourist consumption.

The end of the journey allows us to return to the models suggested in the opening of part 3 in order to reengage the question of their applicability. Appadurai's mediascapes and ethnoscapes gesture suggestively in the direction of the "experience" of tourists/pilgrims; the media event of *Roots* helps generate a narrative of connection brought to us by global capital and the cultural frames provided through global cultural flows. They also, however, reveal themselves as not sufficient for this analysis. Perhaps if we instead consider history and memory as themselves a transnationally circulating "scape," we will get closer to the "Africa" imagined by and for the Black Atlantic. Meanwhile, the idea of circuits of culture reminds us of the need to think about the intertwined relationship between culture and economy in the making of such scapes. Taken together, we are drawn to questions about immigration and travel, and about First World and Third World positionality in these travel encounters.

September 26, 2000. Protestors stage another action aimed against the agenda of globalization as promoted through the policies of wealthy Northern countries and corporations. The scene: the World Economic summit held in Prague, Czechoslovakia. With their persistent outcries and violent confrontations, demonstrators capture the attention of the powerful leaders and global financiers and the world spectatorship. They express their outrage. Among the protestors, Bono, the lead singer of the prominent Irish rock band U2, manages to gain the ear of The World Bank's president, James Wolfensohn. He requests a meeting with Wolfensohn for the purpose of stressing the urgent need of First World countries to alleviate poverty around the world. Dubbed an activist by news reporters, Bono raises the problem of the enormous discrepancy between the world's rich and poor areas. Wolfensohn himself confirms the problem: 80 percent of the world's gross domestic product is controlled by 20 percent of the world's wealthiest countries. Bono, drawing on his ability to coax and cajole an audience, dubs Wolfensohn "the Elvis of development and a moral man" ("Winners and Losers," *Prague Post*, September 27, 2000). Much like a jali, Bono seems convinced that it was worth trying to build leadership through praise. Unlike jali, however, the highest praise Bono can concoct is to call Wolfensohn a musician: a charismatic communicator.

The affinity between musicians and prominent public officials is not new. Many African musicians, particularly in Nigeria and the Republic of the Congo, are outspoken about national politics they find unpalatable. The jali I focus on in this project were not directly identified as political agitators at the national level. Jali may be critics, but they also may shore up the positions of their elite patrons, as my friends in Banjul stressed. They also share the ambiguous influence of musicians elsewhere, including Bono. They can gain the ear of important figures, locally and internationally.

This book has traced connections made by jali who act as articulators, the makers of links through which various projects and agendas make their way. In one instance jali are the interlocutors for their Gambian patrons, including those who speak for the state. In another instance, their international performances create an ever-expanding arena for patrons who use the symbolic importance of the jali for their own programs. African Americans link with them in efforts to know the "real" Africa.

World music enthusiasts seek alternative music forms to enlist signs of a world citizenry. Jali are linkers and speakers. Similarly, in this ethnography I disturb the segregation of cultural phenomena into distinctive domains: culture and politics, political economy and aesthetics, the local and the global. I show jali activities that are at once about performative artistry, development strategy, and personal aggrandizement for professional gain. Jali use these activities to link diverse regimes of power and influence interpersonally, at the level of the community and the nation, and in global networks. Because music is a form that enables Africa to travel as an idea around the world, jali become symbolically significant interlocutors in globally diverse sites and projects.

A set of dilemmas and concerns have provided a piercing critique of anthropology since the mid-1980s. These criticisms have left certain challenges for those who follow after the implosion of the field over the past twenty to thirty years. The most immediate problem is how to write into a disciplinary space when, as the saying goes, the emperor has no clothes. Related concerns question the contours of anthropology in a postcolonial era, not to speak of an era characterized by the end of grand narratives. Once, it seems, great theories were enough. We might glimpse the layered designs of structuralism, or, alternatively, probe deep recesses of the psyche by psychoanalysis, or, instead, chart the dialectical trajectory of history through Marxism. What are we left to do when for many of us the all-encompassing theoretical paradigms seem themselves too ethnocentric, regional, and historically particular and thus unable to describe culture, regionality, and history? Without the hegemony of an all-encompassing master theory, I have mobilized an eclectic set of analytic frameworks that have played an important role in anthropology since the crisis in representation catalyzed the great debates of the 1980s. The key, I argue, is to acknowledge the groundedness of theories in regional histories and debates and yet to use them analytically. Thus performance: a concept that engages our attention both because and beyond the fact that it is a stereotype of embodied Africa. We should use it but should not forget, as many theorists do, how and why it is of use. And thus, too, no one theory is sufficient. All are regionally contaminated—powerful and limited.

Performing Africa has revisited the recent history of anthropology by acknowledging the critical impact of certain debates in shaping both the form and the content of our studies. How do we fully take in the problems raised about representation while engaged in representation? Johannes Fabian's book, *Time and the Other* (1983), argued against the tendency of anthropologists to describe cultures in the ethnographic present, which, Fabian reminded us, takes the subjects of our research outside of our common history. But what if we take this insight farther? Don't our *theo-*

ries always appear in the equivalent of the ethnographic present: the time-less space of transcendent analysis? My goal has been to put theory as well as description in a marked time and space. Theories speak from the cultural and historical context of their emergence. When they are carried to new contexts, culture and history do not disappear, even as they are transformed. The anthropologically savvy cultural theorist must mark the cultural, regional, and historical engagement of theory as well as data.

One way to mark theory is to critically interrupt it even while using it. In this book, I have asked the chapters to interrupt as well as comple-ment each other. The chapters can be said to perform as active agents who speak back and comment on themselves. The chapters engage issues of representation and performance in ways that necessarily call into question their very tools of analysis.

What are the interruptions? In the first chapter, "Music," my aim is to engage the possibilities offered by a most exciting moment for cultural analysts, the discovery of Edward Said's critique of orientalism. His work allowed us to appreciate the intimate relationship between power and discourse in constructing a region. I use this moment of theoretical insight to describe the regional configuration of music and the musical configu-ration of Africa. But then a disruption occurs in the following chapter, "Performance," as it offers a critique of the limits of the type of formation put forth in the chapter 1. My turn to performance allows us to see the limits of a purely text-oriented analysis. Taken together, these chapters show how the tensions of textual and agential analysis can be produc-tively juxtaposed.

The focus of part 2 takes the postindependence Gambian nation-state as an object of interest and traces the building of Gambian history and national culture. Two different theoretical interruptions mark this sec-tion. First, I juxtapose history and performance to show history as perfor-mance. Performance inserts itself most obviously into African history be-cause of the centrality of oral traditions in gathering data on the past. Yet don't all scholars write and narrate with an audience in mind? Historians assemble facts in a way that generates narratives and creates truth-making effects through the representation of cultures and societies. History as historians practice it, positioned up close to performative traditions, can itself be seen as a performative tradition.

Second, I juxtapose debates about culture and the culture of debates. In the first of the three chapters of part 3, "Curators of Tradition," I argue that cultural assumptions about the national past are tentative positions within ongoing disagreements and dialogue linking Western and African scholars, government officials, jali and village elders, and anthropologists and cultural entrepreneurs. In the following two chapters, however, I argue that Gambian cultural assumptions about political agency motivate and guide the negotiations among these very kinds of players. Is culture political, or politics cultural? I argue that we must have it both ways. Thus, too, I advocate an area studies that is both self-conscious about cultural presuppositions and shows how these come to life in global interactions.

Part 3, "Culture as Commodity," is even more explicit about the simultaneous need for insider and outsider points of view. The study of tourism has seemed most promising for our understanding of culture in global interactions, and yet it has been limited by its dichotomous focus. Either analysts study the sociology of tourism, or they study the tourist point of view. In either case, they too rarely position themselves both inside and outside the traveler's perspective. In this section, I show the productiveness of this liminal analytic position: If I were to abandon my ability to read the cultural landscape as a traveler, I would miss the purpose and passion of the exercise; if I were to give myself up to traveling, and refuse to make a few ironic jokes about the situations they inspire, I would lose the ability to describe their movement in a heterogeneous world. The juxtaposition of empathetic understandings and ironic jokes is particularly important in considering race- and gender-marked travels; here, analysts have been conventionally divided between sympathizers, who join the analysis with the travelers' point of view, and critics, who objectify them as sociological ciphers. Instead, I argue for an analysis that interrupts itself to allow the travelers both intelligibility and context. The travelers are motivated and agential performers; they create and are created by institutionalized practices and legacies of representation. We must attend to both.

Consider once more the multiplicitous production of "Africa." International development agencies and musicians, historians and tourists, and of course anthropologists are implicated in the making of Africa. I have tried to show how Africa comes to life as an object in their interconnections.

OVERTURE: **Where and When I Enter**

1. Since the 1980s anthropologists have expanded their ideas about those who write ethnographies. While critical accounts sometimes imply that only white men wrote ethnographies before the 1980s, this has been proven otherwise. The issue, however, is not that women and to a lesser extent minorities were not writing ethnographies; rather, people who occupied these subject positions had to make their claims in relation to the legitimacy of white male authority as knowledge-making. My "arrival story" joins others in refiguring this terrain.

2. This point is nicely developed in Hartigan's (1999) *Racial Situations*. He suggests, "For most Americans, racialness as an order of clear identity, the privilege and the disadvantages, are presented on the spatialization of epidermal difference, which, in turn, informs and reproduces modes of social differentiation" (86).

3. My research assistant, Ms. Jammeh, learned about African Americans in history class, which included viewing *Roots*. She and I had never discussed race in the United States before engaging in a conversation in which the people with whom we were speaking had not heard of African Americans. Once she explained the plight of African Americans, our hosts immediately started offering prayers in response to Mariama's account of the predicament of African Americans in the United States.

4. A thought-provoking consideration of the distortion of "Africa" generated through longing and loss is found in a fictionalized autobiographical account by Senegalese author Ken Bugul (1991) in *The Abandoned Baobab*.

5. One of my interlocutors was particularly puzzled by the term "African American" because he thought it referred to Africans who had recently migrated to the United States. He was a young Gambian who had little knowledge of the social context in which this term emerged. He was unaware that black people living in America also claimed the word "Africa," and thus found it curious that we prefaced the "American" with "African"; after all, he pointed out, we had not been born in Africa. His surprise underlined the problem of how one separates the diaspora into various cohorts and moments, contrasting those transported centuries ago and those who have recently migrated. Recent efforts that complicate the notion of diaspora include Philippe Wamba's (1999) *Kinship*, a work that discusses the cultural negotiations of self and identity through his experience of moving back and forth between Africa and the United States, and Paul Stoller's (1999) novel *Jaguar*, also an effort that addresses the relative lack of attention to the contemporary African diaspora, in this case, of traders from Niger to New York.

6. While African Americans visit Africa with a range of objectives, and while for some this connection makes room for further romanticizations of the continent, others use their voyages to turn against the continent in disgust. This equally passionate view finds proponents running to the other extreme as they frame their experience in terms of being ever-so-pleased to be an American. See Keith Richburg (1997) and Eddie Harris (1992) for examples. What is disturbing in both instances is the inability to engage the continent in a way that makes its significance of consequence except in its role to service the personal identity struggles of African Americans.

7. Manthia Diawara's (1998) book *In Search of Africa* provides a compelling discussion of the cultural exchange between Africa and the United States and the influences of African American popular culture on cosmopolitan African communities. But he is also insightful in his comments about the figure of the jali. See in particular the chapter "Return Narratives" for a discussion of jaliya.

8. Richard Schroeder (1999) discusses the importance of gender to the gathering of information for his research in The Gambia. His discussion of how his position was directly affected by expectations about his role as a man is refreshing. Unlike many male researchers, he views gender as a system of relations, rather than one in which women are gender marked and men are, by omission, unmarked.

9. See Sinduhije's (1999) essay, "Welcome to America," for an in-depth look at African American ideas about Africa.

10. For a penetrating look at Hollywood's creation of stereotypic roles for African Americans, see Robert Townsend's film *Hollywood Shuffle* (1987).

INTRODUCTION: **Performing Africa**

1. Said's book became a lightning rod, stimulating both elaboration and criticism. Many recent critics insist that Said's formula is too simplistic, and that his ideas fail to capture the diversity of approaches and uses of the Orient by failing to show the historical transformations of the meaning of Orientalism. (See, for example, MacKenzie 1995.) Others have suggested that Said merely reinscribed Europe in a critical place as the maker of history while presenting inhabitants of the Near East as mere victims of imperial dreams. Despite these critiques, the text sparked and continues to generate intense debate and discussion. *Orientalism* has created a truly productive conversation.

2. Mudimbe's (1988) *Invention of Africa* would soon be joined by Appiah's (1992) *In My Father's House* in offering another engagement with the question of Africa's place in relationship to Europe. Both texts do so within the rubric of philosophy, tracing the collaborative frame of "African" / "Western" encounters. Notably, both works mark a particular entrée of African scholars that is at once engaged with social worlds generated by colonialism and at the same time makes a critical inquiry on philosophical grounds.

3. One of the striking aspects of recent publications about Africa is ethnographers' acknowledgment of the image-making that frames Africa. Interestingly

enough, one of the first strategies is to acknowledge the fields of imagery that engulf the continent, or more specifically, sub-Saharan Africa. The influence of Said's engagement with representation! Many scholars also move from discourses about Africa and the problem of representation to consider the power of these representations to configure events. Notable among these works are Martin-Shaw (1995), Piot (1999), and Roe (1999).

4. The "Diallo case" has raised awareness on the part of the general public of Africans in the United States. Amadou Diallo was an immigrant from Guinea who in February 1999 was shot forty-one times by New York City policemen who feared, they reported, that Diallo had a concealed weapon. The case has forged a closer bridge among Africans from a number of countries as well as with African Americans, one that brings communities into a debate over the meaning of citizenship and political struggle in the United States. Through the Diallo incident recently migrated Africans have been alerted and socialized into what race means in the United States for African Americans; meanwhile, African Americans have had to become more aware of the dilemmas of immigrants.

5. When I asked a friend unfamiliar with the kora what the instrument sounded like, after she had listened for a while, she suggested that it was like water falling over rocks. Evocative—but does this convey a sense of recognition in my readers? I wondered.

6. For a more extensive history of performance and Africa, see Lindfors (1999).

7. A number of studies that focus on performance in Africa provide analyses that bring to life cultural categories in the enactment of everyday life. They are attentive to questions of agency, joining the more general turn toward performance and away from more rigid structural models. Notable among these works are Kratz (1994), Fabian (1990), and Klein (2000).

8. Many questions of the facticity of the tale have been raised; see Gamble (2000).

9. I extensively address issues of status difference and power in chapters 3–5. See also Camara (1976).

10. This is a term coined by Richard Johnson (1986) and popularized by the Birmingham school of cultural studies. The concept is discussed in greater detail in the introduction to part 3, "Culture As Commodity."

CHAPTER 1: **Music: Europe and Africa**

1. For a more extended discussion of stories in social science, see Kreiswirth (1995).

2. Agawu (1995) points out that rhythm has been a striking feature in accounts of African music since the eleventh century. He further notes that the 1950s saw a reemergence—a reinvention—of the importance of rhythm in studies of African music.

3. The continuing importance of this book is demonstrated by the fact that it was reissued in 1997.

4. See Agawu (1991) for the "prehistory" of this period.

5. A number of critical musicologists have intervened in ways that radically reshape the ideological formation of Western art music history. The work of Subotnick (1996, 1991), McClary (1993), and Leppert (1988) are just three important sites through which to appreciate the complicated history of Western art music. Penelope Gouk (1999), for example, in *Music, Science and Natural Magic in Seventeenth Century England*, traces the connections among science, magic, and music before the Enlightenment.

CHAPTER 2: **Performances**

1. For an extended history of Jacob's Pillow, see Ted Shawn's (1947) *How Beautiful Upon the Mountain*.
2. Christine Arieta (personal communication).
3. Festac, Festival of Arts and Culture, is a pan-African event that links Africans across the continent and throughout the diaspora for a celebration of culture. The first festival occurred in Dakar in 1966, and a second in Lagos in 1977. A few jali interviewed in this project spoke of their involvement in the 1977 festival.

PART 2: **Professional Dreams**

1. For an excellent assessment of the recent history of The Gambia and its financial predicaments, see Abdoulaye Saine (1997), "Vision 2020. The Gambia's Neo-Liberal Strategy for Social and Economic Development: A Critique."

CHAPTER 3: **Curators of Tradition**

1. A number of Sidibe's written contributions to the oral history project appear as papers published under the auspices of OHAD. Many of OHAD's publications are co-authored with American-trained historian Winifred Galloway. She has also written papers on oral history methodology and historical place names of The Gambia (1978, 1980).
2. Philosopher of history Hayden White (1987, 1978) has presented a competing school of thought about history and the important use of language and the establishment of genre conventions in constructing historical narratives.
3. Donald Wright's steady engagement with the quality of history produced about precolonial Senegambia provides a methodology for how one should problematize both the categories and the context of historical data. His work offers the kind of critical challenges that insist upon taking African history as seriously as other histories that can depend more heavily and even exclusively on written documents.
4. According to the director of OHAD, a representative from the Ford Foundation worked very closely with OHAD in the 1970s. In addition to assisting

with the activities connected to OHAD in The Gambia, sponsorship was also provided for jali to tour the United States on short-term visas.

5. Other institutions were involved as well. The German government for a number of years partially supported the salary of a researcher from Germany based at OHAD, with the rest of the salary contributed by the Gambian government.

CHAPTER 5: **Interview Encounters: The Performance of Profession**

1. Jali form an endogamous caste, with only a few surnames. In this chapter, I identify individual jali only, at most, by these common surnames to protect their privacy. "Jali musaloo" refers to a woman jali.

2. The notion of biomythography combines a sense of the temporal dislocation of narrating life events after the fact and the art of pulling those elements into a coherent story. Some have referred to the process of creating life stories or biography as "fabricating life." As in biomythography, the merging of spatial and temporal realignments creates a sense of what a life is.

PART 3: **Culture as Commodity**

1. Ahmed and Shore (1995) argue that tourism will be the largest industry world wide in the twenty-first century. The Gambia is dependent upon its possibilities, which helps explain the need for culture to be crafted into an object for exchange. Garcia Canclini's (1993) discussion of the process of making culture into commodity in the tourist sector of Mexico provides a nice parallel.

CHAPTER 6: **Travel Stories**

1. Marilyn Ivy (1995) analyzes a parallel development in Japanese travel advertising as women became the model travelers of the industry; her insights are also relevant to changes in North American and European images and ideals of travel.

2. On the surface, bumpsters fashion themselves after Rastafarians, adopting a cosmopolitan style of dreadlocks and urban sophistication. The international image of Rastas as oppositional men thus becomes a model of masculinity in transnational configurations of race and desire. Yet scholarly models have ignored the importance of emergent local versions of this transnational masculinity.

3. The demonstration of the mothers but not fathers, in contrast to the lobbying of state officials by male elders, who urged the officials to control their sons, suggests that male elders are more likely to feel threatened and displaced by the young male independence that comes with bumpster activities. Male elders are less involved in the family strategies of which bumpster activity plays a part.

4. Worth noting here is the overlap with other transnational sex literatures. Analogous to what many have suggested about female prostitution in Southeast Asia, bumpsters' behavior can be seen as part of a family strategy for gathering resources. As bumpster "John" recounts his initial involvement in bumpster-like activity, he reports that he and his brother started going to the beach in search of tourists when his mother could not provide for all of her children and their father was too old to provide adequate support for the family through farming. John and his brother Simon began neglecting school to follow tourists as one way to funnel back money and resources to the family (Aziz 1994,12).

5. These are pseudonyms to protect the identities of the tellers.

6. *Polite Society* (Sumner 1995) is one fictional white woman's account of a voyage of self-discovery in Africa that includes sex with the local men. The novel shows some of the elements most central to the allegorical white female journey: the inability to feel self-respect, beauty, or power at home, and the frustrating search elsewhere among what seems to white people to be native anarchy.

CHAPTER 7: **Tourists as Pilgrims**

1. Tejumola Olanyian (1996) describes how Africans in diaspora read the political situations of nation-states with little appreciation of the range of their internal debates.

2. Joan Scott's (1994) essay on experience makes the important point that the process by which experience is formed cannot be taken for granted; experience is socially constructed. Hall (1990) points to the intricate process of memory in identity formation in diasporic communities. The idea of subjective experience as described in this chapter also draws from Appadurai's (1996) scapes model. "Experience" is constituted, in part, through various kinds of media.

3. Victor Turner's (1969) discussion of processual ritual and communities lays some of the groundwork for an interpretation of the tour. Although a great deal of his work addressed the ritual processes in precapitalist societies, in later years Turner also turned his lens to what he refers to as spontaneous communities. A spontaneous community, he offers, is a "phase, a moment, not a permanent condition. . . . What one seeks is a transformative experience that goes to the root of each person's being." (Turner 1969, 138). Obviously moved by moments of deep encounter with "remembered" pasts, many people on the McDonald's tour expressed a sense of belonging.

4. A colleague and I—both of us having previously conducted research in The Gambia—traveled along with the tour but without the sponsorship of McDonald's. I joined the tour almost accidentally, in the course of inquiring about a magazine.

5. Olga Idriss Davis (1997) also analyzes Goree Island as a Turnerian pilgrimage site. She sees Goree as a place ripe for the transformation of self, and her analysis traces the rhetorical ways that the tour captures African Americans' needs of (re)connection to Africa. The coincidence in our use of Turner confirms my assertion that the tour guides promoted this homeland site as a ritual place,

strategically aimed at creating a powerfully moving experience for African Americans. The trope of the ritual return journey works at once as a marketing tool and as an effective strategy for forging identity. This overlap reminds us of the impossibility under contemporary conditions of capitalism of separating culture and economy into distinctive domains.

6. Edward Bruner's (1996) discussion of the development of tourism and diasporic imagining in Ghana is also an exploration of the distinctive niche of homeland tours.

7. In the context of a long debate over the number of people taken as part of the slave trade, historian Philip Curtin has argued that Goree Island never amounted to one of the significant sites (see Magner 1995). Barry (1998, 61–65) argues that Curtin ignores the symbolic significance of Goree to African diasporic history.

8. That each winner received $1,000 in prize money facilitated shopping. One of the winners, interestingly, refused to spend her prize money on souvenirs; she held tight with the hopes of paying off bills once she returned to the United States.

9. Gilroy (1993) and Bauman (1989) note the significance of the slave trade and the Holocaust to modernity. The parallels in the ways that Jewish history and African American history record horrors are striking. One might look at the categories and narrative conventions that frame Holocaust history and the parallels in African American discussions of historical recovery and memory (Saidiya Hartman 1997; Antze and Lambek 1996).

10. Alice Walker's (1993) efforts to render Africa in various forms, including fiction and human rights campaigns such as that promoted in the film *Warrior Marks*, illuminates many of the dilemmas of representation that I have been discussing, as these involve African Americans in search of Africa.

11. The white participants were even more awkwardly positioned after the visit to Goree. Two courageous people sat in the middle of the bus and showed their sense of solidarity with African Americans, although this was not easy because the African Americans had just traveled though something unique that they experienced as emotionally draining, an experience that bonded African Americans in such a way that white Americans were at least for a time excluded. The remaining five sat in the front of the bus. Although she chose not to sit in the back of the bus, the biographer, a white woman long involved in civil rights and a pivotal person in the Haley project, was perceived as an ally. But during one of the stops along the way, one of the "minority" white passengers fell to the ground and when some African Americans offered to help him up, he showed the strain of the emotional stress of the trip; rejecting the efforts of those who would be helpful, he preferred to struggle on his own.

12. The itinerary was followed by a number of tour agencies. Spector Travel is one such agency in Boston whose itinerary is quite similar to that of the McDonald's tour.

13. *Abandoned Baobab* (Bugul 1992), mentioned previously, is a compelling "fictional autobiography" of a Senegalese woman who is estranged from her mother and eventually her family. She moves to Europe, longing to address her sense of loss of home and family. This work captures some of the emotional ten-

sions of separation and loss that seem to parallel that imagined sense for some African Americans.

14. The tour was much like a trip to a demonstration factory, in that each one has a tourist-relations person who anticipates all questions and demonstrates the excellent conditions provided for the people under their supervision.

15. For a more extended discussion of African Americans' political activism in relationship to Africa see Penny M. Von Eschen's (1997) work on African American involvement in anticolonialism during the period between 1937 and 1957.

16. One critical place is in the marketing of the environment and eco-buying. Note also Anita Roddick's ad-campaign slogan for her chain of stores, "The Body Shop": " Trade not aid" is the new global strategy of "progressive" businesses.

17. Thomas Frank (1997) points out that this imagined chasm did not in fact correspond to social practices. Youth culture in the 1960s was a commodified culture.

18. For extended discussions of the social projects of the 1960s see Rozsak (1995) and Jameson (1988).

19. These include texts such as George James's (1985) *Stolen Legacy*, J. A. Rogers's (1961) *Africa's Gift to America*, Chancellor Williams's (1974) *Destruction of Black Civilization*, Walter Rodney's (1972) *How Europe Underdeveloped Africa*, and Robert Allen's (1969) *Black Awaking in Capitalist America*.

20. Harry Elam's (1998) discussion of the theatre arts of the 1960s and particularly Amiri Baraka's role in combining political consciousness raising through community theatre productions is useful.

Agawu, V. Kofi. 1995. "The Invention of 'African Rhythm.'" *Journal of American Musicological Society* 49 (3): 380–95.

———. 1991. *Playing with Signs*. Princeton, New Jersey: Princeton University Press.

———. 1992. "Representing African Music." *Critical Inquiry* 18 (1): 245–66.

Ahmed, Akbar, and Cris Shore. 1995. *The Future of Anthropology*. London: Athlone.

Allen, Robert. 1969. *Black Awakening in Capitalist America*. Garden City, N.Y.: Anchor Books.

Amselle, Jean Loup. 1998. *Mestizo Logics*. Stanford: Stanford University Press.

Anderson, Benedict. 1990. *Language and Power*. Ithaca, N.Y.: Cornell University Press.

———. 1992. *Imagined Communities*. New York: Verso.

———. 1992a. "The Changing Ecology of Southeast Asian Studies in the U.S. 1950–1990." In *Southeast Asian Studies in the Balance*, edited by Charles Hirschman, Charles F. Keyes, and Karl Hutterer. Ann Arbor, Mich.: Association for Asian Studies. Pp. 25–40.

Antze, Paul, and Michael Lambek. 1996. *Tense Past*. New York: Routledge.

Appadurai, Arjun. 1988. "Putting Hierarchy in Its Place." *Cultural Anthropology* 3 (1): 36–49.

———. 1996. *Modernity at Large*. Minneapolis: Minnesota University Press.

Appiah, Kwame Anthony. 1992. *In My Father's House: Africa in the Philosophy of Culture*. New York: Oxford University Press.

Arrighi, Giovanni. 1973. *Essays On the Political Economy of Africa*. New York: Monthly Review Press.

Asante, Molefi K. 1987. *Afrocentric Idea*. Philadelphia: Temple University Press.

Austen, Ralph, ed. 1999. *In Search of Sunjata: The Mande Oral Epic as History, Literary, and Performance*. Bloomington: Indiana University Press.

Aziz, Christine. 1994. "Seeking Sex in The Gambia." *Marie Claire*, May 12–18.

Barry, Boubacar. 1981. "Economic Anthropology of Precolonial Senegambia from the Fifteenth Through the Nineteenth Centuries." In *Uprooted In The Western Sahel: Migrants' Quest for Cash in Senegambia*, edited by Lucie Colvin, Cheikh Ba, Boubacar Barry, Jacques Faye, Alice Hamer, Moussa Soumah, and Fatou Sow. New York: Praeger. Pp. 287–313.

———. 1998. *Senegambia and the Atlantic Slave Trade*. New York: Cambridge University Press.

Barry, Kathleen. 1984. *Female Sexual Slavery*. New York: New York University Press.

Barth, Fredrik. 1969. *Ethnic Groups and Boundaries*. London: Allen and Unwin.

Barz, Gregory, and Timothy Cooley. 1997. *Shadows in the Field*. New York: Oxford University Press.

Baudrillard, Jean. 1981. *For the Political Economy of the Sign*. St. Louis: Teleo.

Bauman, Richard. 1992. *Folklore, Cultural Performances, and Popular Entertainments*. New York: Oxford University Press.

Bauman, Zyamut. 1989. *Modernity and the Holocaust*. Ithaca, N.Y.: Cornell University Press.

Bayart, Jean-Francois. 1993. *State of Africa*. London; New York: Longman.

Bebey, Francis. 1975. *African Music: A People's Art*. New York: Lawrence Hill.

Bellman, Beryl. 1984. *The Language of Secrecy*. New Brunswick, N.J.: Rutgers University Press.

Berliner, Paul F. 1978. *Soul of Mbira*. Berkeley: University of California Press.

———. 1994. *Thinking in Jazz: The Infinite Art of Improvisation*. Chicago: University of Chicago Press.

Berry, Sara. 1984. *Father's Work for Their Sons*. Berkeley: University of California Press.

Bhabha, Homi. 1983. "Difference, Discrimination and the Discourse of Colonialism." In *The Politics of Theory*, edited by Francis Barker, Peter Hulme, Margaret Iverson, and Diane Loxley. Colchester, U.K.: University of Essex Press.

———. 1990. *Nation and Narration*. London: Routledge.

Biggart, Nicole. 1989. *Charismatic Capitalism*. Chicago: University of Chicago.

Born, Georgia. 1991. "Music, Modernism and Signification." In *Thinking Art: Beyond Traditional Aesthetics*, edited by Andrew Benjamin and Peter Osborn. London: Institute of Contemporary Arts. Pp. 157–76.

Bourdieu, Pierre. 1984. *Distinction*. Cambridge: Harvard University Press.

———. 1990. *The Logic of Practice*. Stanford: Stanford University Press.

Bowman, Glenn. 1989. "Fucking Tourists: Sexual Relations and Tourism in Jerusalem's Old City." *Critique of Anthropology* 9 (2): 77–93.

Brooks, George. 1980. "Kola Trade and State-Building: Upper Guinea Coast and Senegambia, 15–17 Centuries." BUASCWP, no. 38.

Brown, Naomi. 1992. "Beach Boys as Cultural Brokers in Bakau Town, The Gambia." *Community Development Journal* 27 (4): 361–70.

Bruner, Edward M. 1996. "Tourism in Ghana: The Representation of Slavery and the Return of the Black Diaspora." *American Anthropologist* 98 (2): 290–305.

Bugul, Ken. 1991. *Abandoned Baobab: Autobiography of a Senegalese Woman*, translated by Marjolijn de Jager. Chicago: Lawrence Hill.

Butler, Judith. 1989. *Gender Trouble*. New York: Routledge.

Camara, Laye.1980. *Guardian of the Word*. London: Fontana.

Camara, Sory. 1976. *Gens des Parole: Essai sur la condition et le rôle des griots dans la société malinké*. Paris: Mouton.

Chakrabarty, Dispesh. 2000. *Provincializing Europe*. Princeton, N.J.: Princeton University Press.

Chapell, Peter. 1997. *Our Friends at the Bank*. 84 min. New York: First Run / Icarus Films. Videocassette.

Charry, Eric. 2000. *Mande Music*. Chicago: University of Chicago Press.

Chernoff, John M. 1979. *African Rhythm and African Sensibility: Aesthetics and Social Action in African Musical Idioms.* Chicago: Chicago University Press.

———. 1991. "The Rhythmic Medium in African Music." *New Literary History* 22 (4): 1093–1102.

Clifford, James. 1986. "Introduction: Partial Truths." In *Writing Culture.* Berkeley: University of California Press. Pp. 1–26.

Cohen, Erik. 1971. "Arab Boys and Tourist Girls in a Mixed Jewish-Arab Community." *International Journal of Comparative Sociology* 12 (4): 217–33.

Cohn, Bernard. 1996. *Colonialism and Its Forms of Knowledge.* Princeton, N.J.: Princeton University Press.

Comaroff, John, and Jean Comaroff. 1992. *Ethnography and the Historical Imagination.* Boulder: Westview Press.

———. 1998. *Occult Economies and the Violence of Abstraction.* Chicago: American Bar Foundation.

Copland, David. 1985. *In Township Tonight.* London: Longman.

Curtin, Phillip. 1975. *Economic Change in Pre-Colonial Africa.* Madison: University of Wisconsin Press.

Darbo, Seni. 1976. "A Griot's Self-Portrait." Banjul, Gambia: Occasional Papers Gambia Cultural Archives, no. 2.

Davila, Arlene. *Sponsored Identities.* Philadelphia: Temple University Press.

Davis, Olga Idriss. 1997. "The Door of No Return: Reclaiming the Past Through the Rhetoric of Pilgrimage." *Western Journal of Black Studies* 21 (3): 156–61.

de Certeau, Michel. 1984. *Practice of Everyday Life*, translated by Steven Randall. Berkeley: University of California.

Debord, Guy. 1977. *Society of the Spectacle.* Detroit: Black and Red Books.

Diawara, Manthia. 1998. *In Search of Africa.* Cambridge: Harvard University Press.

Dirks, Nicolas. 1992. *Colonialism and Culture.* Ann Arbor: University of Michigan Press.

Drewal, Henry John, and Margaret Drewel. 1983. *Gelede: Art and Female Power among the Yoruba.* Bloomington: Indiana University Press.

Drewal, Margaret. 1991. "State of Research on Performance in Africa." *African Studies Review* 34 (3): 1–64.

du Gay, Paul, Stuart Hall, Linda Janes, Hugh Mackay, and Keith Negus. 1997. *Doing Cultural Studies.* London: Sage.

Dusan Bulman, Stephen. 1990. "Interpreting Sunjata: A Comparative Analysis and Exegesis of the Malinke Epic." Ph.D. thesis, University of Birmingham.

Elam, Harry. 1998. *Taking it to the Streets.* Ann Arbor: University of Michigan Press.

Enloe, Cynthia. 1990. *Bananas, Beaches, and Bases: Making Feminist Sense of International Politics.* Berkeley: University of California Press.

Escobar, Arturo. 1994. *Encountering Development.* Princeton, N.J.: Princeton University Press.

Fabian, Johannes. 1983. *Time and the Other.* New York: Columbia University Press.

———. 1990. *Power and Performance.* Madison: University of Wisconsin Press.

Fabre, Geneviève, and Robert O'Meally, eds. 1994. *History and Memory in African-American Culture*. New York: Oxford University Press.

Fardon, Richard. 1985. *Power and Knowledge*. Edinburgh: Scottish Academic Press.

Favret-Saada, Jeanne. 1980. *Deadly Words*. Cambridge: Cambridge University Press.

Feld, Steven. 1989. "Notes on World Beat." *Public Culture* 1 (1): 31–38.

Ferguson, James. 1994. *Anti-Politics Machine*. Minneapolis: University of Minnesota Press.

Ford Foundation. 1958. Ford Foundation annual report. New York: Ford Foundation.

Frank, Thomas. 1997. *The Conquest of Cool*. Chicago: University of Chicago Press.

Frank, Thomas, and Matt Weiland. 1997. *Commodify Your Dissent*. New York: Norton.

Fujimura, Joan. 1992. " 'Crafting Science': Standardized Packages, Boundary Objects, and Translation." In *Science as Practice and Culture*, edited by Andrew. Pickering. Chicago: University of Chicago.

Gal, Susan. 1995. "Language and the 'Arts of Resistance'." *Cultural Anthropology* 3: 407–24.

Galloway, Winifred. 1978. *James Island: A Background with Historical Notes on Juffure, Allbreda, San Domingo, Dog Island*. Banjul, The Gambia: Oral History and Antiquities Division, for the Gambian National Monuments and Relics Commission.

———. 1980. "Analysis, Interpretation and Presentation of Oral Traditions As Historical Sources." Banjul, The Gambia: Oral History and Antiquities Division.[1]

Gamble, David P. 1967 [1957]. *The Wolof of Senegambia*. London: International African Institute.

———. 1988. *The Gambia*. Oxford: Clio Press.

———. 2000. *Postmortem: A Study of The Gambia Section of Alex Haley's Roots*. Brisbane, Calif.: Gambia Studies, no. 39.

Garcia Canclini, Nestor. 1993. *Transforming Modernity*. Austin: University of Texas Press.

Gibson-Graham, J. K. 1996. *The End of Capitalism (As We Knew It)*. Oxford: Basil Blackwell.

Giddings, Paula. 1984. *When and Where I Enter*. New York: Morrow.

Gilroy, Paul. 1993. *The Black Atlantic*. Cambridge: Harvard University Press.

Giovanni, Nikki. 1992. "Preface." In *Abandoned Baobab* by Ken Bugul. Chicago: Lawrence Hill.

Goffman, Erving. 1959. *The Presentation of Self in Everyday Life*. Garden City, N.Y.: Doubleday.

———. 1961. *Asylums*. Garden City, N.J.: Doubleday.

———. 1976. *Gender Advertisements*. Cambridge: Harvard University Press.

Goody, Jack. 1976. *Production and Reproduction: A Comparative Study of the Domestic Domain*. New York: Cambridge University Press.

Gouk, Penelope. 1999. *Music, Science, and Natural Magic in Seventeenth-Century England*. New Haven, Conn.: Yale University Press.

Grenier, Line. 1989. "From Diversity to Difference: The Case of Sociocultural Studies of Music." *New Formations* 9: 125–42.

Guyer, Jane. 1984. *Family and Farm in Southern Cameroon*. Boston: Boston University, African Studies Center.

Haardt, Caroline. 1992. "Goree, Island of Slaves." *UNESCO Courier*, October, 48–50.

Hale, Thomas. 1998. *Griots and Griottes*. Bloomington: Indiana University Press.

Haley, Alex. 1976. *Roots*. Garden City, N.Y.: Doubleday.

Hall, C. Michael. 1994. "Gender and Economic Interests in Tourism Prostitution: The Nature, Development, and Implications of Sex Tourism in South-East Asia." *Tourism: A Gender Analysis*, edited by Vivian Kinnaird and Derek Hall. New York: John Wiley.

Hall, Stuart. 1990. "Cultural Identity and Diaspora." In *Identity: Community, Culture, Difference*, edited by Jonathan Rutherford. London: Lawrence and Wishart. Pp. 222–37.

Hall, Stuart, ed. 1997. *Representation: Cultural Representations and Signifying Practices*. Thousand Oaks, Cal.: Sage.

Harding, Susan. 2000. *The Book of Jerry Falwell*. Princeton, N.J.: Princeton University Press.

Harris, Eddie L. 1992. *Native Stranger: A Black American's Journey into the Heart of Africa*. New York: Simon and Schuster.

Hart, Keith. 1985. "The Social Anthropology of West Africa." *Annual Review of Anthropology* 14: 243–72.

Hartigan, John. 1999. *Racial Situations*. Princeton, N.J.: Princeton University Press.

Hartman, Saidiya. 1997. *Scenes of Subjection*. New York: Oxford University Press.

Hecht, D., and A. M. Simone. 1994. *Invisible Governance: The Art of African Micro-Politics*. Brooklyn, N.Y.: Autonomedia.

Hilgartner, Stephen. 2000. *Science on Stage*. Stanford: Stanford University Press.

Innes, Gordon. 1974. *Sunjata: Three Mandinka Three Versions*. London: SOAS.

Irvine, Judith. 1973. "Caste and Communication in a Wolof Village." Ph.D. thesis, University of Pennsylvania.

———. 1989. "When Talk Isn't Cheap: Language and Political Economy." *American Ethnologist* 16 (2): 248–67.

Ivy, Marilyn. 1995. *Discourses of the Vanishing: Modernity, Phantasm, Japan*. Chicago: University of Chicago Press.

Jackson, Shannon. 2000. *Lines of Activity*. Ann Arbor: University of Michigan Press.

James, Allison, Jenny Hockey, and Andrew Dawson, eds. 1997. *After Writing Culture*. New York: Routledge.

James, George. 1985. *Stolen Legacy*. San Francisco: Julian Richardson Associates.

Jameson, Fredric. 1988. "Periodizing the 60s." In *The Ideologies of Theory*, volume II. Minneapolis: University of Minnesota. Pp. 178–208.

Jameson, Fredric. 1991. *Postmodernism, or The Cultural Logic of Late Capitalism*. Durham, N.C.: Duke University Press.

Johnson, Richard. 1986. "What Is Cultural Studies Anyway?" *Social Text*. Winter 86/87: 38–80.

Kant, Immanuel. 1951 [1790]. *Critique of Judgment*. New York: Hafer.

Kaplan, Robert. 1994. "The Coming Anarchy: How Scarcity, Crime, Overpopulation, Tribalism and Disease Are Rapidly Destroying the Social Fabric of Our Planet." *Atlantic Monthly* 273 (2): 44–76.

Karenga, Maulana. 1982. *Introduction to Black Studies*. Inglewood, Cal.: Kawaida.

Karp, Ivan. 1997. "Does Theory Travel? Area Studies and Cultural Studies." *Africa Today* 44 (3): 281–95.

Klein, Debra. 2000. "Yoruba Bata: Politics of Pop Tradition in Erin Asun and Overseas." Ph.D. thesis, University of California, Santa Cruz.

Knight, Roderick. 1973. "Mandinka Jaliya: Professional Music of the Gambia." 2 vols. Ph.D. thesis, University of California, Los Angeles.

Kondo, Dorinne. 1997. *About Face*. New York: Routledge.

Kopka, Matthew, and Iris Brooks. 1996. *Jali Kunda: Griots of West Africa and Beyond*. Rosylyn, N.Y.: Ellipsis Arts.

Kouyate, Dani. 1994. *Keïta!: l'héritage du griot* [The Heritage of the Griot]. 94 min. San Francisco: California Newsreel. Videocassette.

Kratz, Corinne. 1994. *Affecting Performance: Meaning, Movement and Experience in Okiek Women's Initiation*. Washington, D.C.: Smithsonian.

Kreiswirth, Martin. 1995. "Tell Me a Story: The Narrative Turn in the Human Sciences." In *Constructive Criticism: The Human Sciences in the Age of Theory*, edited by Martin Kreiswirth and Thomas Carmichael. Toronto: University of Toronto Press. Pp. 61–87.

Latham, Michael. 2000. *Modernization as Ideology*. Chapel Hill: University of North Carolina Press.

Laye, Camara. 1980. *Guardian of the Word*, translated by James Kirkup. London: Fontana.

Lee, Wendy. 1991. "Prostitution and Tourism in South-east Asia." In *Working Women International Perspectives on Labor and Gender Ideology*, edited by Nanneke Redclift and M. Thea Sinclaire. New York: Routledge. Pp.79–103

Leppert, Richard. 1988. *Music and Image*. Cambridge: Cambridge University Press.

Lindfors, Bernth, ed. 1999. *Africans on Stage*. Bloomington: Indiana University Press.

Lorde, Audre. 1982. *Zami*. Trumansburg, N.Y.: Crossing.

M'Bow, Amadou Mahtar. 1985. *UNESCO 1984–1985*. Paris: UNESCO.

MacCormack, Carol, and Marilyn Strathern. 1980. *Nature, Culture, and Gender*. Cambridge: Cambridge University Press.

MacKenzie, John. 1995. *Orientalism: History, Theory, and the Arts*. Manchester, U.K.: Manchester University Press.

Magner, Denise. 1995. "Debate in African Studies." *Chronicle of Higher Education* 42 (11): 19–20.

Mansson, Sven-Axel. 1993. *Cultural Conflict and the Swedish Sexual Myth: The Male Immigrant's Encounter with Swedish Sexual and Cohabitation Culture.* New York: Hanover House.

Marcus, George, and Dick Cushman. 1982. "Ethnographies As Texts." *Annual Review of Anthropology* 11: 25–69.

Marcus, George, and Michael Fisher. 1986. *Anthropology as Cultural Critique.* Chicago: University of Chicago Press.

Martin-Shaw, Carolyn. 1995. *Colonial Inscriptions.* Minneapolis: University of Minnesota Press.

Mbembe, Achille. 1992. "The Banality of Power and the Aesthetics of Vulgarity." *Public Culture* 4 (2): 1–30.

McClary, Susan. 1993. "Reshaping the Discipline: Musicology and Feminism in the 1990s." *Feminist Studies* 19 (2): 399–423.

McClintock, Ann. 1995. *Imperial Leather.* New York: Routledge.

Meillassoux, Claude. 1981. *Maidens, Meals, and Money.* New York: Cambridge University Press.

Mercer, Kobena. 1994. *Welcome to the Jungle.* New York: Routledge.

Mez, Adam. 1937. *Renaissance of Islam,* translated by Salahuddin Khuda Bukhsh and D. S. Margoliouth. London: Patnas, Jubilee Printing and Publishing House.

Miller, Christopher. 1985. *Blank Darkness: Africanist Discourse in French.* Chicago: University of Chicago Press.

———. 1990. *Theories of Africans: Francophone Literature and Anthropology in Africa.* Chicago: University of Chicago.

Mkandawire, Thandika, and Charles Soludo. 1999. *Our Continent, Our Future.* Trenton, N.J.: Africa World Press.

Mohanty, Chandra. 1984. "Under Western Eyes." *Boundary* 2 (12 / 13): 333–58.

Mudimbe, Valentine Y. 1988. *The Invention of Africa.* Bloomington: Indiana University Press.

Mudimbe, Valentine, and Bogumil Jewsiewicki. 1990. "African History Finds Its Voice. (In Pursuit of the Past: History and Memory)." *Unesco Courier* March: 40.

———. 1993. "Africans' Memories and Contemporary History of Africa." *History and Theory* 32 (4): 1–11

Niana, D. T. 1965. *Epic of Old Mali,* translated by G. D. Pickett. London: Longman.

Nketia, J. H. 1974. *Music in Africa.* New York: W. W. Norton.

Odzer, Cleo. 1994. *Patpong Sisters.* New York: Blue Moon Books.

Olaniyan, Tejumola. 1996. "The Return of the Native Son." *Transition* 72 (4): 50–63.

Ortner, Sherry, and Harriet Whitehead. 1981. *Sexual Meanings.* Cambridge: Cambridge University Press.

Paolini, Albert. 1997. "The Place of Africa in Discourses About the Post Colonial, the Global, the Modern." *New Formations* 31: 83–106.

Pearson, Michael, and Michael Shanks. 2001. *Theatre Archaeology.* New York: Routledge.

Pickering, H. J., D. Todd, J. Dunn, J. Pepin, and A. Wilkins. 1992. "Prostitutes and Their Clients: A Gambian Survey." *Social Science and Medicine* 34 (1): 75–88.

Piot, Charles. 1999. *Remotely Global.* Chicago: University of Chicago Press.

Pollack, Della, ed. 1998. *Exceptional Spaces.* Chapel Hill: University of North Carolina Press.

Pratt, Mary Louise. 1992. *Imperial Eyes.* New York: Routledge.

Quinn, Charolette. 1972. *Mandingo Kingdoms of the Senegambia.* Evanston, Ill.: Northwestern University Press.

Rahier, Jean Muteba, ed. 1999. *Representations of Blackness and the Performance of Identities.* Westport, Conn.: Bergin and Garvey.

Reuters News Service. August 16, 1994 and August 20, 1994. http://www.reuters.com/news.

Rice, Berkeley. 1967. *Enter Gambia: The Birth of an Improbable Nation.* Boston: Houghton Mifflin.

Richburg, Keith. 1997. *Out of America.* New York: Basic Books.

Ricoeur, Paul. 1991. "Narrative Identity." In *On Paul Ricoeur: Narrative and Interpretation*, edited by David Wood. New York: Routledge. Pp. 188–99.

Roach, Joseph. 1996. *Cities of the Dead: Circum-Atlantic Performance.* New York: Columbia University Press.

Roberts, Richard L. 1996. *Two Worlds of Cotton: Colonialism and the Regional Economy in the French Soudan, 1800–1946.* Stanford: Stanford University Press.

Robinson, David. 1985. *The Holy War of Umar Tall: The Western Sudan in the Mid-Nineteenth Century.* New York: Oxford University Press.

Roddick, Anita. 1991. *Body and Soul.* New York: Crown.

Rodney, Walter. 1972. *How Europe Underdeveloped Africa.* London: Bogue-Louverture.

Roe, Emery. 1999. *Except-Africa.* New Brunswick, N.J.: Transaction.

Rogers, J.A.. 1961. *Africa's Gift to America.* New York: H. M. Rogers.

Rosaldo, Renato. 1989. *Culture and Truth.* Boston: Beacon.

Rozak, Theodore. 1995. *The Making of a Counter Culture.* Minneapolis: University of Minnesota Press.

Rubin, Gayle. 1975. "Traffic in Women: Notes on the Political Economy of Sex." In *Toward and Anthropology of Women*, edited by Rayna Reiter. New York: Monthly Review Press. Pp. 157–210.

Said, Edward W. 1978. *Orientalism.* New York: Pantheon.

———. 1983. *The World, the Text, and the Critic.* Cambridge: Harvard University Press.

———. 1991. *Musical Elaborations.* New York: Columbia University Press.

———. 1993. *Culture and Imperialism.* New York: Pantheon.

Saine, Abdoulaye. 1997. "Vision 2020. The Gambia's Neo-Liberal Strategy for Social and Economic Development: A Critique." *Western Journal of Black Studies* 21 (2): 92–97.

———. 2000. "The Gambia's Foreign Policy since the Coup, 1994–99. *Journal of Commonwealth and Comparative Politics* 38 (2): 73–88.

Sawyer, Akilagpa. 1999. "Globalization and Social Sciences in Africa." *African Sociological Review* 3 (1): 1–19.

Schroeder, Richard. 1999. *Shady Practices*. Berkeley: University of California Press.

Scott, James. 1990. *Domination and the Arts of Resistance*. New Haven, Conn.: Yale University Press.

Scott, Joan W. 1994. "Evidence of Experience." In *Questions of Evidence: Proof, Practice, and Persuasion across the Disciplines*, edited by James Chandler, Arnold Davidson, and Harry Harootunian. Chicago: University of Chicago Press. Pp. 773–97.

Shawn, Ted. 1947. *How Beautiful upon the Mountain: A History of Jacob's Pillow*. 3rd ed. New York: Jacob's Pillow Dance Festival, Inc.

Sher, Steven Paul, ed. 1992. *Music and Text: Critical Inquiries*. New York: Cambridge University Press.

Sidibe, B. K. 1980. *Sunjata*. Banjul, The Gambia: Oral History and Antiquities Division, Vice President's Office.

Sinduhije, Alexis. 1999. "Welcome to America." *Transition* 78: 4–23.

Spivak, Gayatri. 1988. "Can the Subaltern Speak?" In *Marxism and the Interpretation of Culture*, edited by Cary Nelson and Lawrence Grossberg. Urbana: University of Illinois Press. Pp. 271–313.

Star, S. L., and Griesemer, J. 1989. "Institutional Ecology, Translations and Boundary Objects. *Social Studies of Science* 1, 387–420.

Stoler, Ann. 1995. *Race and the Education of Desire*. Durham, N.C.: Duke University Press.

Stoller, Paul. 1989. *The Taste of Ethnographic Things: The Senses in Anthropology*. Philadelphia: University of Pennsylvania Press.

———. 1999. *Jaguar*. Chicago: University of Chicago Press.

Subotnik, Rose Rosengard. 1991. *Developing Variations: Style and Ideology in Western Music*. Minneapolis: University of Minnesota Press.

———. 1996. *Deconstructive Variations: Music and Reason in Western Society*. Minneapolis: University of Minnesota Press.

Sumner, Melanie. 1995. *Polite Society*. Boston: Houghton Mifflin.

Suso, Bamba, and Banna Kanute. 1999. *Sunjata: Gambian Versions of the Mande Epic*, translated and annotated by Gordon Innes with assistance of Bakery Sidibe; edited with new introduction by Lucy Duran and Graham Furniss. London: Penguin.

Thompson, E. P. 1963. *The Making of the English Working Class*. New York: Vintage Books.

Thompson, Robert Farris. 1983. *Flash of the Spirit*. New York: Random House.

Townsend, Robert. 1987. *Hollywood Shuffle*. 81 min. Los Angeles: Samuel Goldwyn Co. and Virgin Vision. Videocassette.

Trinh Minh-ha. 1982. *Reassemblage: From the Firelight to the Screen*. video cassette. 40 minutes New York: Women Make Movies.

———. 1985. *Naked Spaces: Living Is Round*. 135 min. New York: Women Make Movies. 16mm film.

———. 1992. *Framer Framed*. New York: Routledge.

Tsing, Anna Lowenhaupt. 1993. *In the Realm of the Diamond Queen.* Princeton, N.J.: Princeton University Press.

Turner, Victor. 1967. *Forest of Symbols.* Ithaca, N.Y.: Cornell University Press.

———. 1969. *Ritual Process.* Ithaca, N.Y.: Cornell University Press.

Van Gennep, Arnold. 1960 [1909]. *Rites of Passage,* translated by Monika Vizedom and Gabrielle L. Caffee. Chicago: University of Chicago Press.

Vancina, Jan. 1985. *Oral Traditions as History.* Madison: University of Wisconsin Press.

Von Eschen, Penny. 1997. *Race Against Empire: Black Americans and Anticolonialism 1937–1957.* Ithaca, N.Y.: Cornell University Press.

Wagner, Ulla. 1981. "Tourism and the Gambia: Dependency." *Ethnos* 46 (3-4): 190–206.

———. 1982. *Catching the Tourists: Women Handicraft Traders in the Gambia.* Stockholm, Sweden: Department of Social Anthropology, University of Stockholm.

———. 1987. "Out of Time and Space—Mass Tourism and Charter Trips." *Ethnos* 42 (1-2): 38–52.

Wagner, Ulla, and Bawa Yamba. 1986. "Going North and Getting Attached: The Case of the Gambia." *Ethnos* 51 (3-4): 199–222.

Walker, Alice, and Pratibha Parma.1993. *Warrior Marks.* New York: Harcourt Brace.

Wallerstein, Immanuel. 1979. *The Capitalist World-Economy.* Cambridge: Cambridge University Press.

Wamba, Philippe. 1999. *Kinship: A Family's Journey in Africa and America.* New York: Plume.

Waterman, Christopher. 1990. *Juju: A Social History and Ethnography of an African Popular Music.* Chicago: University of Chicago Press.

White, E. Frances. 1987. *Sierra Leone Settler Women Traders.* Ann Arbor: University of Michigan Press.

White, E. Frances. 1991. "Africa on My Mind: Gender, Counter Discourse and African American Cultural Nationalism." *Journal of Women's History* 2 (1): 73–97.

White, Hayden. 1978. *Tropics of Discourse.* Baltimore, Md.: The Johns Hopkins University Press.

———. 1987. *Content of the Form*: Baltimore, Md.: The Johns Hopkins University Press.

White, Luise. 1994. "Alien Nation." *Transition* 63: 24–33.

———. 2000. *Speaking with Vampires.* Berkeley: University of California Press.

Williams, Chancellor. 1974. *Destruction of Black Civilization: Great Issues of a Race from 4500 B.C. to 2000 A.D.* Chicago: Third World Press.

Williams, Raymond. 1966. *The Long Revolution.* New York: Harper.

"Winners and Losers." 2000. *Prague Post* September 27.

Wiseman, John A. 1990. *Democracry in Black Africa: Survival and Revival.* New York: Paragon House.

Wolf, Eric. 1982. *Europe and the People Without History.* Berkeley: University of California Press.

Wolff, Janet. 1987 "Forward: The Ideology of Autonomous Art." In *Music and Society: The Politics of Composition, Performance and Reception*, edited by Richard Leppert and Susan McClary. New York: Cambridge University Press. Pp. 1–12.

———. 1995. "On the Road Again: Metaphors of Travel in Cultural Criticism." In *Resident Alien: Feminist Cultural Criticism*. New Haven, Conn.: Yale University Press. Pp. 115–34.

Wright, Bonnie L. 1989. "The Power of Articulation." In *Creativity and Power*, edited by Ivan Karp. Washington, D.C.: Smithsonian. Pp. 39–57.

Wright, Donald R. 1976. *The Early History of Niumi: Settlement and Foundation of a Mandinka State on the Gambia River*. Papers in International Studies: Africa series, no. 32. Athens: Ohio University Center for International Studies.

———. 1979–80. *Oral Traditions from The Gambia*. Papers in International Studies: Africa series, no. 37–38. Athens: Ohio University Center for International Studies.

———.1991. "Requiem for the Use of Oral Tradition to Reconstruct the Precolonial History of the Lower Gambia." *History on Africa* 18: 399–408.

———. 1997. *The World and a Very Small Place in Africa*. Armonk, N.Y.: M. E. Sharpe.